Stock Market Short-Termism

Kim M. Willey

Stock Market Short-Termism

Law, Regulation, and Reform

Foreword by Martin Lipton

palgrave
macmillan

Kim M. Willey
Faculty of Law
University of Victoria
Victoria, BC, Canada

ISBN 978-3-030-22902-3 ISBN 978-3-030-22903-0 (eBook)
https://doi.org/10.1007/978-3-030-22903-0

This Palgrave Macmillan imprint is published by the registered company Springer Nature Switzerland AG
The registered company address is: Gewerbestrasse 11, 6330 Cham, Switzerland

Foreword

I have been waiting for Kim Willey's comprehensive analysis of short-termism for more than 40 years. In Takeover Bids in the Target's Boardroom, published in *The Business Lawyer* in 1979 [Lipton, Martin. 1979. "Takeover Bids in the Target Boardroom." November 1979. 35. *The Business Lawyer*. 101–134], I argued for the rejection of short-termism, recognition of the interests of all stakeholders in a public company and that the market was not so efficient that it adequately valued all public companies at all times. This kicked off a debate that continues today—a debate which has long suffered from the absence of Kim Willey's comprehensive study and analysis of the empirical and pragmatic evidence of the economic and societal impact of short-termism and the counter-arguments of agency-cost, shareholder-democracy academics. With deep insight and reference to research on both sides, this book will be of great value to a wide range of interested parties, including asset managers, institutional investors, corporate directors and executives, market analysts, investment advisors, investment bankers, legal counsel, accountants and academics.

The importance of this comprehensive study of short-termism is shown by the recognition of the impact short-termism on wages, gross domestic product (GDP) and inequality, and by the growing efforts to combat short-termism. On the other hand, the hedge funds and stock market crowd, supported by a still vociferous group of academics, deny that short-termism is a problem. As one who has long rejected Nobel Laureate, Milton Friedman's *ex cathedra* pronouncement that the purpose of the business corporation is to maximize, within the limits of the law, profits for the shareholders, and the related efficient market theory of Nobel Laureate, Eugene Fama, I found it very useful to have these and other theories discussed in relationship to the debate on short-termism.

There is also a full discussion of the efforts to combat short-termism and promote environmental, social and governance (ESG) factors and sustainable long-term investment by corporations, and to curb activism and attacks by activist hedge funds. *The New Paradigm: A Roadmap for an Implicit Corporate Governance Partnership Between Corporations and Investors to Achieve Sustainable Long-Term Investment and Growth* [Lipton, Martin et al. 2019. "It's Time to Adopt the New Paradigm." Harvard Law School Forum on Corporate Governance and Financial Regulation. 11 February 2019. https://corpgov.law.harvard.edu/2019/02/11/its-time-to-adopt-the-new-paradigm/] that I and my colleagues prepared for the International Business Council of the World Economic Forum is discussed—as is the underlying proposition that the economic impact of a short-term myopic approach to managing and investing in businesses has become abundantly clear and has been generating rising levels of concern across a broad spectrum of stakeholders and policymakers.

On the legislative front, the Accountable Capitalism Act [S.3348—Accountable Capitalism Act 115th Congress (2017–2018)], a federal bill that would make all corporations with US$1 billion or more of annual revenue subject to a federal corporate governance regime (by requiring them to be chartered as a United States corporation), was introduced this past August by Senator Elizabeth Warren. Among other things, this regime would mandate that not less than 40% of the directors of a United States corporation must be elected by employees, and that directors must consider the interests of all corporate stakeholders—including employees, customers, suppliers, investors and the communities in which the corporation operates. Although the passage of such a bill in the United States currently seems highly unlikely, its introduction serves as a warning that legislative solutions could be imposed over time if the issues of sustainability and stakeholder interests are not adequately addressed by the private sector.

In addition, the British Academy has undertaken a study to create a framework for "The Future of the Corporation." [Mayer, Colin. 11 October 2018. "The Future of the Corporation: Towards Humane

Business." https://www.wlrk.com/docs/TheFutureoftheCorporation TowardsHumaneBusiness.pdf] The project is led by Oxford Professor, Colin Mayer, who presents a radical reinterpretation of the nature of the corporation that focuses on the corporate purpose, its alignment with social purpose, the trustworthiness of companies and the role of corporate culture in promoting purpose and trust. This view of the corporation rejects shareholder primacy as the corporation's sole goal.

Mayer argues that corporate purpose is distinct from the consequential implications for the corporation's profitability and shareholder returns. The purpose of corporations is not to produce profits. The purpose of corporations is to produce profitable solutions for the problems of people and planet. In the process, it produces profits, but profits are not per se the purpose of corporations. This view of the corporation of the future would be implemented by establishing a regulatory system that would promote alignment of corporate conduct with social purposes and ensure that companies' ownership, governance, measurement and incentive systems are appropriate for these purposes.

These and other developments suggest that legislative and regulatory reforms are a distinct possibility and that meaningful change is inevitable through one means or another. Kim Willey's work will be essential in dealing with these developments.

New York, USA
April 2019

Martin Lipton
Founding partner of Wachtell
Lipton, Rosen & Katz

Acknowledgements

I am grateful to my family for their enduring support and encouragement and to Professor Brian Cheffins for his guidance and insightful comments.

Contents

Abbreviations

AUM	Assets Under Management
CAPM	Capital-Asset Pricing Model
CCA	Comparable Company Analysis
CEO	Chief Executive Officer
CFA	Chartered Financial Analyst
CHI	Corporate Horizons Index
CPPIB	Canada Pension Plan Investment Board
CREST	Certificateless Registry for Electronic Share Transfer
CSD	Central Securities Depository
CSR	Corporate Social Responsibility
EC	European Commission
ECMH	Efficient Capital Market Hypothesis
EPS	Earnings Per Share
ESG	Environmental, Social and Governance
EU	European Union
EU UCITS	EU Undertakings for Collective Investment in Transferable Securities
FCA	UK Financial Conduct Authority
FCLT	Focusing Capital on the Long Term
FRC	Financial Reporting Council
FTT	Financial Transaction Tax
GAAP	Generally Accepted Accounting Principles
GDP	Gross Domestic Product
GFC	2007–2009 Global Financial Crisis
HFT	High Frequency Trading
IIRC	International Integrated Reporting Council

IMA	UK Investment Management Association
IPO	Initial Public Offering
ISS	Institutional Shareholder Services
LSE	London Stock Exchange
LTI	Long-Term Incentives
LTIP	Long-Term Incentives Plan
M&A	Merger and Acquisition
MiFID II	EU Markets in Financial Instruments Directive (2014/65/EU) and the Markets in Financial Instruments Regulation (Regulation 600/2014)
NAPF	UK National Association of Pension Funds
NASDAQ	National Association of Securities Dealers Automated Quotations
NGO	Non-Governmental Organization
NPV	Net Present Value
NYSE	New York Stock Exchange
PRI	Principles for Responsible Investment
R&D	Research and Development
SEC	United States Securities and Exchange Commission
SGX	Singapore Stock Exchange
SMST	Stock Market Short-Termism
SVM	Shareholder Value Maximization
UK	United Kingdom
UKIA	UK Investment Association
UN	United Nations
UNEP	United Nations Environment Program
US	United States of America
VBM	Value Based Management

List of Figures

List of Tables

CHAPTER 1

Introduction

The role of modern companies, and, more precisely, the functioning of the world's largest publicly listed companies, has been cast into the spotlight after the global financial crisis of 2007–2009 (GFC).[1] Central to this conversation is the proposition that listed companies and their financial intermediaries and investors are far too focused on short-term financial objectives, and corrective measures are urgently needed. This short-term financial focus hinders the development of sustainable long-term oriented listed companies that create employment, further stakeholder interests, develop valuable products and services, generate earnings, and return profits to shareholders. It has been widely asserted that such short-termism was a contributing factor in the GFC, and continues to jeopardize the operations of listed companies, and consequently erode the long-term growth potential of modern markets. Alarming claims have been made that short-termism in stock markets is increasing drastically, and the "destructive impact of short-termism has reached crisis proportions",[2] and that "[t]he ongoing short-termism in the business world is undermining corporate investment, holding back economic growth, and lowering returns for savers."[3]

[1] For example, see The Modern Corporation and Lipton et al. (2019).

[2] Rappaport (2011, 3).

[3] Barton and Wiseman (2014, 3).

K. M. Willey, *Stock Market Short-Termism*,
https://doi.org/10.1007/978-3-030-22903-0_1

This book provides a comprehensive review of the causes and effects of stock market short-termism (SMST) and offers a tangible framework for reform.

A. Rationale for This Book

The research in this book has been undertaken primarily as a result of the countless calls for regulatory and financial industry reform to address SMST, and the resulting need to analyze whether implemented reforms conceptually address such concerns. Demonstrating that allegations of short-termism in financial markets have increased significantly since the GFC, Fig. 1 illustrates the increased use of the term 'short-termism' in major international business papers from 1999 to 2018. As illustrated by the results of each of the *Wall Street Journal* and the narrowed definition searches in Fig. 1, the use of the term short-termism has followed a steady upward trend.

This book explores the extent to which this increased attention to the SMST problem involving public companies has generated reforms by regulators and the financial industry. Jurisdiction-specific academic analysis of short-termism has been previously conducted, particularly in the United States (US), the United Kingdom (UK) and the

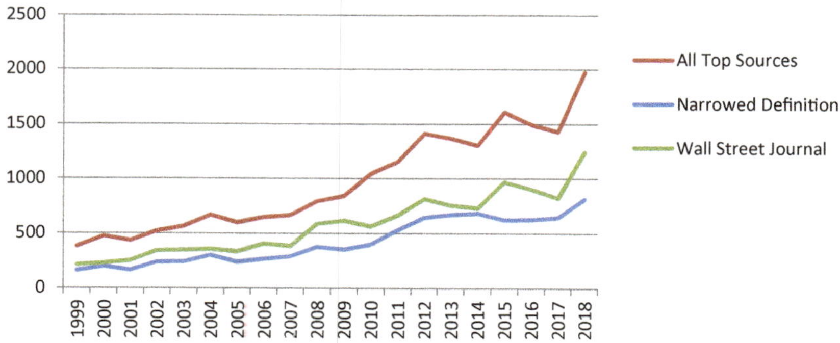

Fig. 1 Citations of the term 'short-termism' (*Source* Compiled from data available on Factiva as at 31 December 2018)

European Union (EU).[4] However, to date there has not been a comprehensive academic analysis of all implemented—or seriously considered—short-termism reform efforts. This broader analysis is warranted because, as discussed further in Chapter 3, short-termism concerns are raised in markets around the world and modern capital markets are increasingly interconnected. This interconnectedness, which was highlighted by the GFC,[5] has the potential to further the globalization of issues such short-termism.

Although 'western' stock markets, specifically the US and the UK, have been the primary focus of the discussion,[6] capital market short-termism has been discussed by policymakers outside the US and the UK, notably in the EU. As an example, commenting on the Swedish capital market, Sophie Nachemson-Ekwall of the Stockholm School of Economics, discusses how after years of high taxes, family ownership has been falling, and with domestic institutional investors continuing to act in a markedly passive manner, the opportunities for private equity, foreign industrial owners and foreign—passive and short-term—institutional investors have grown.[7] According to Nachemson-Ekwall, this trend has resulted in the Swedish capital market generally having features associated with 'value-destructive short-termism'.[8]

[4]See for example, Dallas (2012) summarizing US reform proposals after the GFC, which focuses mostly on reforms to the US banking industry, Kay (2012) assessing short-termism in the context of UK capital markets and Bowdren (2016) further examining short-termism in the UK context, and Johnston and Morrow (2014), considering whether amendments to the 2007/36/EC as regards the encouragement of long-term shareholder engagement (effective as of 9 June 2017) (EU Amended Shareholder Rights Directive) address short-termism.

[5]The total and country by country statistics provided by the World Federation of Exchanges Database, 'Market capitalization of domestic listed companies – all countries and economies' (current US$). Online: http://data.worldbank.org, provides demonstrates the impact of the GFC on market capitalization, as the total statistics and statistics for most of the countries included in the database show a significant decline during the time of the GFC.

[6]For example, see Thornhill (2016), in which the author observes that "[o]ne of the startling features of Anglo-American capitalism is that corporate investment remains so low when profits are so high", and Barton (2011, 86), in which Dominic Barton sees the issues in terms 'East' v. 'West', with Eastern countries favouring longer term investment and the West, US and Europe focused on near-term returns

[7]Nachemson-Ekwall (2017, 267).

[8]Ibid.

Short-termism may not presently be a significant concern outside the Anglo-American capital market model. However, it is, and arguably should be, of interest globally. Equity market interconnectivity facilitated primarily by US investors diversifying risk and looking for high growth by seeking investment opportunities outside of their home jurisdictions[9] could further issues of short-termism.[10] Relevant to the short-termism discussion is foreign portfolio investment (FPI), rather than foreign direct investment (FDI). FPI is defined by the European Commission (EC) as where "an investor buys equity in or debt of a foreign company<but>[t]he investor does not necessarily have a long-term interest in the company or an influence over its management."[11] Unlike FDI, which involves buying a controlling interest in a business,[12] FPI is highly liquid and passive—i.e. in the equity context, the investment is generally under 10% of the voting rights.[13] Despite declines in FPI in 2008 due to the GFC and 2015 due to global political uncertainty, FPI is generally following an upward trend,[14] which is particularly evident in the Euro-area.[15] Therefore, policymakers outside of the US and the UK are, and should continue to be, alive to the issue of short-termism, and there is merit in a global analysis whereby regulators and the financial industry can learn from what is being done outside their respective jurisdictions.

There are undoubtedly differences in financial markets around the globe, particularly with respect to operating cultures and regulatory frameworks. As a result, any definitive reform efforts will need to be

[9] 'International Investing' US Securities and Exchange Commission (7 December 2016). Online: https://www.sec.gov/reportspubs/investor-publications/investorpubsininvesthtm.html.

[10] Atkins and Williamson (2007).

[11] European Commission, Trade Policy, Definition of 'Investment'. Online: http://ec.europa.eu/trade/policy/accessing-markets/investment/.

[12] See the definition of 'foreign direct investment' in www.Investopedia.com.

[13] 'Balance of Payments and International Investment Position Manual' International Monetary Fund Sixth Edition (BPM6) (2009) 110. Online: http://www.imf.org/external/pubs/ft/bop/2007/pdf/bpm6.pdf.

[14] World Investment Report, 2017, 'Investment and the Digital Economy', UNCTAD. Online: http://unctad.org/en/PublicationsLibrary/wir2017_en.pdf, 'Investment and the Digital Economy', UNCTAD, 13, Figure I.12. Online: http://unctad.org/en/PublicationsLibrary/wir2017_en.pdf.

[15] Portfolio Investment, net (BoP, current US$), Euro Area, The World Bank. Online: https://data.worldbank.org/indicator/BN.KLT.PTXL.CD?locations=XC.

tailored to the relevant implementing jurisdiction. Illustrating these differences, Anglo-American corporate governance systems, such as the US, UK, Canada and Australia, are seen to have a similar approach based on prioritizing shareholder value, often with a dispersed shareholder base.[16] In contrast, in the EU—excluding the UK—a greater reliance generally on bank lending and debt, rather than equity, has been identified.[17] Also, in the EU, listed companies have traditionally not been widely-held as share ownership has been concentrated in a limited number of resident shareholders, such as, for example, family groups or the state.[18]

In Asia, concentrated ownership of listed companies is also a common feature.[19] For example, the Chinese government holds a significant portion of the equity of Chinese listed companies, and approximately 75% of Hong Kong listed companies have a dominant shareholder.[20] However, many listed companies appear to be moving towards an Anglo-American shareholder capitalism model, with its distinctive features of a dispersed and globalized shareholding structure.[21] As explored further in this book, short-termism may be more or less pronounced depending on the corporate structure, and particularly, the presence of a dominant shareholder. The analysis in this book is not meant to be a panacea or to offer a set of reform proposals for all concerns relating to the short-termism issue world-wide. Instead, it is hoped that this analysis may prove useful to policymakers and the financial industry as the ongoing impact of the current implemented short-termism-driven reforms and the need for further reforms are considered. Any future reforms meant to address short-termism must of course be tailored to the specific regulatory framework and capital market requirements of each jurisdiction.

[16] Kraakman et al. (2009, 29–30).

[17] Brecht (2015).

[18] Grant and Kirchmaier (2004) and Kraakman et al. (2009, 29–30).

[19] Kraakman et al. (2009, 30).

[20] OECD Survey of Corporate Governance Frameworks in Asia (2017). Online: https://www.oecd.org/daf/ca/OECD-Survey-Corporate-Governance-Frameworks-Asia.pdf.

[21] Bena et al. (2017, 123), and the discussion generally in Hansman and Kraakman (2017).

B. Short-Termism—A Real Problem or a Red Herring?

Despite claims that short-termism is an alarming destructive force in modern capital markets, there is considerable debate on whether short-termism is in fact a real problem. Notable proponents asserting that there is a short-termism problem justifying a regulatory and financial industry response include UK economics professor John Kay—commissioned by the UK Government in 2011 to investigate UK capital market short-termism—,[22] Bank of England economist Andrew Haldane,[23] Delaware Supreme Court Chief Justice Leo Strine,[24] noted US economist Alfred Rappaport,[25] former US Democratic Presidential Candidate, Hillary Clinton,[26] and renowned US corporate lawyer and market commentator, Martin Lipton.[27] Adding weight to the argument that there is problem requiring correction, short-termism concerns have also been raised by the financial industry itself, most prominently by Larry Fink—Chief Executive Officer (CEO) of BlackRock, Inc. (BlackRock), which one of the world's largest asset management firms.[28]

Despite an extensive dialogue led by these financial market heavy weights, not all agree that a harmful short-termism problem exists. The commonplace assumption that stock markets are too obsessed with short-term financial returns has been questioned in the popular press. In *The New Yorker*, James Surowiecki acknowledged the political appeal of calls to make stock markets less short-term focused, and that certain investors may be myopic, but argued that markets on the whole are not short-term focused.[29] Additionally, Harvard Law professor Mark Roe acknowledges that US markets may be net short-termist. However, he asserts that this SMST is mitigated in the US economy as a whole—e.g. by non-stock market capital structures such as venture capital markets,

[22] Kay (2012).

[23] Haldane and Davies (2011).

[24] Strine (2015).

[25] Rappaport (2011).

[26] Jacobs (2015).

[27] Lipton et al. (2019) and Lipton (2006).

[28] Turner (2016), Oyedele (2017), and Fink (2018).

[29] Surowiecki (2015).

private equity markets, and other non-traded means of raising capital.[30] Roe argues that there is currently no justification for regulation to correct the SMST problem. If listed companies feel they are not properly valued in public markets, they can look to private sources of capital, and thus no more than 'watchful waiting' is required.[31]

As discussed further in Chapter 5,[32] evidence of a short-termism problem in stock markets, which evidence includes survey results, analysis of investor bias, evidence of increasing discounting of long-term cash flows, and proxies used to measure short-termism, is undoubtedly mixed. There are also questions on what exactly constitutes short-termism behaviour: is it duration of shareholding or short-term financial gains—, or rather is it corporate behaviour or objectives—i.e. short-term projects or financial returns. Regardless of this uncertainty, it is highly probable that policymakers and the financial industry will maintain their drive for longer-term sustainable investment in and by listed companies, and that short-termism will continue to be viewed as a contributing factor hindering such longer-term investment. Clarity around these issues is crucial before short-term reform measures can be properly assessed and further implemented.

This book aims to provide much needed clarity on this unclear and politically charged area of capital market reform. As discussed further in this book, many of the calls for reform and the resulting reform efforts are based on an unsubstantiated assumption that short-termism is a problem. To address this lacuna, I investigate further into what is causing such short-termism in stock markets and whether in fact such short-termism is problematic, through vigorously and systematically assessing the most probable causes, transmission methods and harms of short-termism. As the analysis in Chapter 3 demonstrates, short-termism is a recurring theme, and is prone to re-emerge in force with the next round of market turmoil. Further, if short-termism is the genuine problem it is alleged to be, effective reform to correct the problem is justified now in the absence of any triggering event. The intent of the analysis in this book is, therefore, to provide a useful framework for assessing whether current or future reform proposals, in theory at least, may conceptually

[30] Roe (2013, 977).

[31] Ibid., 1005.

[32] See Chapter 5, Sect. A.

act to reduce the short-termism issue. It is hoped that this objective framework, and the supporting analysis provided in this book, may be of use to policymakers and the financial industry—particularly investors and those who manage money on their behalf—as they continue to grapple with how best to address this slippery and complicated concept.

C. Structure of This Book

This book examines the short-termism discussion and conducts a comprehensive multi-jurisdictional examination of regulatory and financial industry measures meant to contend with the short-termism problem. This analysis indicates that despite the significant level of attention given to the short-termism issue, the anticipated surge of reform has not occurred. Having shown that the reform output is less than would be expected, this book then explores why the substantial discussion of short-termism has not resulted in greater reform efforts. To properly determine the body of reforms meant to address the short-termism issue, and thereby assess the validity of the hypothesis, the first step is to adequately identify and rigorously define the concept of SMST.

To do so, Chapter 2 opens the discussion with a detailed examination of the term 'short-termism' and its narrower application to the context of stock market investing. SMST is defined in this book as asset owners and intermediaries in the chain of parties connecting listed companies with their ultimate investors, weighing near-term financial outcomes too heavily at the expense of more profitable longer-term investment opportunities. In other words, less now is better than more later. This weighing is reflected in share pricing as short-term financial actions by company managers have positive impacts on share price and longer-term objectives are undervalued. The resulting impact to share prices causes company managers of listed companies to take actions that prioritize short-term financial returns to the detriment of listed companies, which by extension includes such listed companies' investors and broader stakeholder elements.

Terms relevant to the definition of SMST are also considered in Chapter 2. These include the terms 'stock market', 'listed company', 'equity security', and the 'financial intermediation chain'—defined in this chapter as the 'equity ownership chain'. Each of the key components of the equity ownership chain—articulated as asset owners, intermediaries and company managers—and their relationship to SMST, are then separately analyzed in this chapter. Further, as the focus of this book is on regulatory—and to a lesser degree, financial industry—reforms aimed at correcting the SMST problem so defined, the difference between 'hard' and 'soft' law and is examined as this distinction is particularly relevant to regulatory reform. The concept of 'light' touch regulation is also presented as it forms the basis for the recommendation in Chapter 8, that a 'light' touch approach is the optimal approach to 'nudge' capital markets away from their current short-termism focus. A 'light' touch approach is recommended given the complexities around defining SMST and proving that it is problematic and harmful, and in implementing 'hard' law reform. These definitions guide the analysis provided in the remainder of the book.

Chapter 3 examines the development of the SMST concept from when it was first clearly articulated as an issue in the 1970s in response to concerns of hostile takeovers of primarily US companies, to its widespread usage post-GFC. This examination of the development of the SMST concept brings to the forefront the question of whether SMST is a substantive issue or if it is instead merely compelling rhetoric that overlaps with the capital market concerns of the day. This chapter considers the SMST concerns raised during the US takeover boom of the 1970s and 1980s by US corporate lawyer and market commentator, Martin Lipton, the dialogue in the 1990s and 2000s around SMST and national competitiveness, and the changing market conditions known as the rise of agency capitalism. Also considered are the SMST concerns raised in the corporate scandals of the early 2000s, and in the GFC itself. The key aspects of the SMST discussion post-GFC are also examined. Chapter 3 hypothesizes that although SMST rhetoric appears to have been used in the development of the discussion, the SMST concern may have developed because of the increasing financial intermediation of public markets and the corresponding increased reliance on short-term performance of asset managers rather than the underlying performance of an investment. The substantive evidence of the existence of a real SMST problem is then considered further in Chapter 5.

Before assessing whether SMST is in fact a problem, Chapter 4 examines the most significant regulatory and financial industry reforms proposed or implemented to date meant to address the SMST problem. These reforms are categorized into asset owner, intermediary and company manager reforms on the basis that each of these groups serves a distinct role within stock markets, and SMST manifests differently in each role. The reforms directed at correcting the SMST of asset owners, intermediaries and company managers are each discussed in this chapter, and separately summarized in Appendix 'A' (Tables 1, and 3), respectively. Each of the reforms in these tables is color-coded to indicate which are 'hard' and 'soft' law reforms and voluntary initiatives. A summary of all the SMST reforms which have actually been implemented are included in Appendix 'B', Table 4. The results of this analysis indicate that despite the significant discussion and many proposals, the actual output of SMST reform in all jurisdictions surveyed has been relatively modest, and of the implemented reforms, many are 'light' touch in that they are disclosure or 'comply or explain' based or contain an 'opt-out' mechanism. The complexity of the SMST problem and the inconclusive evidence on the harms of SMST may help explain why there has been so little substantive reform, despite significant discussion on SMST and calls for reform. The basis for this complexity and inconclusive evidence of the harms of SMST is explored further in the following chapters.

Chapter 5 delves into the financial and legal discussion around whether SMST is a problem, and if so, what is causing SMST. This chapter considers the evidence presented supporting the argument that there is a SMST problem. After assessing the strength of this evidence and accepting that there is at least some basis for concern, this chapter then considers how SMST may be evident in share pricing, as share prices are an important communication mechanism between listed companies and the market. The primary question then considered in this analysis is whether there can be a short-termism problem at all if share pricing is an adequate indicator of long-term corporate value. This analysis requires a consideration of market efficiency theory. I consider whether share prices are informationally efficient—meaning that all publicly available information is reflected in the share price—, or fundamentally efficient—meaning that share prices are a decent measure of the underlying long-term value of the listed company. Accepting that stock markets are generally informationally efficient, I question the basis of their fundamental efficiency, given the apparent excessive discounting of future returns by asset owners and intermediaries. This apparent excessive discounting, and the resulting impact on share prices, is known to company managers and, accordingly, there is a strong incentive to prioritize short-term financial results of listed companies. Consequently, this chapter questions if share prices are a decent measure of the long-term value of listed companies.

The next two chapters look at two fundamental issues stemming from the conclusions drawn on the cause of SMST in Chapter 5. The first of these issues is analyzed in Chapter 6 and is that SMST requires a transmission mechanism through the equity ownership chain into the listed company. For the excessive discounting identified in Chapter 5 to be a problem, it must somehow result in short-termism actions of listed companies. The main argument in this respect is that the short-term interests of asset owners and intermediaries, primarily asset managers, are transmitted into listed companies mainly through shareholder activism and executive compensation and the resulting actual or perceived impact of such practices on share prices of listed companies. Consequently, the upstream short-term interests impact the actions of listed companies by causing company managers to forgo longer-term value maximization in favour shorter-term returns. As considered in Chapter 8, if SMST is transmitted into the listed company in this manner, any remedy to the SMST problem requires either addressing the excessive discounting issues around share pricing or cutting off these transmission mechanisms.

The second issue stemming from the conclusions drawn in Chapter 5 is that for SMST to be a material problem there needs to be some demonstrable harm. Particularly, why does it matter if company managers are consistently saying that they prioritize short-term returns? How is such prioritizing harmful? Chapter 7 discusses the difficulties around measuring the impacts of SMST, and analyzes the research conducted demonstrating the harms caused by SMST. This research identifies four key categories of harm: (1) reduced firm productivity, (2) reduced trust in the stock market, (3) societal costs, and (4) wealth transfer from future to current asset owners. Based on an assessment of the research in each category, the arguments (1) reduced firm productivity and (3) societal costs are rejected as a sufficiently viable basis justifying reform.

Although questions remain around the evidence presented in support of the arguments (2) reduced trust in the stock market, and (4) wealth transfer from future to current asset owners, these two arguments are the more probable areas of harm from SMST. Reduce trust in the stock market appears to occur due to the perception that investors unduly discount future returns. The wealth transfer concern is that short term financial gains are paid out to current shareholders. This payout is at the expense of developing sustainable long-term focused listed companies that create employment, develop valuable products and services, generate earnings, and return profits to shareholders. Consequently, Chapter 7 concludes that SMST appears to be detrimental, even if some investors may benefit in the short-term, as it results in executives failing to make decisions that yield financial success over the longer-term, to the detriment of employees, customers and the community at large. The analysis provided in Chapter 7, together with Chapters 5 and 6 provides the basis for the examination of the SMST reforms provided in Chapter 8.

Chapter 8 analyzes if the reforms identified in Chapter 4 solve the SMST issue. Based on the analysis in the previous chapters, this chapter presents a dual pathway for reform. This dual pathway provides that an effective remedy to the SMST problem involves either: (1) minimizing the excessive discounting of future returns; or (2) cutting off the transmission mechanisms of SMST into the listed company. Option (2) of this dual pathway requires 'hard' law reform. After examining the reforms, this chapter concludes that few of the SMST reforms set out in Chapter 4 adequately hit the mark and address the SMST issue. Further, of the implemented SMST reforms that do employ one of these options, most are disclosure-based, voluntary or limited in scope and proceed via Option (1) of the dual pathway either by reducing performance uncertainty or helping investors appreciate the harms of SMST. Given the inherent difficulty in effectively regulating to correct SMST, it is not surprising that the few implemented SMST reforms to date have been minimal and relatively 'light' touch. This chapter goes on to explore whether a focused 'light' touch approach may not be a bad idea, as 'light' touch measures are easier to implement than 'hard' law, and, in the case of regulatory reforms, provide scope for flexibility to minimize some of the many harms which may be associated with 'hard' law measures. This chapter advocates for a 'light' touch approach focused on Option (1) of the dual pathway.

Chapter 9 concludes that SMST reform should be considered in the context of the dual pathway for reform identified in Chapter 8. This analysis identifies Option (1) of the dual pathway, and in particular the two sub-paths in Option (1), namely Option 1(a)—reducing performance uncertainty, and Option 1(b) 'improving' asset owners discussed in Chapter 8, as the reform methods which employ a 'light' touch approach. This chapter concludes that a 'light' touch approach focused on Option (1) of the dual pathway guided by policymakers and implemented and supported by the financial industry may be the most effective method of 'nudging' capital markets away from their current short-term focus.

D. Limitations

This book focuses on short-termism in the context of capital markets. As discussed further in Chapter 2, short-termism is, however, a broad and nebulous concept. Short-termism has been considered generally in respect of human behaviour—i.e. the natural human tendency to seek out instant gratification[33]—, and in the context of numerous fields including, for example, politics,[34] sports[35] and marketing strategy.[36] The examination of short-termism as it relates to financial markets in this book is an important—but albeit only one—branch of inquiry. This research in this book is also further constrained by each of the limitations detailed below.

1. *Listed Companies Instead of Banking or Non-listed Companies*

The research in this book is intentionally limited to SMST in the context of publicly traded companies—also known as listed companies—, the equity securities of which are listed for trading on a recognized stock market. Each of the terms 'equity securities', 'listed company' and 'recognized stock market' are defined in Chapter 2. With respect to financial markets, short-termism has also been a significant part of the discussion resulting in enhanced regulation of the banking sector post-GFC.[37] The impact of short-termism of the banking industry raises special issues unique to the banking industry[38] that are beyond the scope of this book. Instead, the focus of this book has been on the short-termism of listed companies, which would include banks that list their equity securities on a stock market—for example, the Bank of New York Mellon Corporation the shares of which are listed on the New York Stock Exchange.

[33] Baumeister and Bushman (2010).

[34] For example, see Kuper (2012) and 'Now for the Long Term', The Report of the Oxford Martin Commission for Future Generations (October 2013). Online: http://www.oxfordmartin.ox.ac.uk/downloads/commission/Oxford_Martin_Now_for_the_Long_Term.pdf, which looks generally at short-termism in politics and business.

[35] Cooper (2014).

[36] Pate (2014).

[37] For example, see the discussion in Blair (2011).

[38] See the discussion in Dallas (2012) and Blair (2011).

The rationale for focusing on SMST in the context of the equity securities of listed companies rather than on private, semi-public, or public but non-listed companies[39]—referred to collectively in this book as 'non-listed companies'—is because, as will be demonstrated in Chapters 5 and 6, the SMST issue, at least conceptually, is transmitted through market pricing of the equity securities of listed companies. Non-listed companies lack a dynamic and liquid public market for their equity securities and, consequently, are not included in the research in this book.

2. *Equity Securities Rather Than Derivatives or Debt Instruments*

This book deliberately focuses on the equity securities of listed companies rather than debt instruments—i.e. bonds or debt-like preferred shares. A bond is a debt security that represents a fixed-income claim on the cash flows and assets of a company.[40] Bonds have considerable importance in global capital markets. The global bond market was worth approximately US$80 trillion in 2012.[41] By comparison, the equity market capitalization of listed companies in the same period was less, at approximately US$60 trillion during the same period.[42] Despite the significance of debt markets, short-termism is arguably not as significant a concern with these instruments, as it is with equity securities. Publicly traded debt securities—and debt-like preference shares—have clearly defined parameters, namely repayment timeframes and amounts and are generally non-voting. These securities appear less likely to have the same long-term valuation concerns that may arise with respect to equity securities which are discussed in Chapter 5, and also lack the requisite transmission mechanism into the listed company, which mechanisms are discussed in Chapter 6.

[39] There are public companies that are not listed on a recognized stock exchange and semi-public companies that elect to stay just under the shareholder number threshold which attracts public company reporting requirements. For a discussion of these distinctions in the US, see Coffee (2013).

[40] Thakor (2015, 1).

[41] Ibid.

[42] World Federation of Exchanges Database, 'Market capitalization of domestic listed companies – all countries and economies' (current US$). Online: http://data.worldbank.org/indicator/CM.MKT.LCAP.CD?end=2016&start=1975.

Like bonds, derivatives are also an additional important component of public capital markets. The value of over-the-counter derivatives at the end of 2013 was about US$710.2 trillion globally,[43] which is considerably higher than the combined amount of bond and equity global markets. A derivative in its simplest form is a security, the price of which is derived from an underlying asset—i.e. an equity security of a listed company.[44] A common example of a derivative is a futures contract, whereby one party wants security on the future price of equity securities of a listed company—e.g. 100 Apple shares—, and another party agrees to buy those 100 Apple shares at a set price on a pre-determined future date. However, despite the significance of the derivative market, trading in derivative instruments does not generally impact the prices of the listed company shares underlying such derivatives. Therefore, the interests of such derivative holders—and similarly non-voting debt instruments and preference shares—lack the requisite direct transmission mechanism into the listed company, which mechanisms are discussed in Chapter 6. Although SMST may manifest as pricing issues of derivatives, these issues would stem from the pricing issues inherent in the underlying equity securities. Consequently, derivatives are not excluded from this study, but rather focusing on SMST in respect of equity securities is the most feasible and logical method of tackling any potential SMST issues with derivatives, and derivatives instruments are not separately considered in this research. The focus of the research in this book is therefore on SMST in the context of equity securities of listed companies.

3. *Jurisdictional Limitations*

Of the US$65 trillion global market capitalization in 2016, approximately US$27.5 trillion was attributed to companies listed in the US, and a further approximately US$8 trillion was attributed to companies listed in the EU—of which approximately US$3 trillion was attributable to UK listed companies.[45] Although the survey in Chapter 4 has

[43] Thakor (2015, 1).

[44] See the definition of 'related party transaction' in Investopedia. Online: http://www.investopedia.com/terms/d/derivative.asp.

[45] World Federation of Exchanges Database, 'Market capitalization of domestic listed companies' (current US$). Online: http://data.worldbank.org/indicator/CM.MKT.LCAP.CD?end=2016&start=1975.

intentionally been as made broad as possible to capture all efforts to correct the SMST problem worldwide, the significant market capitalization of the US, the UK and the EU justifies an increased focus and analysis of the SMST discussion and the resulting SMST-driven financial industry and regulatory reforms in these jurisdictions.

4. *Rhetoric Not Substance*

Financial industry and regulatory reforms in which SMST rhetoric appears to be used in a manner unconnected to the intention of the reform are not included in the compilation of reforms in Chapter 4. As an example, the EU Amended Shareholder Rights Directive contains provisions meant to increase minority shareholder oversight on related party transactions.[46] Related party transactions are business transactions between one or more connected parties, which in the listed company context often involve deals between a listed company and its majority shareholders.[47] Such transactions may negatively impact minority shareholders.

The EU Amended Shareholder Rights Directive reforms are generally meant to strengthen long-term shareholder engagement and address the behaviour of institutional investors and asset managers who 'often do not engage properly with companies…and…exert pressure on companies to perform in the short term, which jeopardizes the long-term financial and non-financial performances of companies'.[48] Article 9c of the EU Amended Shareholder Rights Directive provides institutional investors and asset managers—parties which the EU has identified have short term interests—with additional rights in related party transactions. While providing such rights may serve a valid corporate governance function, doing so does not appear to be in any way connected to correcting the short-termism of such actors. Therefore, these EU related party transaction reforms, and other similar reforms which appear to use short-termism as rhetoric, are not included in the analysis in this book. Where

[46] See Article 9c of the EU Amended Shareholder Rights Directive regarding the voting, disclosure and third-party appraisal rights of minority shareholders in a related party transaction.

[47] See the definition of 'related party transaction' in www.investopedia.com.

[48] EU Amended Shareholder Rights Directive, Whereas Clause (9).

the impacts of the reforms on the SMST issue are less easy to discount—for example, with depositaries and proxy advisors—they are included in the consideration of SMST-driven reforms in Chapter 4.

5. *Intra-Company Operations*

It is certainly logical that the listed company response to the apparent short-termism of investors does not stop at company managers—i.e. the top-level decision makers in a listed company. The success of an organization depends on its activities at the operating level.[49] It follows that the actions of company managers and employees at the operating level may contribute to the perceived short-termism of listed companies, and this level of operations of a listed company would need to be included in any effective corrective efforts. However, intra-company relationships are unlikely to pursue short-term goals without a queue from the senior management of a listed company. Consequently, SMST implications of intra-company operations are intentionally excluded from the scope of analysis of this book.

6. *Time Limitations*

Of necessity, the analysis in this book has been restricted to reforms in place, or proposed, at the time of writing. The rapid pace of change in modern financial markets, and ongoing political uncertainty, in particular the UK's decision to exit the EU, may drastically impact the focus of financial market reform. As a result, the heightened attention given to SMST in the years since the GFC may wane as a motivator for financial market reform. However, as demonstrated in Chapter 3, the SMST conversation has been developing for over forty years and is unlikely to disappear entirely from policymaker and boardroom agendas. Consequently, it is intended that the analysis in this book will be helpful to analyze current SMST-driven reforms and reform proposals, and when SMST is inevitably raised in the future as a rationale for financial industry or regulatory reform.

[49] See the discussion of the significant of operating units in Rappaport (2011, 114–116), and generally in Koller (1994).

References

Atkins, Ralph and Williamson, Hugh. 2007. "Call to Resist Anglo-American Model of 'Short-termism'." 26 April. *Financial Times.*

Barton, Dominic. 2011. "Capitalism for the Long Term." March. *Harvard Business Review.* 84–90.

Barton, Dominic and Wiseman, Mark. 2014. "Focusing Capital on the Long Term." January–February. *Harvard Business Review.* 44–51.

Baumeister Roy, F. and Bushman, Brad J. 2010. *Social Psychology and Human Nature.* 2nd ed. Wadworth.

Bena, Jan, Ferreia, Miguel A., Matos, Pedro, and Pires, Pedro. 2017. "Are Foreign Investors Locusts? The Long-Term Effects of Foreign Institutional Ownership." 126 *Journal of Financial Economics.* 122–146.

Blair, Shelia. 2011. "Lessons of the Financial Crisis: The Dangers of Short-Termism." 4 July. *Harvard Law School Forum on Corporate Governance and Financial Regulation.* https://corpgov.law.harvard.edu/2011/07/04/lessons-of-the-financial-crisis-the-dangers-of-short-termism/.

Bowdren, Andrea. 2016. "Contextualising Short-Termism: Does the Corporate Legal Landscape Facilitate Managerial Myopia?" 5:2 *UCL Journal of Law and Jurisprudence.* 285–312.

Brecht, Kira. 2015. "How U.S. and EU Capital Markets are Different." 29 October. http://openmarkets.cmegroup.com/10431/how-u-s-and-eu-capital-markets-are-different.

Coffee, John C. 2013. "The Challenge of the Semi-Public Companies." 1 April. *The CLS Blue Sky Blog.* http://clsbluesky.law.columbia.edu/2013/04/01/the-challenge-of-the-semi-public-company/.

Cooper, Joe. 2014. "Short-Termism's Damaging Effect on the Premier League." 7 May. *HuffPost.* http://www.huffingtonpost.co.uk/joe-cooper/premier-league-short-termism_b_4904887.html.

Dallas, Lynne L. 2012. "Short-Termism, the Financial Crisis, and Corporate Governance" 2011–2012. 37:2 *The Journal of Corporation Law.* 265–364.

Fink, Larry. 2018. CEO Letter, BlackRock, Inc. January. https://www.blackrock.com/corporate/investor-relations/larry-fink-ceo-letter.

Grant, Jeremy and Kirchmaier, Thomas. 2004. "Corporate Ownership and Performance in Europe." April. Centre for Economic Performance, CEP Discussion Paper No. 632.

Haldane, Andrew and Richards, Davies. 2011. "The Short-Long". Speech at the 29th Société Universitaire Européene de Recherches Financières Colloquium: New Paradigms in Money and Finance? May. Brussels.

Hansmann, Henry and Kraakman, Reinier. 2017. "Chapter 3: The End of History for Corporate Law." In Mitchell, Lawrence E. (ed.). *Corporate Governance: Values Ethics and Leadership.* Taylor & Francis Group.

Jacobs, Ben. 2015. "Hillary Clinton Decries Wall Street's 'Quarterly Capitalism' in Tax Reform Pitch." 24 July. *The Guardian.*

Johnston, Andrew and Morrow, Paige. 2014. "Commentary on the Shareholder Rights Directive." University of Oslo Faculty of Law Research Paper No. 2014-41.

Kay, John. 2012. "The Kay Review of UK Equity Markets and Long-Term Decision Making." Final Report. July.

Koller, Timothy. 1994. "What Is Value-Based Management?" August. *McKinsey Quarterly*. http://www.mckinsey.com/business-functions/strategy-and-corporate-finance/our-insights/what-is-value-based-management.

Kraakman, Reinier, et al. 2009. *The Anatomy of Corporate Law: A Comparative and Functional Approach.* 2nd ed. Oxford University Press: Oxford.

Kuper, Jeremy. 2012. "Working Lives: Political Short-Termism Perpetuates the Housing Crisis." 3 October. *The Guardian.* https://www.theguardian.com/housing-network/2012/oct/03/jeremy-kuper-shelter-political-short-termism.

Lipton, Martin. 2006. "Taking Short-Termism Seriously: A Response to Charles Nathan." *Harvard Law School Forum on Corporate Governance and Financial Regulation.* 13 September. https://corpgov.law.harvard.edu/2016/09/13/taking-short-termism-seriously-a-response-to-charles-nathan/.

Lipton, Martin, et al. 2019. "It's Time to Adopt the New Paradigm." *Harvard Law School Forum on Corporate Governance and Financial Regulation.* 11 February. https://corpgov.law.harvard.edu/2019/02/11/its-time-to-adopt-the-new-paradigm/.

Nachemson-Ekwall, Sophie. 2017. "Swedish Institutional Investors as Large Stake Owners: Enhancing Sustainable Stakeholder Capitalism." 255–276. In Kallifatides, M. and Lerpold, L. (eds.). *Sustainable Development and Business.* SSE Institute for Research (SIR).

Oyedele, Akin. 2017. "Here Is the Letter the World's Largest Investor, BlackRock CEO Larry Fink, Just Sent to CEOs Everywhere." 24 January. *Business Insider UK.* http://uk.businessinsider.com/blackrock-ceo-larry-fink-letter-to-ceos-2017-1?r=US&IR=T.

Pate, Neil. 2014. "The Psychology of Instant Gratification and How It Will Revolutionize Your Marketing Approach." 24 June. *The Entrepreneur.* https://www.entrepreneur.com/article/235088.

Rappaport, Alfred. 2011. *Saving Capitalism from Short-Termism: How to Build Long-Term Value and Take Back our Financial Future.* New York: McGraw-Hill.

Roe, Mark J. 2013. "Corporate Short-Termism—In the Boardroom and in the Courtroom." August. 68. *Business Lawyer.* 977–1006.

Strine, Leo E., Jr. 2015. "Securing Our Nation's Economic Future: A Sensible, Nonpartisan Agenda to Increase Long-Term Investment and Job Creation in The United States." University of Pennsylvania Institute for Law & Economics Research Paper No. 15–41.

Surowiecki, James. 2015. "The Short-Termism Myth." 24 August 2015. *The New Yorker.* http://www.newyorker.com/magazine/2015/08/24/the-short-termism-myth.

Thakor, Anjan. 2015. "International Financial Markets: A Diverse System Is the Key to Commerce." Winter. Center for Capital Market Competitiveness. http://www.centerforcapitalmarkets.com/wp-content/uploads/2013/08/021881_SourcesofCapital_fin.pdf.

The Modern Corporation: Corporate Governance for the 21st Century. Statement on Economics. https://themoderncorporation.wordpress.com/economics-and-msv/.

Thornhill, John. 2016. "Rewrite Tax Regimes to Spur Greater Investment." 6 December 2016. *Financial Times.*

Turner, Matt. 2016. "Here Is the Letter the World's Largest Investor, BlackRock CEO Larry Fink, Just Sent to CEOs Everywhere." 2 February. *Business Insider UK.* http://uk.businessinsider.com/blackrock-ceo-larry-fink-letter-to-sp-500-ceos-2016-2?r=US&IR=T.

CHAPTER 2

Defining the Issues

This chapter provides a detailed definition of perceived short-termism in the context of stock market equity investing and defines terms relevant to such short-termism. Articulations of the term 'short-termism' generally, and its narrower form of short-termism in the context of stock market investing, are first examined, and a definition of the 'stock market short-termism' (SMST) problem is then provided. There is considerable discussion amongst academics, policy makers and the financial industry and in the popular press about SMST, and why and if SMST is in fact problematic. There have been some efforts to define the concept. However, further efforts to define the term with precision are warranted. Therefore, this chapter attempts to attempts to narrow the discussion of short-termism into a precise articulation of the short-termism issue. This definition is then used to identify and analyze the SMST-driven reforms in Chapter 4.

Salient terms relevant to the definition of SMST including 'stock market', 'listed company', 'equity security', and the financial intermediation chain—defined in this chapter as the 'equity ownership chain'—are considered and defined in this chapter. Each of the key components of the equity ownership chain—articulated as asset owners, intermediaries and company managers—and their relationship to the definition of SMST, are separately analyzed. Though there is undoubtedly overlap of the SMST issues in each component, this separation facilitates an examination of how the SMST problem manifests in each main element of the equity ownership chain. Further, the focus of the study in this book is

K. M. Willey, *Stock Market Short-Termism*,
https://doi.org/10.1007/978-3-030-22903-0_2

on regulatory—and to a lesser degree, financial industry—reforms aimed at correcting the SMST problem so defined. Therefore, I also examine a distinction particularly relevant to regulatory reform, namely the difference between 'hard' and 'soft' law. Each of the definitions provided in this chapter frame the analysis of the SMST-driven reforms set out in the following chapters.

A. Defining SMST

Many articles in the popular and financial press accept as a given that short termism behaviour in stock markets is not only occurring, but that it is problematic. Headlines such as 'Short-Termism is a Wolf Stalking the Equity Market'[1] are emblematic of this pervasive popular opinion. For the third year running, Larry Fink, Chief Executive Officer (CEO) of BlackRock Inc. (BlackRock), the world's largest asset management firm, denounced short-termism, and put out a call to action against SMST which has generated considerable press.[2]

Despite the popularity of this opinion, many questions have been raised about SMST.[3] These questions include: Is there short-termism in capital markets at all? If so, who is receiving the benefits of management's focus on short-term financial returns? Who is harmed by this short-term focus? If short-termism is occurring, what is driving this short-term behaviour in stock markets? Is it company managers, intermediaries, or asset owners, or a combination of some or all of them, causing the short-term focus? If SMST is primarily caused by asset owner pressure—as is often argued by company managers[4]—why are asset owners with long-term investment horizons encouraging short-term investment

[1] Walker (2014).

[2] Turner (2016), Oyedele (2017), and Fink (2018).

[3] Most notably see Roe (2013, 977), where Harvard Law Professor Mark Roe acknowledges that US markets may be net short-termist—although Roe finds the evidence unconvincing as stock markets often value the long-term—, but that this short-termism is mitigated in the US economy as a whole—e.g. by private equity. Consequently, Roe argues that there is no justification for regulation to correct SMST.

[4] For example, see CPP and McKinsey (2013), referencing a Canada Pension Plan (CPP) and McKinsey & Company (McKinsey) international survey of directors and CEOs where 79% of directors and senior executives said they felt the most pressure to demonstrate strong financial performance over a time period of less than two years.

strategies, which strategies appear ultimately harmful to their own long-term interests?[5] This chapter examines questions around the SMST issue and clarifies what SMST means in the context of this book.

1. *Short-Termism Generally*

As observed in Chapter 1,[6] short-termism is a broad and nebulous concept based on the natural human predisposition to seek out instant gratification. Quick decision-making undoubtedly has its merits, but the problematic behaviour identified is the human propensity to make impulsive decisions for immediate benefit at the expense of our longer-term best interests. Professor John Kay describes this behaviour as our "natural human tendency to make decisions in search of immediate gratification at the expense of future returns: decisions we subsequently regret."[7] Generally, Kay claims that this tendency manifests in actions where "[w]e speak and act in the heat of the moment, we eat and drink too much, and we do not save enough."[8]

Warnings of the perils of short-termism abound in literature—e.g. the fables of the Tortoise and the Hare and the Boy Who Cried Wolf. Kay provided the example of Ulysses tied to the masts to avoid the calls of the sirens as an illustration of the difficulties humans face in overcoming alluring short-term rewards.[9] This apparent inclination for short-term reward is perhaps most noticeable in the behaviour of young children. It may be said that a common objective of most parents is to encourage children to appreciate longer-term value—e.g. the benefits of eating a healthy meal over the immediate gratification of sweet treats. The Stanford marshmallow experiment,[10] and the resulting adorable videos of young children fighting their primal instincts for instant gratification when faced with the choice of eating "one marshmallow now in place of

[5] Question asked by in a discussion paper of the Initiative for Responsible Investment (2016, 2), which paper also asserts that institutional investors help create the short-termism problem by rewarding managers and companies for short-term behaviour.

[6] See Chapter 1, Sect. D.

[7] Kay (2012, 14).

[8] Ibid.

[9] Ibid.

[10] Walter et al. (1972).

two later",[11] is a popular illustration of the parental challenge of the difficulty of overcoming natural human short-term impulses. Though most evident in children, adults are not immune to short-termism behaviours, particularly when it comes to the time pay-offs of stock market investing.

Andrew Haldane, Chief Economist of the Bank of England, observed that allegations of short-termism in capital markets are certainly not new, and classical economists such as William Stanley Jevons, Alfred Marshall, Arthur Pigou and John Maynard Keynes have all grappled with the implications of the human tendency to prefer instant gratification and discount future outcomes.[12] Arthur Pigou, for example, stated that humans have a "defective telescopic faculty" such that "we see future pleasures on a diminished scale."[13]

More recently, neuroscientists have attempted to place this 'defective telescopic faculty' in an anatomical context, and have identified that different parts of the brain are responsible for valuing short-term and long-term monetary payoffs.[14] Using magnetic resonance imaging, neuroscientists have observed that from a neuroscience perspective, when the choice involves an immediate gain, the medial pre-frontal cortex—a part of the brain associated with automatic, emotional thinking that is connected to the mid-brain dopamine system—is used disproportionately, in other words, it feels good to obtain short-term results. The same process reveals that when the decision involves a delayed reward, a different calculating part of the brain—the parietal cortex—is used to make a more rational and patient choice. This part of the brain does not produce the same good feeling. Consequently, it may be said that our brains are 'hard-wired' to cause us to prefer short-term results.[15]

But this 'hard-wiring' in our brains does not mean that we cannot overcome our supposedly anatomically driven human inclinations towards short-term gratification. Behavioural economics theory attempts to understand these natural inclinations—often termed biases—and adjust such undesirable behaviour through a variety of means including legal and financial industry reforms. Behavioural economics is essentially

[11] For example, see the IntegratedMedia.com video (24 September 2009) available on YouTube. Online: https://www.youtube.com/watch?v=QX_oy9614HQ.

[12] Haldane and Davies (2011, 2).

[13] Ibid.

[14] See Knustson et al. (2005) and Onoda et al. (2011).

[15] See the summary of these neurological studies in Behavioural Finance (2015).

a field of study in the social and behavioural sciences developed from cognitive psychology, which field of research has gained traction in inter-disciplinary research in recent years. Based primarily on psychological experimentation, research in this area aims to develop theories on human decision-making, which are based largely around biases inherent in human behaviour and apply such theories to real world circumstances—for example, personal and public finance, health, energy, and marketing.[16]

As considered further in Chapter 8,[17] behavioural economists have discussed how law can be used to de-bias certain behaviours, either by restricting undesirable behaviours—e.g. the controls on gambling—, or by reducing undesirable behaviours by offering guidance towards the desired outcome—e.g. compelling disclosure on boardroom diversity.[18] Consequently, although a bias towards instant gratification in decision-making may be hard-wired, there is hope that any negative effects in the context of stock market investing could be corrected or at least 'nudged' through appropriately structured regulatory or financial industry actions.

Translated generally into a business context, Kay asserted in the Kay Review[19] that "short-termism occurs when companies invest too little, either in the physical assets of their business or in the intangibles which are generally the course of their competitive advantage – their reputation, their capacity for innovation, and in skills and capabilities of their employees."[20] The question is how this natural human tendency to prefer short-term rewards translates into the type of short-termism seen in capital markets and railed against by financial industry leaders such as Larry Fink, CEO of BlackRock, Ronald O'Hanley, president and CEO of State Street Investors, and William McNabb, Chairman and CEO of Vanguard.[21] It is possible that these asset management giants may want to be seen to be doing something about an area of growing public concern, rather than be substantially invested in resolving the issue. Regardless of such intentions, answering the question about how the

[16] See further discussion in Loewenstein (2014).

[17] Chapter 8, Sect. C.

[18] Jolls and Sunstein (2006).

[19] Kay (2012).

[20] Ibid., 14.

[21] Tulay (2017).

human tendency for short-term reward translates into the context of stock market investing is at the crux of satisfactorily defining and assessing the SMST problem.

2. *Short-Termism in Equity Capital Markets*

This subsection analyzes how short-termism has been defined in relation to equity capital markets. As demonstrated below, many definitions of short-termism in stock markets have been presented and examples of short-term behaviour provided. However, considerable uncertainty still exists on what constitutes short-termism in equity capital markets. For example, Charles Nathan, of the financial services consultancy firm, Finsbury, observed that a complicating factor in this discussion on short-termism is the uncertainty on whether the debate should be about investor behaviour or objectives, or corporate behaviour or objectives.[22] Is it investors that are behaving in a short-term manner by holding shares for shorter time periods, or is it companies that are prioritizing short-term financial objectives, such as quarterly earnings per share? As an example of the wide range of activities that fall under the short-termism umbrella, the US Trustee Leadership Forum offered a list of short-term activities which included trading practices such as high frequency trading (HFT),[23] pressure from activist investors, leveraged buy-outs, short-selling, CEO pay tied to share price, and money manager incentives based on short-term performance.[24]

Given the broad assortment of activities associated with short-termism—which arguably constitutes many of the features of modern capital markets—, it is necessary to pin down a workable definition of SMST that concisely articulates the perceived problem and its causation. Having greater clarity around what constitutes stock market short-termism is an essential cornerstone for analyzing if there is in fact a

[22] Nathan (2015).

[23] HFT includes a number of characteristics, but essentially means using sophisticated technological tools and computer algorithms to rapidly trade securities (Dallas 2012, 299). The short-termism concerns of HFT have been articulated as the costs of such trades which erode ultimate saver value (Aspen Institute 2009, 2), and create a negative trend in equity markets favoring securities trading over building trust relationships (Kay 2012, 39).

[24] Initiative for Responsible Investment (2016, 1).

SMST problem and whether the reforms discussed in chapter do at least conceptually address the perceived SMST issue.

As set out above, broad allegations of short-termism in capital markets are certainly not new, although there has been a spike of interest since the global financial crisis (GFC).[25] The profile of the short-termism problem as it relates to equity capital markets has arguably been raised post-GFC given the increased inter-connectedness and rapid pace of change in modern equity capital markets,[26] which was highlighted by the GFC. As will be demonstrated in Chapter 3, there has been much discussion on short-termism and why short-termism has been seen as problematic in the context of capital markets. These discussions have undoubtedly been influenced by the relevant political issues of the day—e.g. takeovers in the 1980s, national competitiveness in the 1990s, and concerns about market vulnerability post-GFC—which is explored further in Chapter 3. Although short-termism was discussed vaguely prior to the GFC, numerous broad definitions have been articled post-GFC, possibly in response to the widespread nature of the harms caused by the GFC. For example, the *Financial Times* defines it as "an excessive focus on short-term results at the expense of long-term interests."[27] A Barclays' report on short-termism defines it as "our tendency to constantly be solving today's problems rather than taking a long-term view."[28] These definitions have captured the imagination of corporate commentators, but are not particularly helpful in articulating the harms or causation of short-termism.

Lynne Dallas offered a more detailed definition of short-termism as it relates to capital markets. She defined SMST as "the excessive focus of corporate managers, asset managers, investors, and analysts on short-term results, whether quarterly earnings or short-term portfolio returns, and a repudiation of concern for long-term value creation and the fundamental value of firms."[29] Similarly, J. W. Mason released a report with the Roosevelt Institute defining short-termism as "the focus on short-term horizons by both corporate managers and financial markets, prioritizing near-term shareholder interests over the long-term growth of

[25] See the search results in Fig. 1, in Chapter 1.

[26] See opening remarks in the speech by Haldane and Davies (2011, 1).

[27] http://lexicon.ft.com.

[28] Barclays (2015, 3).

[29] Dallas (2012, 268).

the firm."[30] Both Dallas and Mason's definitions articulate that the perceived problem is the excessive focus on short-term results, but neither explain exactly what is problematic about doing so that jeopardizes long-term growth of the firm. Further, Dallas's definition suggests that the long-term and fundamental values of listed companies are 'repudiated'. Arguably this is an unhelpful value judgment on the behaviour of corporate managers, which would be difficult, if not impossible to substantiate, as doing so would require demonstrating that corporate managers are unconcerned about long-term value or have taken the effort to 'repudiate' such long-term and fundamental values.

Harvard Law Professor Mark Roe, noted for his claims that SMST is exaggerated,[31] offered clarity around what is problematic about favouring short-term returns. He articulates the SMST issue as corporate directors and managers favoring 'immediate but *lower-value* results over *more profitable* long-term results'[32]—emphasis mine. Authors from *The Economist*—Richard Davies—and the Bank of England—including Andrew Haldane, Chief Economist—bulk up Roe's definition and provide additional clarity on how this short-term preference translates into behaviours at the firm level. Davies et al. claim that the problem is caused by "agents in the financial intermediation chain weighing *near-term outcomes too heavily* at the expense of longer-term opportunities and *thus forgoing valuable investment projects and potential output*"[33]—emphasis mine. They provide evidence in support of this reasoning demonstrating systematic and increasing excessive discounting of future returns in United States (US) and United Kingdom (UK) stock markets.[34] This evidence, and the harms of SMST, are assessed further in Chapters 5 and 7. However, the heart of the argument presented by Davies et al., and included in Roe's articulation of the SMST issue, is that short-termism results in investors as a whole receiving lower financial return in the short-term over greater financial benefit in the future.

Assuming that short-termism is harmful to listed companies, and by extension to their investors and broader constituent elements, such as

[30] Mason (2015, 4).

[31] Roe (2013, 2016), in which Mr. Roe claims that short-termism is a chimera, which has turned into a bigger political issue than it deserves to be.

[32] Roe (2013, 981).

[33] Davies et al. (2014, 16).

[34] See Chapter 5, Sect. A.3.

employees and customers, the definition of SMST also needs to identify causation. There is considerable discussion about what is driving short-termism in capital markets, which is considered in Chapter 5. However, the basis of the argument presented in this book is that if a short-termism problem exists, it is mainly caused by asset owners, and intermediaries who act on asset owner's behalf, preferring short-term returns. This preference is then transmitted to company managers through a variety of methods, as explored in Chapter 6. Consequently, SMST is defined in this book as asset owners and intermediaries in the equity ownership chain—as is defined below[35]—weighing near-term financial outcomes too heavily at the expense of more profitable longer-term investment opportunities. This weighing causes company managers of listed companies to take actions that prioritize short-term financial returns to the detriment of the listed company and by extension its broader constituent elements. Though certain activities in capital markets may be short-term oriented in a temporal sense—such as HFT—the capital market reforms meant to address short-termism are only analyzed against the definition of SMST provided in this book. Such analysis of the SMST reforms also requires further explanation of the salient stock market terminology discussed below.

B. Stock Market Terminology

1. *Stock Markets*

This book focuses on perceived short-termism as it relates to organizations that have equity securities listed for public trading on a 'recognized' stock market—defined in this book as a 'stock market'—, which are also known as 'stock exchanges' or 'equity markets.' The complete list of 'recognized' stock markets varies from jurisdiction to jurisdiction.[36] However, 'recognized' stock exchanges essentially include all of the major stock markets in the world, most of which—other than the

[35] See Sect. B.

[36] See for example, the list of designated recognized exchanges provided by the UK Government in respect of Section 1005 of the UK Income Tax Act 2007. Online: https://www.gov.uk/government/uploads/system/uploads/attachment_data/file/552552/table1-rse2016.pdf.

London Stock Exchange (LSE)[37]—are members of the World Federation of Stock Exchanges.[38] The majority of the largest stock markets[39] are private sectors enterprises that compete nationally and globally for business.

The two primary functions of a stock market are to: (1) provide liquidity to investors based on reasonably reliable pricing; and, (2) facilitate the raising of capital by listed companies.[40] The reliability of share prices of listed companies is discussed in detail in Chapter 5.[41] For the purpose of defining stock markets, it suffices here to say that stock markets facilitate their two primary functions—liquidity and capital raising—by providing a trading platform whereby investors can achieve liquidity for their investments, and also companies with appealing growth prospects may be able to raise significant amounts of capital in the primary market from a large pool of public investors.[42] Evidencing their commitment to this trading role, two of the world's largest stock markets, the New York Stock Exchange (NYSE) and National Association of Securities Dealers Automated Quotations (NASDAQ),[43] each have corporate strategic objectives focused on providing technology, products and services to facilitate trading. The existence of a large number of investors, at least theoretically, is meant to lower the investment risk for all investors in the listed company and, thus, the cost of capital for the listed company, as each investor is not required to invest as much as they would need to do in a non-listed company.[44] Given this large pool of investors and a liquid secondary market among such investors, listed companies are, theoretically at least, able to raise large amounts of capital

[37] Stafford (2013).

[38] www.world-exchanges.org.

[39] Of the top ten stock markets based on market capitalization, only the Chinese stock markets (Shanghai Stock Exchange and Shenzhen Stock Exchange) were government owned. The remaining stock markets are themselves publicly listed (e.g. LSE and NYSE) or owned by a group of private investors (e.g. Tokyo Stock Exchange)—Simpson (2011).

[40] Cleary (2015, 6), and see definition of 'stock exchange' at www.businessdictionary.com.

[41] See Chapter 5, Sect. B.

[42] Ibid.

[43] The NYSE and NASDAQ are the first and second largest stock exchanges in the world, respectively, based on market capitalization as at 31 January 2015 (www.world-exchanges.org).

[44] Cleary (2015, 6).

for activities with time horizons that may exceed the horizons of individual investors.[45]

Arguably the role of stock markets as a capital raising mechanism is diminishing in importance.[46] However, the liquidity function based on reliable pricing continues to serve a valid purpose. Properly functioning stock markets may reduce investing risk by providing liquidity for asset owners and asset managers.[47] and a viable exit option for company founders and other early stage investors.[48] Another useful, but perhaps often over-looked function of stock markets, is that listed companies provide a benchmarking tool for private company valuations. Consequently, though the focus of this book is on listed companies, it is worth briefly highlighting the contribution made to the economy generally by private companies, to demonstrate the benefits that a well-functioning public equities market provides to non-listed companies in the private sector.

Non-listed companies are important because they contribute significantly to employment and gross domestic product (GDP) growth in most developed countries. In the US, for example, out of the 27 million US businesses, less than 6300[49] were publicly traded on the major US exchanges in 2012.[50] The remainder of US business was privately held, and these businesses generated a majority of new jobs and more than half of the US GDP in 2012.[51] Stock markets play an important role in

[45] Ibid.

[46] See the Kay (2012, 22), where Professor Kay observes that "[e]quity markets have not been an important source of capital for new investment in British business for many years…[l]arge UK companies are self-financing – the cash flow they obtain from operations through profits and depreciation is more than sufficient for their investment needs". Also, in the US, which accounts for almost half of global market capitalization, the number of listed companies has fallen from 8090 in 1996 to 4331 in 2016 World Federation of Exchanges database, 'Listed domestic companies, total'. Online: http://data.worldbank.org/indicator/CM.MKT.LDOM.NO?locations=US&name_desc=true.

[47] Arestis et al. (2001, 18).

[48] See the Kay (2012, 28), where Professor Kay observes that "[e]quity markets today should primarily be seen as a means of getting money out of companies rather than a means of putting it in".

[49] There were 4331 domestic US companies publicly trading on recognized US stock exchanges in 2016 World Federation of Exchanges Database, Total US Listed Domestic Companies. Online: http://data.worldbank.org/indicator/CM.MKT.LDOM.NO?locations=US.

[50] Biery (2012).

[51] Ibid.

ensuring that the private sector is viable. In addition to the capital raising and liquidity—including exit options for early investors—functions, a liquid, properly functioning stock market is also useful as a benchmarking tool for non-listed companies.

The simplest method of estimating non-listed company value is to use comparable company analysis (CCA).[52] CCA involves finding public markets for firms which most closely resemble the private firm, and basing valuation estimates on the values at which the private company's publicly-traded peers are traded.[53] CCA assists with accurately valuing private companies, which valuations are useful in a range of private company financial transactions including share and debt issuances, credit facilities and merger and acquisitions transactions. The impact of the SMST problem on proper stock market functioning is considered further in the following chapters. In particular, Chapter 7 examines whether SMST is degrading the quality of stock markets, consequently impacting the ability of stock markets to fulfill their primary liquidity and capital raising functions, as well as their important valuation role.[54]

2. *Listed Company*

As discussed in Chapter 1,[55] this book focuses on short-termism exclusively as it relates to listed companies rather than non-listed companies. As will be demonstrated in Chapters 5 and 6, this focus is because the SMST issue, at least conceptually, is transmitted through market pricing of the equity securities of listed companies. Non-listed companies lack a dynamic and liquid public market for their equity securities and, consequently, are not specifically included in the research in this book. Listed companies go by various names in different jurisdictions—e.g. quoted companies or publicly-traded or publicly-quoted companies. However, the term 'listed company' is used in this book to specifically mean a legal entity the equity securities of which are listed—or quoted—for public trading on a stock market, as defined above.[56]

[52] 'Valuing Private Companies' Investopedia. 16 November 2016. Online: http://www.investopedia.com/articles/fundamental-analysis/11/valuing-private-companies.asp.

[53] Ibid.

[54] See Chapter 7, Sect. B.

[55] See Chapter 1, Sect. D.1.

[56] See http://lexicon.ft.com/Term?term=listed-company.

Listed companies are materially significant to most major national economies, and the global economy. The combined global market capitalization of listed companies has been increasing—with fluctuations most notably during the GFC—, and the total market capitalization of all listed companies had risen to almost US$65 trillion in 2016.[57] On a national level, domestically listed companies also have considerable economic impact. For example, UK listed companies employed approximately 3.7 million people—equating to about 16% of private sector employment—, and also accounted for approximately 47% of domestic investment in 2011.[58] In the US, statistics on the cumulative impact of listed companies are not as readily accessible. However, employment by S&P 500 companies[59] increased as a share of US non-farm payroll employment, from 15% in 1990 to 17.3% in 2015—although such increase may include non-US based employees. Regardless, the financial significance of US listed companies—for example, Apple Inc. (NASDAQ: AAPL), Microsoft Corporation (NASDAQ: MSFT), Exxon Mobile Corporation (NYSE: XOM) and General Electric (NYSE: GE)—to the US national economy, and globally, is apparent. Assessing the impact of short-termism on listed companies is, therefore, a meritorious endeavour.

3. *Equity Securities*

Investors may hold a wide range of publicly tradable interests in listed companies—generally classed as debt,[60] equity, and derivative[61] securities. However, it is the equity securities of listed companies that are of particular interest in the short-termism discussion, and specifically voting common shares, also known as common stock. The term 'equity security' as used in this book refers to this type of equity securities. Equity securities are essentially a publicly traded contractual and statutory

[57] World Federation of Exchanges Database, 'Market capitalization of domestic listed companies – all countries and economies' (current US$). Online: http://data.worldbank.org/indicator/CM.MKT.LCAP.CD?end=2016&start=1975.

[58] Promoting Long-Term Wealth (2017, 7).

[59] The S&P 500 is an index of 500 stocks seen by Standard & Poor's, a US financial analysis firm, as a leading indicator of US equities (Investopedia, Online: http://www.investopedia.com/terms/s/sp500.asp).

[60] See the discussion of debt securities and the definition of 'bond' in Chapter 1.

[61] See the definition of 'derivative' in Chapter 1.

interest in a listed company comprising a bundle of rights. These rights most typically include voting rights in respect of significant matters of the listed company—such as the election of the board of directors—, rights to receive dividends out of earnings of the listed company as declared by the board of directors, and a right to receive a proportional interest in any assets of the listed company remaining after payment to all creditors upon dissolution or liquidation of the listed company.[62]

The prices at which equity securities are bought or sold on a stock market are—at least theoretically—linked to the stock market's expectation of the present value of the risk-adjusted future returns of the listed company—i.e. the expected future value of any payments to the holders of the equity securities.[63] As set out in Chapter 5, it is this assessment of the future value of payments by the listed company, and the resulting impact on the trading prices of equity securities, that raises potential SMST concerns. Consequently, as discussed further in Chapter 1,[64] the analysis in this book is limited to the equity securities of listed companies. Debt instruments, including preference shares with debt-like terms,[65] commonly have their payment parameters fixed at the time of issuance, and are, therefore, less likely to generate the same SMST concerns discussed in this book. Furthermore, short-termism related to derivative instruments—and non-voting debt instruments and preference shares—are excluded as such short-termism lacks a clear transmission mechanism into the listed company given that these instruments generally do not have voting rights.

[62] See http://www.investopedia.com/terms/c/commonstock.asp for a discussion of the term 'equity securities'. Also, see Berle and Means (1932) as discussed at Alces (2010, 791), where the author describes Berle & Means identification of shareholders as the 'owners' of the residual interest in the firm. This identification by Berle & Means forms the basis for the influential—although much debated—shareholder primacy theory. This theory provides that the goal of corporate management should be to maximize value for shareholders given that in doing so the value of the firm's wealth, which equates to the residual claim, will increase and is discussed further in Chapters 3 and 6.

[63] Articulations of this concept abound, but it is perhaps best summarized by noted US economist Burton Malkiel (2016, 31–33).

[64] See Chapter 1, Sect. D.2.

[65] Preference shares may be structured with defined dividend payments, redemption prices and a specified liquidation preference, which makes these types of financial instruments less susceptible to the valuation concerns raised in Chapter 5 in respect of equity securities generally.

C. Equity Ownership Chain

The equity ownership chain connecting listed companies with their ultimate investors is complex. In order to explain how the main elements of this equity ownership chain create the SMST concerns, I have divided the equity ownership chain into three functional sub-sets. As illustrated in Fig. 1, these three functional sub-sets may generally be classed as:

1. asset owners;
2. intermediaries; and
3. company managers.

The activities of individual market participants admittedly may not perfectly delineate into these three orderly sub-sets, as a single firm in the equity ownership chain may supply more than one role. For example, asset owners may serve an intermediary function by also providing asset management services in-house—e g. Blackrock is an asset owner, but it also provides a significant asset management role to third parties. The division of the equity ownership chain into these three functional sub-sets is beneficial, however, as it facilitates further analysis on how the SMST issue may impact each role.

Understanding how this equity ownership chain functions is important, because, as aptly stated by the UK governance think-tank, Tomorrow's Company, this intermediation chain "does not simply allocate savers' funds, it also helps determine how the assets owned on their

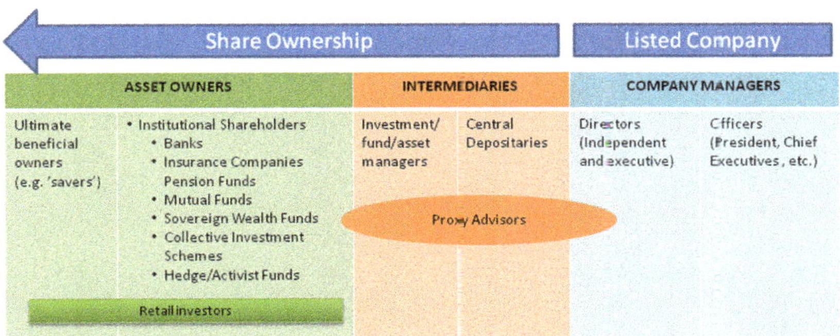

Fig. 1 Equity ownership chain

behalf are run."[66] In the equity ownership chain, asset owners cede control to asset managers, who in turn do not hold shares of a listed company directly. Rather, shares are generally registered in the name of a central depositary, and instructions to the listed company on significant voting matters may need to flow through this central depositary. This equity ownership chain undoubtedly has benefits for asset owners. Kay observed that financial intermediation serves a valuable purpose as it, "enables savers to achieve diversification and liquidity."[67] Particularly, asset managers can pool multiple clients' funds, purchase a wide range of securities and offer clients the ability to quickly redeem their investment based on their own liquidity needs. Theoretically, at least, the ultimate purpose of this equity ownership chain is to achieve the best possible financial returns for asset owners.

The benefits provided by financial intermediation are, however, not without a cost. Kay argued that "[t]he price for diversification and liquidity is a loss of information and control."[68] Observations have also been made that "[o]ver the past few decades, the link between individual savers and the companies that ultimately benefit from their capital has become tenuous as the chain of intermediation has lengthened considerably."[69] It is this increasing disconnection and complexity between ownership and control which may create or exacerbate short-termism concerns, as discussed further in this book.

1. *Asset Owners*

The term 'asset owners', often called shareholders, investors or asset holders,[70] describes the parties holding the economic ownership interest in the equity securities. Asset owners may be institutional investors—including sovereign wealth funds, mutual funds, insurance companies,

[66] Promoting Long-Term Wealth (2017, 19).

[67] Kay (2012, 22).

[68] Ibid.

[69] Garratt and Hamilton (2016, 797), where the authors provide an example of individual pension savers who entrust their savings to a fiduciary, who then selects an investment committee, which in turn appoints potentially dozens of investment managers, which each then engage brokers and advisors.

[70] The used in Kay (2012, 31) to refer to parties (e.g. pension funds) which may hold legal title to shares but often act as pooling agents for 'savers'.

pension funds, hedge funds and collective investment schemes—or individual retail investors. Institutional investors are by far the most significant of this group as they hold the largest percentage of equity securities in most major stock markets.[71] There is no accepted definition of the term 'institutional investor' and they come in many forms and serve a wide variety of interests. However, institutional investors are generally synonymous with 'intermediary investors', as they are "an institution that manages and invests other people's money."[72] Examples of prominent institutional investors include California Public Employees, the pension fund of the State of California, and companies which also have a notable asset management role, e.g. Legal & General Group plc, a British multi-national financial services company based in London, UK and BlackRock, a US asset management firm based in New York.

Although institutional investors come in many different shapes and sizes, the common link is that they hold an economic interest in the equity securities of listed companies for someone else. These persons are termed 'savers' in the Kay Review,[73] and may be ultimate individual owners, or beneficiaries in the case of pension funds. Asset owners may hold equity securities directly on the register of the listed company, or more likely, through a host of intermediaries in the equity ownership chain. The connections between SMST and asset owners and the rationale for why asset owners may excessively discount long-term returns are explored further in the subsequent chapters.

2. *Intermediaries*

Moving along the equity ownership chain, the next set of participants to be considered are intermediaries. The term 'intermediary' is used in this book to refer to all of the entities in the equity ownership chain between

[71] For example, Kay (2012, 29) observes that individuals hold only 11% of UK equities securities. Individual equity security ownership ranges from 2 to 22% across Europe, see 2015 Shareholder's Guide. Retail investment in the US is significantly higher and represented 38% of US market capitalization in 2015 according to the US investor communication firm Broadridge—Broadridge Press Release (1 March 2016) 'Retail Investors Remain an Important "Untapped" Shareholder Segment, Finds New Report from Broadridge and PwC US.' Online: https://www.broadridge.com/press-release/2016/retail-investors-remain-an-important-untapped-shareholder-segment.

[72] Çelik and Isaksson (2014, 96).

[73] 'Savers' are defined in Kay (2012, 31) as "the person … who holds the economic interest, and who will be the ultimate beneficiary of successful investment."

the asset owner and the listed company. The term also encompasses auxiliary intermediaries, most notably proxy advisers. Many variations exist, but the standard intermediary set includes: (1) asset managers—also called investment or fund managers—who manage assets on behalf of investors; (2) auxiliary intermediaries, most notably, proxy voting agencies, vote service providers or shareholder voting research providers, which are referred to collectively as 'proxy advisors' in this book; and (3) central depositaries in whose name the shares of listed companies are registered and held.

Asset managers—arguably the most significant sub-set of intermediaries[74]—are often named as the owners of the equity securities registered on the central depositary's book entry system and hold and manage investments on behalf of their clients, namely asset owners. Asset managers include well-known names such as BlackRock, and other firms including Fidelity Investments, J. P. Morgan Asset Management, and Prudential Financial. Although the lines are blurred and many of these asset managers may also be considered institutional investors in their own right, for the purposes of this book such entities are considered primarily in their role as specialist investment intermediaries for asset owners.

Proxy advisors are third party advisory services that primarily assist asset owners vote their shares in listed companies. They are auxiliary intermediaries as they are not directly in the equity ownership chain, but they have been included in the SMST discussion.[75] Although proxy advisors may not be a priori short-termist, they do play an important role in facilitating the voting of equity securities by asset owners and asset managers, and advising other participants in the equity ownership chain including listed companies.[76] Specifically, third party proxy advisory firms, such as Institutional Shareholder Services (ISS), which covers almost 40,000 shareholder meetings in 115 countries and has over 1600 institutional clients, provide services to asset owners and asset managers to vote their shares at general meetings of listed companies, and may also

[74] Kay (2012, 11), where Kay notes that asset managers are the dominant players in the investment chain, and the Financial Conduct Authority (2017, 3), which describes the vital role of the UK asset management industry, the second largest asset management industry in the world.

[75] European Union Green Paper (2011, 14) and Nathan (2015).

[76] See the discussion generally in Malenko and Shen (2016).

advise listed companies on strategies around shareholder voting.[77] The connection of proxy advisors to the perceived SMST issue is explored further in Chapter 6.[78]

Central depositaries, such as Certificateless Registry for Electronic Share Transfer (CREST) in the UK, Euroclear in the EU, and Cede & Co in the US, are another link in the equity ownership chain which potentially adds complexity to the asset owner/listed company relationship, and contributes to the perceived SMST problem.[79] There are, however, questions on how SMST is transmitted through depositaries, and the role of central depositaries as a contributing factor to the SMST problem is considered further in Chapter 6.[80]

Intermediation is generally significant to the SMST discussion as capital market intermediaries have been accused of contributing to, or exacerbating, short-termism concerns. Allegations have been made that: (1) the short-term incentives of intermediaries, particularly asset managers, may not align well with the long-term interests of their principals, namely asset owners and ultimate investors[81]; and (2) competition among asset managers has caused a short-term focus in the market.[82] Each of these concerns and the links between intermediation and SMST are explored further in the subsequent chapters.

3. *Company Managers*

The term 'company manager' refers to the directors and officers charged with the operation and management of a listed company. Delegated management with a board structure is a core structural characteristic of a listed company.[83] Corporate law by and large vests authority over the operations of a listed company in a board of directors elected by the shareholders.[84] The operations of a listed company are typically then

[77] Ibid., 3394.

[78] Chapter 6, Sect. C.2.

[79] Kay (2012, 84).

[80] Chapter 6, Sect. C.2.

[81] Kay (2012, 33).

[82] Dallas (2012, 295).

[83] Kraakman (2009, 12–14).

[84] Ibid., 13.

delegated by the board of directors to the officers of the listed company, with the ongoing oversight of such management retained by the board of directors. The purpose of an asset owner's ability to elect the board of directors is to ensure that the board remains responsive to the interests of the asset owners.[85] The company managers act, consequently, as agents for the asset owners in an economic sense, although legally they are agents of the listed company.

Company managers are perceived to be short-termist for a myriad of reasons. The basic argument, however, is that they are taking actions which maximize short-term financial returns of the listed company instead of pursuing activities with a longer term investment horizon—i.e. managerial myopia.[86] A contributing fact to this managerial myopia may be short-term focused remuneration structures.[87] Further, as the company manager's employment security and market reputation, in addition to compensation, may often be tied to a listed company's short-term performance metrics, company managers may be incentivized to use the listed company resources to maximize short-term earnings. Speaking to the origins of this behaviour, it has been argued that "[t]he practice of managerial short-termism represents the internal response at the business enterprise level to the external financial-performance demands of the stock market."[88] In other words, the SMST issue may not necessarily originate from a negative behavioural characteristic of company managers, such as greed or self-interest. Rather company managers may merely be responding to the interests of asset owners as communicated via intermediaries. This argument, and the role of company managers generally in the SMST problem, is considered in the subsequent chapters.

D. Hard v. Soft Law

An objective of this book is to analyze the conceptual effectiveness of regulatory and financial industry responses to the perceived SMST problem. Doing so requires assessing and categorizing regulatory as well as

[85] Ibid.

[86] Moore and Walker-Arnott (2014, 427–432), where the authors outline the various ways in which company managers engage in earnings manipulation to produce earnings growth.

[87] For example, see Kay (2012, 77–79).

[88] Moore and Walker-Arnott (2014, 427).

financial industry reforms. Consequently, the SMST reforms discussed in detail in Chapter 4 are categorized into 'hard' and 'soft' law, and financial industry initiatives. The 'hard' verses 'soft' law distinction is admittedly not without debate, and the divide is often in practice a sliding scale.[89] However, in this book 'hard' law generally refers to binding legislation, and the regulations promulgated under such legislation.[90] What constitutes 'soft' law is more complicated, and can cover a wide range of different instruments.[91] Nonetheless, the term 'soft' law is limited in this book to refer to non-statutory measures including codes of conduct or other standard setting documentation. These 'soft' laws are often implemented by regulatory authorities—e.g. the implementation by the UK Financial Reporting Council (FRC) of the UK Stewardship Code[92]—, but such 'soft' laws may also be implemented by legislators—e.g. guidance notes. The central point of this term is that through 'soft' laws regulators attempt to impact behaviour in a more moderated non-statutory form.

Both 'hard' and 'soft' law reforms are undoubtedly significant in governing the operations of listed companies. However, 'hard' law reforms may evidence a stronger intention from legislators to effect change, as they are built into legislation and are legally binding. This position is weakened when the 'hard' law reform is 'light' touch and contains an 'opt out' or is 'comply or explain' or disclosure based, rather than mandating a specific course of action with penalties for failure to comply. Based on this distinction, 'hard' law reforms are further categorized in Appendix 'B', Table 4 into prescriptive versus 'light' touch reforms. The significance of these additional distinctions is considered further in

[89] See the doctrinal discussion generally of 'hard' and 'soft' law in Guzman and Meyer (2010).

[90] Ibid., 180.

[91] Ibid., 173, which states that anything "law-like can be described as a form of soft law".

[92] 'UK Stewardship Code', Financial Reporting Council (September 2012) ('UK Stewardship Code'), which is a good practice code adopted by the FRC in 2010 and revised in 2012, directed at asset owners and asset managers with equity holdings in UK listed companies. The UK Stewardship Code provides seven principles aimed at enhancing the quality of engagement between investors and UK listed companies to help improve long-term risk-adjusted returns to shareholders. The UK Stewardship Code is binding on UK regulated asset managers (FCA Conduct of Business Sourcebook Rule 2.2.3) but demonstrating compliance with the seven principles of the UK Stewardship Code is on a 'comply or explain' basis.

Chapters 4 and 8. Specifically, Chapter 8 analyzes whether a 'light' touch approach using 'soft' or 'hard' law measures and financial industry initiatives is the most viable method of SMST reform as it is easier to implement and provides scope for flexibility to minimize the harms associated with prescriptive 'hard' law measures.

The discussion around each of the issues identified in this Chapter 2 is extensive. In particular, the dialogue on how the SMST issue impacts the equity ownership chain is complex. It suffices to here to set out the main concepts and the debate surrounding such concepts, and to provide the definition of SMST used in this book, which in turn provides the basis for the detailed analysis provided in the following chapters.

References

2015 Shareholder's Guide. Individual Share Ownership in Europe. http://www.plus.airliquide.com/en/ouverture/actionnariat-individuel-europe.html.

Alces, Kelli A. 2010. "Revisiting Berle and Rethinking the Corporate Structure." 33:4 *Seattle University Law Review*. 787–808.

Arestis, Philip, Demetriades, Panicos O., and Luintel, Kul B. 2001. "Financial Development and Economic Growth: The Role of Stock Markets." 33:1 *Journal of Money, Credit and Banking*. 16–41.

Aspen Institute. 2009. "Overcoming Short-Termism: A Call for a More Responsible Approach to Investment and Business Management." 9 September.

Barclays. 2015. "Short-Termism in Business: The Long and Short of It." November. https://www.barclayscorporate.com/content/dam/corppublic/corporate/Documents/research/short-termism-report.pdf.

"Behavioural Finance: Short-Termism." 2015. *Fidelity International*. April. https://www.fidelity.com.au/insights/education/behavioural-finance-short-termism1/.

Biery, Mary Ellen. 2012. "Comparing Private, Public Company Trends." 25 July. *Forbes*. https://www.forbes.com/sites/sageworks/2012/07/25/comparing-private-public-company-trends/#5976ea812bab.

Çelik, Serdar and Isaksson, Mats. 2014. "Institutional Investors and Ownership Engagement." 2013:2 *OECD Journal: Financial Market Trends*. 93–114.

Cleary, Siobhan. 2015. "Stock Exchanges and Sustainability." December. UNEP. Inquiry Working Paper. http://unepinquiry.org/wp-content/uploads/2015/12/Stock_Exchanges_and_Sustainability.pdf.

CPP Investment Board and McKinsey & Company: Global Survey Signals Short-Term Pressures on Business Leaders Are Mounting. 2013. CPP Investment Board and McKinsey & Company. 22 May. Press Release. http://www.marketwired.com/press-release/cpp-investment-board-mckinsey-company-global-survey-signals-short-term-pressures-on-1793872.htm.

Dallas, Lynne L. 2012. "Short-Termism, the Financial Crisis, and Corporate Governance." 2011–2012. 37:2 *The Journal of Corporation Law*. 265–364.

Davies, Richard, Haldane, Andrew G., Nielsen, Mette, and Pezzini, Silvia. 2014. "Measuring the Costs of Short-Termism." 12 *Journal of Financial Stability*. 16–25.

European Union Green Paper. 2011. "The EU Corporate Governance Framework". COM (2011)164. 5 April.

Financial Conduct Authority. 2017. Asset Management Market Study Final Report. MS15/2.3 June.

Fink, Larry. 2018. CEO Letter, BlackRock, Inc. January. https://www.blackrock.com/corporate/investor-relations/larry-fink-ceo-letter.

Garratt, T. and Hamilton, K. 2016. "The Loneliness of the Long-Term Investor: A Comment on Patience in Practice." 2016. 14:4 *Socio-Economic Review*. 789–806.

Guzman, A. and Meyer, T. 2010. "International Soft Law" 2:1 *Journal of Legal Analysis*. 171–225.

Haldane, Andrew and Richards, Davies. 2011. "The Short-Long." Speech at the 29th Société Universitaire Européene de Recherches Financières Colloquium: New Paradigms in Money and Finance? May. Brussels.

Initiative for Responsible Investment at the Hauser Institute for Civil Society, Trustee Leadership Forum for Retirement Security. 2016. Discussion Paper. http://iri.hks.harvard.edu/files/iri/files/tlf-note-on-long-term-investing.pdf.

Jolls, Christine and Sunstein, Cass R. 2006. "Debiasing Through Law." 35:1 *Journal of Legal Studies*. 199–242.

Kay, John. 2012. "The Kay Review of UK Equity Markets and Long-Term Decision Making." Final Report. July.

Knutson, Brian, Taylor, Jonathan, Kaufman, Matthew, Peterson, Richard, and Glover, Gary. 2005. "Distributed Neural Representation of Expected Value." 11 May. 25:19 *Journal of Neuroscience*. 4806–4812.

Kraakman, Reinier, et al. 2009. *The Anatomy of Corporate Law: A Comparative and Functional Approach*. 2nd ed. United Kingdom: Oxford University Press.

Loewenstein, George, Sutherland, Rory, and Samson, Alain. 2014. *Behavioral Economics Guide 2014* (with a foreword by Loewenstein, George and Sutherland, Rory).

Malenko, Nadya and Shen, Yao. 2016. "The Role of Proxy Advisory Firms: Evidence from a Regression-Discontinuity Design." 29:12 *Review of Financial Studies*. 3394–3427.

Malkiel, Burton. 2016. *A Random Walk Down Wall Street*. W. W. Norton: New York.

Mason, J. W. 2015. "Understanding Short-Termism: Questions and Consequences." 6 November. *The Roosevelt Institute*.

Moore, Marc T. and Walker-Arnott, Edward. 2014. "A Fresh Look at Stock Market Short-Termism." 41:3 *Journal of Law and Society*. 416–445.

Nathan, Charles. 2015. "Observations on Short-Termism and Long-Termism." 12 October. *Harvard Law School Forum on Corporate Governance and Financial Regulation*. https://corpgov.law.harvard.edu/2015/10/12/observations-on-short-termism-and-long-termism/.

Onoda, Keiichi, Okamoto, Yasumasa, Kunisato, Yoshihiko, Aoyama, Siori, Shishida, Kazuhiro, Okada, Go, Tanaka, Saori, Schweighofer, Nicolas, Yamaguchi, Shuhei, Doya, Kenji, and Yamawaki, Shigeto. 2011. "Inter-individual Discount Factor Differences in Reward Prediction Are Topographically Associated with Caudate Activation." 212 *Experimental Brain Research*. Experimentelle Hirnforschung. Expérimentation cérébrale. 593–601.

Oyedele, Akin. 2017. "Here Is the Letter the World's Largest Investor, BlackRock CEO Larry Fink, Just Sent to CEOs Everywhere." 24 January. *Business Insider UK*. http://uk.businessinsider.com/blackrock-ceo-larry-fink-letter-to-ceos-2017-1?r=US&IR=T.

"Promoting Long-Term Wealth: Reshaping Corporate Governance." 2017. A Report by Tomorrow's Company for the All-Party Parliamentary Corporate Governance Group. January.

Roe, Mark J. 2013. "Corporate Short-Termism—In the Boardroom and in the Courtroom." August. 68 *Business Lawyer*. 977–1006.

Roe, Mark J. 2016. "The Chimera of Stock-Market Short-Termism." 17 October. Project Syndicate. https://www.project-syndicate.org/commentary/clinton-proposal-capital-gains-tax-by-mark-roe-2016-10.

Simpson, Stephen. 2011. "Who Owns the Stock Exchanges." 9 March. *Investopedia*. http://www.investopedia.com/financial-edge/0311/who-owns-the-stock-exchanges.aspx.

Stafford, Phillip. 2013. "London Stock Exchange to Quit World Federation of Exchanges." 28 November. *Financial Times*. https://www.ft.com/content/584714e4-582a-11e3-82fc-00144feabdc0.

Tulay, Mark. 2017. "Why the World's Largest Asset Managers Are Pushing Long-Term Thinking." 27 July. *GreenBiz*. https://www.greenbiz.com/article/why-worlds-largest-asset-managers-are-pushing-long-term-thinking.

Turner, Matt. 2016. "Here Is the Letter the World's Largest Investor, BlackRock CEO Larry Fink, Just Sent to CEOs Everywhere." 2 February. *Business Insider UK*. http://uk.businessinsider.com/blackrock-ceo-larry-fink-letter-to-sp-500-ceos-2016-2?r=US&IR=T.

Walker, Simon. 2014. "Short-Termism Is a Wolf Stalking the Equity Market." 13 November. *The Telegraph*.

Walter, Mischel, et al. 1972. "Cognitive and Attentional Mechanisms in Delay of Gratification." 21:2 *Journal of Personality and Social Psychology*. 204–218.

CHAPTER 3

Short-Termism, an Evolving Concern?

This chapter traces the development of the concept of 'short-termism' in capital markets from when it was first articulated as a material concern in the 1970s in response to concerns over an influx of hostile takeovers of US companies, to the 'in vogue' phrase used post-global financial crisis (GFC) with abandon by the popular press, academics and the financial industry. Market commentators have said that during this time period, "[i]n the business community, short-termism has gone from a simmer to a boil."[1] As a result, this chapter examines how the perceived short-termism problem intersects with significant trends in capital markets, initially predominantly in the United States (US), and often appearing to overlap with market disruptions. I then consider how this primarily US discussion subsequently spread into capital markets in other jurisdictions in the fallout of the GFC, and captured the attention of policymakers worldwide, though most notably in the United Kingdom (UK) and the European Union (EU).

The historical analysis in this chapter places the current short-termism discussion into a larger social and economic context. In doing so it brings to the forefront the question of whether short-termism is actually a substantive issue, or if it is instead simply compelling rhetoric that overlaps with the dominant capital market concerns of the day. If stock market short-termism (SMST) concerns are merely rhetoric, regulatory

[1] Rappaport (2011, 5).

K. M. Willey, *Stock Market Short-Termism*,
https://doi.org/10.1007/978-3-030-22903-0_3

and financial industry reform efforts may not be justified solely on the basis of SMST concerns. If, however, there is substance underlying the concerns, regulatory and financial industry reform is warranted.

Arguing that there is at least some substance to the SMST concerns, this chapter presents the argument that SMST emerged as an issue during this time period due to changing dynamics in public markets—more precisely, the move towards financial intermediation by investors, with a corresponding focus on short-term investment parameters meant to hold asset managers to account. Answering the question of whether short-termism is rhetoric or substance also necessitates a review of the reforms themselves—which is done in Chapter 4—, and further examination of whether SMST is a real and harmful problem, and if the reforms implemented at least conceptually address SMST, which analysis is provided in the remainder of the book.

A. 1970s/1980s—Articulation of a SMST Problem

Concerns about short-termism in stock markets may have been around long before,[2] but the most notable first articulation of the current day version of the SMST issue was in 1979 by the renowned US corporate lawyer and market commentator, Martin Lipton.[3] Speaking prophetically as the US takeover boom of the 1980s that generated much of the discussion on stock market short-termism had not yet kicked into gear, Lipton asked if, "[i]t would not be unfair to pose the policy issue as: Whether the long-term interests of the nation's corporate system and economy should be jeopardized in order to benefit speculators interested…only in a quick profit…?"[4] Subsequent shake-ups of large, primarily US, listed companies in the 1980s[5] sent shock

[2] See Haldane and Davies (2011, 2), which refers to historical examples of classical economists such as William Stanley Jevons, Alfred Marshall, Arthur Pigou and John Maynard Keynes grappling with the short-termism concept.

[3] Roe (2013, 979).

[4] Lipton (1979, 104).

[5] For example, these shake ups included the hostile takeovers of TWA in 1985 and Gulf Oil in 1984 respectively, by so called 'corporate raiders' Carl Ichan and T. Boone Pickens, and the leveraged buyouts which followed thereafter, including most notably the management buyout of RJR Nabisco in 1988.

waves through the stock markets, and elevated Lipton's question on short-termism to prominence, at least in the US. Lipton's query—which suggested that distributing earnings out of a listed company to a select few was at odds with long-term value generation and national interests—spawned decades of analysis not only on the precise merits of US corporate takeover policies and regulation, but more broadly on US stock market structure and the purpose of listed companies.[6]

Lipton specifically called out the short-term perspective of "certain arbitrageurs and professional investors",[7] and opined that the "overall health of the economy should not in the slightest degree be made subservient to the interests of certain shareholders in realizing a profit on a takeover."[8] His definition of the market problem did not, however, focus exclusively on the actions of certain bad actors. Rather, Lipton claimed that the threat of hostile takeovers themselves would have a negative impact on the stock market as a whole, as company managers would endeavor to pre-empt such takeovers by foregoing long-term planning.[9] This concern may have been part of the policy rationale for subsequent takeover protection measures implemented in the US. These measures included the 'poison pill',[10] and the Delaware Supreme Court's development of case law on takeover defenses, essentially

[6] See Gilson and Kraakman (2005), in which the authors reviewed the impact of Mr. Lipton's 1979 paper.

[7] Lipton (1979, 104).

[8] Ibid.

[9] Ibid., 109–110.

[10] 'Shareholder rights plans', known colloquially as 'poison pills', are a takeover defense mechanism developed by Martin Lipton in 1982 which, when adopted by a company, provide for existing shareholders to purchase significant additional shares at discount if the company is the subject of a takeover offer. A detailed description of poison pills is set out in Gilson and Bernard (1999, 10–18). Client interests, namely the interests of incumbent boards, may have been part of Lipton's motivations in developing this mechanism to prevent takeovers. However, a key position in his 1979 paper (at 105) is that there is a public policy interest in defending against takeovers that would adversely impact corporate long-term planning, and it is not a stretch to argue that this was a rationale for developing the poison pill.

bolstering the ability of boards of directors to fend off hostile takeover bids.[11]

Although Lipton's opinion was to some degree supported among corporate managers and the influential Delaware Supreme Court, this view was not universally accepted. An alternative line of reasoning emphasized that the corporate shakeups of the 1980s were instead driven by a failure of company managers over the preceding decades to effectively manage for shareholder value.[12] In direct response to Lipton's 1979 paper, two noted US law professors, Frank Easterbrook and Daniel Fischel, criticized Lipton's claim that such takeover activity was harmful to society. Instead they argued that "[s]ociety benefits from an active takeover market… because it simultaneously provides an incentive to all corporate managers to operate efficiently and a mechanism for displacing inefficient managers."[13]

These two opposing lines of argument are further considered in Chapter 5. As discussed in Chapters 5 and 7, there is minimal quantitative evidence of a SMST problem during this period, which may be due to the difficulty of articulating and measuring the issue, but which also gives weight to the position that the SMST discussion during this time was largely rhetoric layered onto the debate over whether hostile takeovers should be restricted. It is also possible that SMST was identified as an issue during this time period as the hostile takeovers necessitated pooled investment by a large number of investors, which was part of trend of using financial intermediation to facilitate large investments in US listed companies. Such financial intermediation meant that investors looked less at the underlying fundamentals of their investments, but rather focused on the short-term financial performance of their asset managers. Regardless, it suffices to say that the SMST problem was first articulated rather narrowly during this period of market disruption in the context of the US market for corporate control. The focus was on short-termist behaviour by certain 'hostile' market actors looking to derive short-term gain, which actions allegedly hindered long-term corporate planning by listed companies.

[11] See Gilson and Kraakman (2005) summarizing the impact of Lipton (1979) on the development of Delaware takeover law, which reviewed the Delaware Chancery and Supreme Court case law and notes at 1430 that "Lipton ultimately persuaded the Supreme Court that the problem of allocating discretion between boards and shareholders in hostile takeovers could be resolved by abstract principles." These abstract principles were adverse impact on corporate long-term planning caused by the threat of hostile takeovers.

[12] Rappaport (2011, 10).

[13] Easterbrook and Fischel (1981, 1184).

B. 1990s–2000s: Short-Termism as a Factor in National Competitiveness, and the Rise of 'Agency Capitalism'

After the takeover boom period of the 1980s, the discussion on short-termism continued in the US, suggesting that SMST was about more than just the market for corporate control and rather was part of a more fundamental concern over market structure. However, the focus moved away from takeovers, and onto why US competitiveness was in decline. Although national competitiveness was certainly on the agenda prior to the 1980s, US commentators in particular were concerned about declining overall market competitiveness relative to their international economic competitors, such as Germany and Japan, in the 1990s.[14] Prominent US business and economics academic Michael Porter presented evidence demonstrating that US listed companies invested at a lower rate and with a shorter time frame than competitors in Japan or Germany.[15]

This was, Porter opined, because "[t]he American system is less supportive of investment overall because of its sensitivity to current returns for many established companies combined with corporate goals that stress current stock price over long-term corporate value."[16] In his book, 'Short-Term America', former US Treasury director of corporate finance, Michael Jacobs, echoed Porter's analysis and argued that 'business myopia' was at the heart of the US competitive problem. Jacobs defined business myopia as "[a] preoccupation with short-term results and instant economic gratification [that] is undermining the long-run viability of American companies, and in some cases, entire industries."[17] This analysis demonstrates how, prior to the GFC, commentary was focused on discussing short-termism, but with an increasing emphasis on attributing industry and national competitiveness to a perceived short-termist mindset in the US markets.

Adding weight to the argument that the SMST concern was really about the move towards financial intermediation, noted economist, Alfred Rappaport, conceptualized this time-period in US history as

[14] See Porter (1992) and Jacobs (1991).

[15] Porter (1992, 67–68).

[16] Ibid., 73.

[17] Jacobs (1991, 7–8).

the rise of 'agency capitalism'.[18] Rappaport observed that from 1986 to 2006 in the US, direct ownership of equity securities of US listed companies dropped from 56 to 27%, with a corresponding increase in institutional—primarily equity mutual fund—ownership.[19] This rise of institutional equity ownership in the US, Rappaport argued, created an era of agency capitalism, which introduced additional agency/principal relationships into the equity ownership chain. 'Agency problems' are said to arise because of conflicts of interest among corporate constituencies, whereby the financial interest of one party—the 'principal'—is dependent on the actions taken by another party—the 'agent'.[20] The core difficulty in the agency relationship is that the principal has handed control over to an agent, who thus often has better information than the principal about the relevant facts.[21] Consequently, the agent has an incentive to act opportunistically—or may be lazy or incompetent—, and the principal must engage in costly monitoring to reduce the agent's opportunistic behaviour or accept the agency costs of the agent.[22]

In the capital structures that rose to prominence during 1986 to 2006 in the US, Rappaport argued that both institutional investors and asset managers appeared to have a common short-term performance agenda, and, therefore, no agency conflicts.[23] Consequently, Rappaport observed that the agency conflict was then between the company managers and the ultimate owners in whose interests the institutional investors and asset managers are supposed to act.[24] The concern was that the short-term interests of institutional investors and asset managers appeared to be dominating the market—including, for example, in the compensation structures of company managers, which were increasingly based on stock options with short-vesting periods.[25] This short-termism problem, supposedly amplified by the agency capital structure, arguably contributed to the decline in relative US national competitiveness, which was discussed above by Jacobs and Porter.

[18] Rappaport (2011, 11).

[19] Ibid.

[20] See the summary in Kraakman et al. (2009, 35–36).

[21] Ibid., 35.

[22] Ibid., 36.

[23] Ibid., 12.

[24] Ibid.

[25] Ibid.

This form of agency capitalism was also observed in the UK during this time period, which in addition to the US, experienced a significant rise in institutional ownership. The Kay Review[26] (Kay Review) noted that by the 1990s insurance companies and pension funds accounted for around half of the holders of equity securities of UK listed companies.[27] Nigel Lawson, Chancellor of the Exchequer of the UK, commented on the short-termism of these institutional investors, when he declared in 1986 that "[t]he big institutional investors nowadays increasingly react to short-term pressure on investment performance…they are unwilling to countenance long-term investment or sufficient expenditure on R&D."[28] Short-termism was routinely cited as a negative consequence of agency capitalism, thereby causing declining national competitiveness.

As will be discussed further in Chapters 5 and 7, convincing quantitative evidence linking such concerns to a SMST problem was not provided during this time period. Consequently, the mention of short-termism may just be largely colorful and intuitively compelling rhetoric, used as part of broader concerns around agency capitalism and declining national competitiveness during this time period. However, financial intermediation evident during this time period may have spawned SMST concerns, and the SMST discussions in both the US and the UK during this time set the ground-work for the renewed focus on short-termism in the fall-out of a wave of high-profile US corporate scandals in the early 2000s.

C. The Early 2000s: Short-Termism and Corporate Scandal

The new millennium opened in the US with a steep market decline and brought with it a number of high profile corporate collapses involving accounting scandals at major US listed companies.[29] The most notorious of these scandals caused the collapses of industry giants, Enron Corporation (Enron) and WorldCom. Using a variety of underhanded accounting loopholes, offshore special purpose vehicles and incorrect

[26] Kay (2012).

[27] Ibid., 30–31.

[28] Cleary (2015, 11).

[29] Rappaport (2011, 13).

reporting, Enron's management managed to hide funds, and deceive its lenders and the investing public. When the dust settled, Enron filed for bankruptcy, its auditors, Arthur Anderson—one of the world's largest auditing firms—were eventually dissolved, Enron's executives were put in jail and employees were out of work, and investors and creditors lost billions of dollars.[30] In 2003, a year after Enron's bankruptcy, another Arthur Anderson client, WorldCom, filed for bankruptcy in the US WorldCom's collapse was also attributed to accounting irregularities and outright fraud. Similar to Enron, the WorldCom scandal exposed fraudulent accounting practices, which involved certain WorldCom executives employing improper accounting practices in order to disguise reduced earnings and bolster declining share prices.[31]

These accounting scandals have been linked with the pursuit of short-term market expectations. For example, as opined by Pawel Bilinski, director of the Centre for Financial Analysis and Reporting Research at Cass Business School, in relation to WorldCom, "[a]ccounting scandals happen because there is pressure to meet short-term market expectations in terms of financial and share price performance."[32] Additionally, Malcolm Salter of the Harvard Business School argued that with regard to such accounting frauds including Enron "short-termism also invites institutional corruption."[33] Although these arguments may hold popular appeal, as discussed further in Chapter 7,[34] and short-termism rhetoric appears to have been used in the examination of these scandals, the real concern was how best to shed light on and to address the accounting frauds underlying these scandals. In the US, the accounting scandals of this era lead to a re-examination of corporate governance and accounting practices.

The culmination of this re-examination process was the introduction of the Sarbanes–Oxley Act of 2002 (SOX Act). The Sox Act was US federal legislation that placed elaborate internal controls on listed companies and imposed direct responsibility for the accuracy of financial reporting of listed

[30] Healy et al. (2003).

[31] "Report of Investigation by The Special Investigative Committee of the Board of Directors of Worldcom, Inc." US Securities and Exchange Commission. Online: https://www.sec.gov/Archives/edgar/data/723527/000093176303001862/dex991.htm.

[32] Farrell (2015).

[33] Salter (2012).

[34] See the discussion on the societal costs of SMST in Chapter 7, Sect. C.

companies on Chief Executive Officers (CEOs) and Chief Financial Officers (CFOs) of listed companies.[35] Rather than a correction of the SMST issue as identified in this book through restricting more subtle attempts by company managers to manipulate accounting through the active management of earnings, the reforms included in the SOX Act attempted instead to address outright accounting fraud by imposing direct obligations on CEOs and CFOs to certify the accuracy of financial disclosure.

Despite increased regulation in the US meant to address accounting manipulation, concerns about the harms of short-term interests in US accounting practices continued. Instead of focusing on short-termism in the context of accounting fraud—which arguably declined after the introduction of the SOX Act—, attention then turned to the more subtle aspects of earnings management by listed companies.[36] Of note, researchers John Graham, Campbell Harvey and Shiva Rajgnopal, conducted a survey of 401 financial executives in the US, and observed that the majority of these executives would avoid initiating a positive net present value (NPV) project if it meant falling short of the current quarter's consensus earnings.[37]

'Net present value' or 'NPV' is defined as the difference between the present value of cash inflows and the present value of cash outflows over a period of time.[38] This involves discounting the expected future cash flows for a project into present dollars. A positive NPV means even at the discounted rate the project would still be financial beneficial to the listed company. This line of research into the connection between short-term interests and earnings management developed post-GFC and is discussed in further detail in Chapter 6.

In the years immediately preceding the GFC, the profile of SMST as a broad threat to capital markets was on the rise. As an example, referring to the research of Graham et al. on earnings management, William H. Donaldson, then Chairman of the US Securities and Exchange Commission (SEC), gave a speech at the Chartered Financial Analyst (CFA) Institute Annual Conference in 2005, on the challenge of moving

[35] Rappaport (2011, 13).

[36] See Dallas (2012, 278) referring to Cohen et al. (2008, 757–759 and 770); and the summary of articles in Dallas (2012, 279 at Note 80).

[37] Graham et al. (2005).

[38] Net Present Value (NPV) Definition, Investopedia. Online: https://www.investopedia.com/terms/n/npv.asp#ixzz5RUe3nec8.

beyond short-termism.[39] The following year, in 2006, the CFA Center for Financial Market Integrity hosted a symposium (2006 CFA Roundtable) on breaking the short-term cycle, which brought together thought leaders from the corporate issuer, analyst, asset and hedge fund manager, institutional investor, and individual investor community.[40] During this time The Conference Board also hosted a corporate/investor summit series on the SMST problem cumulating in a research report released in 2006 with suggestions for future action.[41] The following year, a bipartisan Commission on the Regulation of US Capital Markets in the 21st Century established by the US Chamber of Commerce issued a report and recommendations to reduce earning guidance on the basis that "there is too much focus on the short-term performance of U.S. companies."[42]

The SMST problem had, however, not yet as widely captured the imagination of the popular press or policymakers in the US as it would do in the post-GFC period. It is possible that the short termism discussion had less resonance in the popular press and with policymakers in the US prior to the GFC because many developed countries, including the US and UK, were in a period of relatively consistent Gross Domestic Product (GDP) growth during this time.[43] For example, US and UK Annual GDP increased relatively steadily during the period of 1970 to 2015 with the US increased each of the US and the UK rose relatively steadily in the years leading up to the GFC.[44] When the economy is generally on an upward trend, there may be less interest from the financial industry and the public generally to question the short-termism of capital markets. However, increasing dialogue in the financial industry, academic and popular on the short-termism of market participants during this era of relative prosperity laid the foundations for the explosion of discussion on SMST in the wake of the GFC.

[39] Donaldson (2005).

[40] Krehmeyer et al. (2006).

[41] Tonello (2006).

[42] Commission on the Regulation of Capital Markets (2007, 5).

[43] Jacobs (1991, 2–9), where Jacobs provides evidence of declining US competitiveness relative primarily to Japan and Germany.

[44] Word Data Bank. Online: http://data.worldbank.org (GDP at Current US$ Prices) shows a relatively steady increase of GDP in the UK from US$130 billion in 1970 to pre-GFC peak of US$3.074 trillion in 2007 and in the US from US$1.076 trillion in 1970 to pre-GFC peak of US$14.719 trillion in 2008.

D. 2007 to Current: An Increase of SMST Concern Post-GFC

The GFC was triggered by the collapse of the sub-prime mortgage market in the US in 2007 and developed into a crisis of epic proportions in international financial markets throughout 2008 and 2009. The GFC has been cited as the worst financial crisis since the Great Depression of the 1930s,[45] and the end result was the collapse and eventual government bailouts of large financial institutions, a rout of the US and worldwide stock markets, a significant decline in US housing prices, a 22% drop in average US household savings, and drop in GDP in many countries.[46] The GFC also contributed to the European sovereign debt crisis, and triggered a recession in global markets, which lasted until about 2012.[47]

'Short-termism' rapidly became a buzzword linked to the GFC. Given the historical analysis set out in Sects. A–C above, it is not surprising that short-termism appeared on the agenda with vigor after yet another major capital market disruption. The GFC has a myriad of causes but may generally be said to have originated with the collapse of the US sub-prime housing market.[48] The short-termist behaviour of participants in the US equity markets, mainly guided by Wall Street investment firms, was also entangled in post-GFC analysis. As demonstrated in Fig. 1 in Chapter 1, usage of the term 'short-termism' in the popular press nearly doubled between 2006 and 2010 and has risen in major news and business sources globally significantly and consistently since the GFC. For example, headlines such as 'Short-termism made institutions vulnerable' in the *Financial Times*[49] and 'Wall Street's Mania for

[45] Business Wire (2009).

[46] Farrar and Mayes (2013).

[47] Ibid.

[48] For a comprehensive analysis of the causes of the GFC, see the Dissenting Statement of SEC Commissioners Keith Hennessey, Douglas Holtz-Eakin and Bill Thomas, 'Causes of the Financial and Economic Crisis', Financial Crisis Inquiry Commission (27 January 2011), which statement identifies ten essential causes, namely the credit bubble, the housing bubble, nontraditional mortgages, credit ratings and securitization, financial institutions concentrated correlated risk, leverage and liquidity risk, risk of contagion, common shock, financial shock and panic and that the financial crisis caused an economic crisis.

[49] Jackson (2009).

Short-Term Results Hurts Economy' in the *Washington Post*[50] pinned at least part of the blame for the GFC on the short-term profit focus of market participants in US equity markets. Legal and economic academic commentators affirmed these opinions about the short-termism of US equity markets contributing to the GFC.[51] For example, Professor Lynne Dallas argued that "[t]he financial crisis of 2007-2009 was preceded by a period of financial firms seeking short-term profit regardless of long term consequences."[52]

Although the GFC was primarily linked to the collapse of the US sub-prime housing market, the ramifications of this crisis spread throughout the global financial markets including into the world's equity markets, and the resulting shock waves caused many observers to ask if there were broader capital market failings.[53] The following sections consider this SMST discussion post-GFC, starting with the US in Sect. D.1, which as set out above, dominated the bulk of the short-termism conversation prior to the GFC. Given the Kay Review and the UK Government's response to the recommendations in this review, the following Sect. D.2 then reviews the discussion in the UK, as it has generated the most substantive SMST-driven reform discussions relative to other jurisdictions which have considered the issue and necessitates separate consideration. Next, the remainder of Europe is considered in Sect. D.3, where short-termism has factored into several significant implemented reforms. Section D.4 then considers SMST deliberations in the rest of the

[50] Pearlstein (2009).

[51] For example, Moore and Walker-Arnott (2014), Rappaport (2011), Chapter 2 'Short-Termism Produces a Financial Crisis'; and also see the statement on short-termism in The Modern Corporation: Corporate Governance for the 21st Century, Statement on Economics, para 3. Online: https://themoderncorporation.wordpress.com/economics-and-msv/, signed by over 80 academics. Commenting on the post-GFC state of capital markets, this Statement on Economics asserts that "short-termism prevails and investment in productive capability diminishes".

[52] Dallas (2012, 267).

[53] See Dallas (2012, 281–293), where Dallas reviews the sub-prime mortgage market in the US, and the layers of complexity of the securitization of these products, the collapse of which she argues lead to the financial crisis. Dallas used this financial crisis as a starting point for re-examining the role of short-termism in capital markets. Similarly, Kay 2012 was an examination of broader market failings post-GFC, and Dominic Barton cites the "near meltdown of the financial system" as the reason for his call to re-orient capital markets towards a longer-term approach (Barton 2011, 85).

world, where there is less significant dialogue about reform, and finally discussions by the financial industry and its advisors are considered in Sect. D.5.

1. SMST Discussion in the US

As discussed in Sects. A–C in this chapter, the US has long been a hot bed of academic and financial industry discussion for short-termism reform. These discussions appeared to gather momentum during periods of market disruption, most notably during the hostile takeover boom of the 1970/1980s, the bursting of the market bubble in the early 2000s, and the GFC. The short-termism of market actors as a cause of the GFC was a consideration in the reform of the US banking industry post-GFC. In direct response to the GFC, the Dodd-Frank Wall Street Reform and Consumer Protection Act,[54] known as the 'Dodd-Frank Act', was signed into United States federal law by President Barack Obama on 21 July 2010. The Dodd-Frank Act is a wide sweeping piece of legislation that created oversight agencies for financial institutions, brought in new rules on executive compensation and corporate governance, regulated investment fund advisors, and increased transparency of off-market trading practices.[55] The primary intentions of the reforms as stated in the Dodd-Frank Act itself,[56] and as confirmed by President Barrack Obama when the Dodd-Frank Act was signed into law,[57] were to improve accountability and transparency, end 'too big to fail' and bailouts by taxpayers, and implement stronger consumer protection regulations. However, as is considered further in Chapter 4,[58] at least a few of these changes were also meant to mitigate some of the perceived harmful effects of SMST.

An articulation in the US of short-termism specifically targeting policy change in equity capital markets after the GFC was a report issued by

[54] Pub. L. 111–203, H.R. 4173.

[55] Dallas (2012, 323–358).

[56] The Dodd-Frank Act, Recital.

[57] "Text of Obama Remarks on Dodd-Frank." *Market Watch*. 21 July 2010. Online: https://www.marketwatch.com/story/text-of-obama-remarks-on-dodd-frank-2010-07-21 and "Wall Street Reform: The Dodd-Frank Act" The White House President Barrack Obama. Online: https://obamawhitehouse.archives.gov/economy/middle-class/dodd-frank-wall-street-reform.

[58] See Chapter 4, Sects. A.1.b, B.2, and C.1.

an Aspen Institute think-tank in 2009.[59] During 2007–2009 the Aspen Institute in the US sought input from a wide range of business, labour, investment and political sources, including Martin Lipton and noted financial market guru, Warren Buffet. This resulted in a policy statement which claimed that "short-termism is not limited to the behavior of a few investors or intermediaries."[60] Instead, the statement claimed, "[i]t is system-wide, with contributions by and interdependency among corporate managers, boards, investment advisers, providers of capital, and government."[61]

The agenda for SMST-driven reform as set out in the Aspen Report was enthusiastically endorsed by Delaware Chief Justice, Leo E. Strine.[62] Chief Justice Strine added further specificity to the Aspen Institutes' proposals to promote US long-term growth and counter short-termism, mainly in the form of US tax reform and changes to the incentive structure in the equity ownership chain.[63] Former SEC Commissioner Daniel Gallagher commended Chief Justice Strine on advancing the dialogue towards tangible results, and also observed that the SEC was best placed to facilitate a discussion between all stakeholders on the way forward.[64] Delaware Court Justice Jack B. Jacobs also honed in on the SMST issue, focusing on the decline of patient capital in the US, and how the Delaware Courts and US legislators could best fix the growing problem of impatient capital.[65] Justice Jacobs' solution was to propose laws meant to discourage investors from apply short-term pressure on company managers; specifically by longer directorship terms rather than yearly elections.[66]

Influential US politicians have as well recently condemned short-termism in capital markets—demonstrating just how strongly the topic resonates with the voting public. Both former Democratic Vice President Joe Biden[67] and former Democratic Presidential candidate

[59] Aspen Institute (2009).

[60] Ibid., 3.

[61] Ibid.

[62] Strine (2015, 4). Chief Justice Strine's comments on this topic are significant given Delaware's prominence as a corporate domicile for most US companies.

[63] Ibid., starting at 6.

[64] Gallagher (2015).

[65] Jacobs (2012).

[66] Ibid., 1658.

[67] Biden (2016).

nominee Hillary Clinton[68] called for reforms to address the perceived SMST problem. Given the political tide change in the US in the 2016 Presidential election, the future of SMST reform is uncertain, but SMST may likely take a back seat. President Donald Trump's focus is on reducing corporate tax rates rather than providing tax incentives to reduce SMST. As evidenced in the US tax relief plan announced in September 2017,[69] and enacted effective as of 31 December 2017,[70] the focus of US tax reform is on reducing rates and complexity rather than specific changes meant to address SMST. It is possible that calls from the financial industry for capital gains reform to correct SMST, most notably by the CEO of BlackRock Inc. (BlackRock), Larry Fink supported by other asset managers—as discussed in Sect. D.5 below—may keep the topic of SMST alive on the political agenda in the US. Although not citing SMST concerns, President Trump has also picked up on financial industry concerns around the short-termism pressures inherent in quarterly reporting and asked the SEC to consider reducing the reporting requirement for US listed companies from quarterly to a six-month system.[71] The impact of these tax and quarterly reporting reform initiatives on SMST are discussed further in Chapter 4.[72] The policy agenda in the UK, EU and elsewhere has, however, progressed further towards SMST-driven reforms.

2. *The UK and the Kay Review*

Much of the substantive discussion on SMST reform post-GFC has been in the UK,[73] and the Kay Review is a leading example of how short-termism reform was put on the agenda. In 2011, the UK Secretary

[68] Jacobs (2015).

[69] "President Donald J. Trump Puts American First in Tax Relief." The White House, Office of the Press Secretary. 27 September 2017. Online: https://www.whitehouse.gov/the-press-office/2017/09/27/president-trump-puts-americans-first-in-tax-relief.

[70] Act to provide for reconciliation pursuant to titles II and V of the concurrent resolution on the budget for fiscal year 2018, a congressional revenue act originally introduced in Congress as the Tax Cuts and Jobs Act (TCJA), Public law no. 115–197.

[71] Merced and Phillips (2018).

[72] See Chapter 4, Sect. A.2.a for a discussion of tax related SMST reforms and Sect. A.3.a for a discussion of quarterly reporting SMST initiatives.

[73] See Haldane and Davies (2011), Davies et al. (2014), and commentary on short-termism in the UK by Will Hutton in *How Good We Can Be*, 2015 Little Brown Books Publisher and his opinion pieces in *The Guardian*, including "'Quarterly capitalism' is short-term, myopic, greedy and dysfunctional" *The Guardian* (26 July 2015)

of State for Business, Vince Cable, commissioned economist Professor John Kay to provide an independent report on the UK stock markets and long-term decision-making. Kay formed an advisory board which widely consulted with the UK financial industry. As a result of this consultation, Kay concluded that UK stock markets are not as effective as they should be in supporting the long-term growth of British business and, consequently, long-term sustainable returns on investment for British savers, and that short-termism in UK stock markets was the culprit.[74] Principal causes of short-termism, according to Kay, were the decline of trust, and misalignment of incentives throughout the investment chain.[75] Kay provided 17 recommendations meant to correct the SMST issue, which focused largely on rebuilding trust by changing the behaviour of company managers and asset managers.[76]

The UK government accepted the Kay Review recommendations, at least in principle,[77] with some in the UK government questioning if the soft-touch approach in the Kay Review actually went far enough.[78] As discussed in Chapter 4, however, many specifics of the recommendations have not yet been implemented. Regardless, the Kay Review demonstrates that short-termism has been a significant part of the UK market reform discussion, at least in the years following the GFC. Additionally, the chief economist of the Bank of England, Andrew Haldane, has entered the discussion claiming that "companies risk 'eating themselves' as shareholders and management [are] gripped by a form of short-termism."[79] Demonstrating the extent to which this concept of 'short-termism' has infiltrated popular culture in the UK, the Prince of Wales has also publicly urged UK companies to end short-termism.[80]

Despite all of this attention, perhaps indicative that SMST-driven reform may be dropping off the agenda of UK policymakers, the latest green paper on corporate governance released by the UK

[74] Kay (2012, 5).

[75] Ibid.

[76] Ibid., 13.

[77] Kay Review Government Response (2014) and Implementation (2014).

[78] Kay Review Government Response, Ev4.

[79] Weldon (2015), referencing a speech summarizing Mr. Haldane's position (see Haldane 2015).

[80] White (2013).

government does not pick up the SMST-driven reform thread.[81] Instead, short-termism is only briefly mentioned in the context of executive remuneration packages.[82] However, Tomorrow's Company,[83] a UK non-profit think tank that aims to promote good business, continues to press a general SMST reform agenda. This agenda includes the adoption of a system of long-term capital trusts be established to counter the perceived SMST problem, which would be regulated and overseen by the Financial Conduct Authority (FCA) in the UK.[84] Policymakers in Europe have also, concurrently with the SMST discussion in the UK, called for reform and considered reform measures, meant to correct the perceived SMST issue.

3. *Europe and the EU Amended Shareholder Rights Directive*

Concurrently with the UK review, the European Commission (EC) released a green paper in 2011 assessing the strength of the governance frameworks of EU companies (EU Governance Green Paper).[85] The EU Governance Green Paper was based on a Group of Twenty (G20) call to action meant to ensure sustainable growth and a stronger financial system in the wake of the GFC.[86] The EU Governance Green Paper aligned with the EC's general initiatives on market unification and corporate social responsibility (CSR).[87] The EU Governance Green Paper was the result of interviews by the EC with a large sample of EU companies from different member states, and extensive meetings with corporate governance experts and the representatives of the investor community in the EU.[88] Similar concerns as in the Kay Review were raised by the EC in the EU Governance Green Paper These concerns included that short-termism and excessive risk taking caused by short-term behaviour

[81] Corporate Governance Reform (2016).

[82] Ibid., 24 and 32.

[83] http://tomorrowscompany.com/.

[84] Promoting Long-Term Wealth (2017).

[85] European Union Green Paper (2011).

[86] Ibid., 2.

[87] Ibid.

[88] Ibid., 3.

of market participants were damaging sustainable long-term growth and jeopardizing a strong financial system in the EU.[89]

The EC observed that the majority of shareholders of EU listed companies are passive and often only focused on short-term profits.[90] Consequently, the EC suggested that measures were needed to encourage shareholders of EU listed companies to take an interest in sustainable returns and longer-term performance.[91] The EC also observed that there were issues in the agency relationship between institutional investors and asset managers in EU listed companies requiring correction, and that management short-term performance criteria may be having a negative influence on long-term corporate sustainability in the EU.[92] A wide range of questions for possible reforms were presented by the EC, which set the basis for EU reforms. To the extent that these proposals have been implemented, they are contained in the EU Amended Shareholder Rights Directive,[93] which entered into force on 9 June 2107 and EU Member States had until 10 June 2019 to implement these changes into national legislation. The specifics of the EU Amended Shareholder Rights Directive with regards to SMST reforms is discussed further in Chapter 4. There have also been some country-specific SMST-driven reforms in the European economic zone—namely in France and Switzerland. These reforms appear to have been motivated at least in part by SMST concerns, and these country-specific reforms are also assessed further in Chapter 4.

4. *The SMST Concerns of the Rest of the World*

There has been discussion of short-termism reform post-GFC outside of the UK, Europe and the US. In particular, specific governance organizations in many jurisdictions have advocated a longer-term approach—as discussed further in Chapter 4. Short-termism has also been considered

[89] Ibid., 2 and 12.

[90] Ibid., 3.

[91] Ibid.

[92] Ibid., 12.

[93] Directive (EU) 2017/828 of the European Parliament and of the Council, of 17 May 2017, amending Directive 2007/36/EC as regards the encouragement of long-term shareholder engagement (effective as of 9 June 2017) (EU Amended Shareholder Rights Directive).

by non-governmental organizations (NGOs)—e.g. the United Nations (UN) Global Compact,[94] Organisation for Economic Co-operation and Development (OECD) Long-Term Investment Project[95] and the World Economic Forum—Global Agenda Council on Long-Term Investing.[96] Acknowledging the issue, the UN Global Compact, stated that "[s]hort-termism in investment markets is a major obstacle to companies embedding sustainability in their strategic planning and capital investment decision."[97] The focus of NGO consideration is, however, intertwined with supporting longer-term investments in infrastructure projects and sustainable development, rather than specifically addressing short-termism in public capital markets. There has also been some academic consideration in Singapore[98]—perhaps motivating the Singapore Stock Exchange (SGX) to consider removing mandatory quarterly reporting and prompting changes to the restrictions on listing dual class share structures.[99] However, there is significantly less evidence of substantial short-termism driven reform discussion outside of the US, UK and the EU.

5. *SMST Discussions in the Financial Industry*

Short-termism driven reform has been of considerable interest to the financial industry—including consulting firms auxiliary to the financial industry such as McKinsey & Company (McKinsey) McKinsey is a consulting firm that provides advice to listed companies, intermediaries and asset owners. Dominic Barton, the global head of McKinsey, has been a long-time prominent advocate for financial industry-driven long-termism initiatives. He is credited with coining the phrase 'quarterly capitalism',

[94] UN Global Compact, 'Short-Termism in Financial Markets.' Online: https://www.unglobalcompact.org/take-action/action/long-term (UN Global Compact: Short-Termism).

[95] "Institutional Investors and Long-Term Investment." OECD. Online: http://www.oecd.org/pensions/private-pensions/institutionalinvestorsandlong-terminvestment.htm.

[96] https://www.weforum.org/system-initiatives/long-term-investing-infrastructure-and-development.

[97] UN Global Compact: Short-Termism.

[98] For example, see Chen et al. (2014).

[99] See the discussion in Chapter 4, Sect. A.1.c regarding dual listings and Sect. A.3.a regarding quarterly reporting.

which he defines as the continuing pressure on public companies to maximize short-term results.[100] The phrase 'quarterly capitalism' was given a boost of popularity when it was taken up by Hillary Clinton in her run for the Democratic Party nominee for US president.[101] Barton has also claimed the financial industry must correct the issue or change will be legislated upon it.[102]

Dominic Barton's solution to the quarterly capitalism problem can be summarized as: (1) businesses must revamp rewards towards long-term goals of at least five to seven years; (2) executives must infuse organizations with the objective of serving all major stakeholders, which in turn builds corporate value; and (3), to counter disengaged and dispersed ownership, boards must be bolstered to act like owners. Building on Barton's proposals, the Canada Pension Plan Investment Board (CPPIB) and McKinsey co-founded the online platform titled 'Focusing Capital on the Long Term' (FCLT) in 2013 which developed practical structures, metrics, and approaches for longer-term behaviour in the investment and business worlds.[103] Supported by Mark Wiseman, the President and CEO of CPPIB, Barton reiterated his proposals to counter quarterly capitalism in 2014, and called for the major players in the market, namely asset managers, to join in the fight.[104]

Consistent with Barton and Wiseman's message, for the third year running, Larry Fink, CEO of BlackRock, one of the world's largest asset management firm, has denounced short-termism and put out a call to action against short-termism which has generated considerable press. Arguably as an outcome of the 'secret summits' triggered by Chief Justice Strine's calls for action and Hillary Clinton's decry of short-termism,[105] Fink sent letters to CEOs of S&P 500 and large EU companies first in February 2016,[106] and again in 2017[107] and most recently in 2018[108]

[100] Barton (2011, 86).

[101] Jacobs (2015).

[102] Barton (2011, 87).

[103] http://www.fclt.org.

[104] Barton and Wiseman (2014, 46).

[105] McGee (2016).

[106] Turner (2016).

[107] Oyedele (2017).

[108] Fink (2018).

expressing BlackRock's concerns about increasing short-termism in stock markets. Larry Fink's calls have been echoed by other notable asset management firms. For example, soon after the 2016 letter, Ronald O'Hanley, president and CEO of State Street Investors warned of 'the perils of companies focusing on short-term results at the expense of long-term value creation', and William McNabb, Chairman and CEO of Vanguard, emphasized that good governance is key to long-term value.[109]

In his 2016 letter, Fink called for short-termism to be corrected by: (1) excess cash not being returned to shareholders at the expense of value-creating investments; (2) CEOs clearly laying out an annual strategic framework for long-term value creation; and (3) environmental, social and governance (ESG) issues being focused on by asset managers and handled well by companies.[110] In his 2017 letter to CEOs, Fink reiterated this call to action to S&P 500s, and also commented that "the private sector alone is not capable of shifting the tide of short-termism afflicting our society…[w]e need government policy that supports these goals – including tax reform, infrastructure investment and strengthening retirement system."[111] In his 2018 letter to CEOs, Fink again called on CEOs to "publicly articulate your company's strategic framework for long-term value creation and explicitly affirm that it has been reviewed by your board of directors."[112] "The statement of long-term strategy is essential" Fink said, "to understanding a company's actions and policies, its preparation for potential challenges, and the context of its shorter-term decisions."[113]

Larry Fink was also part of a small group of executives consisting of CEOs of asset managers, activist investors, a public pension plan and several public companies, which included Mary Barra of General Motors, Warren Buffet of Berkshire Hathaway Inc., and Jamie Dimon of JPMorgan Chase, that signed a statement of 'Commonsense Corporate Governance Principles'.[114] These principles were meant to serve as

[109] Tulay (2017).

[110] Turner (2016).

[111] Oyedele (2017).

[112] Fink (2018).

[113] Ibid.

[114] Commonsense Corporate Governance Principles (2016). Online: http://www.governanceprinciples.org/.

guidance for the good governance of public companies, and cover a wide range of governance matters, focusing primarily on the long-term financial health of US public companies. Speaking directly to the SMST issue, these principles encourage asset managers to use voting rights to act in the long-term interest of the public company,[115] and also provide that companies should place quarterly reporting in a broader context and avoid earnings guidance.[116]

It remains to be seen whether SMST will feature as prominently in asset manager communications with CEOs in 2019, or if the momentum around short-termism will fade. As demonstrated in this chapter, SMST is not a new issue but rather an evolving concern, This concern has interwoven with the main issues of the time period but appears to be generally linked to the increasing financial intermediation of public markets and the resulting need to measure asset managers on short-term results. Takeover concerns in the 1970/1980s in the US brought a denunciation of the short-termism of bad actors. Fear of losing pace with national competitors in the subsequent decades resulted in a rally against the short-termism of US companies. The 1990s and early 2000s saw the short-term interests of institutional investors and asset managers raised as a concern, as agency capitalism became the norm in US markets. Around the time of the bursting of the market bubble in the early 2000s, short-termism was cited as a contributing factor to high profile accounts frauds, which set the stage for a broader analysis of the short-term decision making of company managers. Despite the rising profile of SMST, GDP growth during these periods was relatively stable, and arguably it took the catastrophic financial fall out of the GFC to cast SMST definitively into the limelight.

The potential harms of SMST in capital markets have without a doubt been on the radar of academics, the financial industry and policy makers both before and, with renewed vigor, after the GFC. However, GDP growth stability appears to be returning in most major markets[117] and

[115] Ibid., 8.

[116] Ibid., 6.

[117] World Bank Open Data. Online: https://data.worldbank.org/ shows that from its post-GFC low of US$2.383 trillion in 2009, the UK GDP (in current US$) has risen to US$2.622 trillion in 2017 (which growth has presumably been impacted by the UK vote to leave the EU in 2016), and the US GDP has steadily risen from its post-GFC low of US$14.419 trillion in 2009 to US$19.391 trillion in 2017.

the world economy generally.[118] It is possible that interest in SMST may now take a back seat to other more pressing capital market concerns, such as for example, global political uncertainty. Nevertheless, if SMST is indeed the real and harmful problem it is made out to be rather than merely a rhetorical tool, regulatory and financial industry reform is warranted now rather than waiting until the next inevitable capital market disruption. Consequently, Chapter 4 analyzes the SMST reforms which have emerged in the post-GFC period. The remaining chapters of this book then provide further examination of whether SMST is an actual problem, and if the reforms discussed in Chapter 4 at least conceptually address the SMST problem.

References

Aspen Institute. 2009. "Overcoming Short-Termism: A Call for a More Responsible Approach to Investment and Business Management." 9 September.

Barton, Dominic. 2011. "Capitalism for the Long Term." March. *Harvard Business Review*. 84–90.

Barton, Dominic and Wiseman, Mark. 2014. "Focusing Capital on the Long Term." January–February. *Harvard Business Review*. 44–51.

Biden, Joe. 2016. "How Short-Termism Saps the Economy." 27 September. *Wall Street Journal*.

Business Wire. 2009. "Three Top Economists Agree 2009 Worst Financial Crisis Since Great Depression; Risks Increase If Right Steps Are Not Taken." 27 February. *Reuters*. https://www.businesswire.com/news/home/20090213005161/en/Top-Economists-Agree-2009-Worst-Financial-Crisis.

Chen, Xia, Qiang Cheng, Alvis, K. Lo, and Xin, Wang. 2014. "CEO Contractual Protection and Managerial Short-Termism." 5 March. Singapore Management University School of Accountancy Research Paper No. 2014-18.

Cleary, Siobhan. 2015. "Stock Exchanges and Sustainability." December. UNEP. Inquiry Working Paper. http://unepinquiry.org/wp-content/uploads/2015/12/Stock_Exchanges_and_Sustainability.pdf.

Cohen, Daniel A., Dey, Aiyesha, and Lys, Thomas Z. 2008. "Real and Accrual-Based Earnings Management in the Pre- and Post- Sarbanes-Oxley Periods." May. 83 *The Accounting Review*. 757–787.

[118]World Bank Open Data. Online: https://data.worldbank.org/ shows that from a global (current US$) post-GFC low of US$60.267 trillion in 2009, GDP has rise fairly steadily to US$80.738 trillion in 2017.

Commission on the Regulation of U.S Capital Markets in the 21st Century, Report and Recommendations. 2007. An Independent, Bipartisan Commission Established by the US Chamber of Commerce. March. https://www.uschamber.com/commission-regulation-us-capital-markets-21st-century.

"Corporate Governance Reform." 2016. Green Paper. November. UK Government Department for Business, Energy & Industrial Strategy.

Dallas, Lynne L. 2012. "Short-Termism, the Financial Crisis, and Corporate Governance." 2011–2012. 37:2 *The Journal of Corporation Law*. 265–364.

Davies, Richard, Haldane, Andrew G., Nielsen, Mette, and Pezzini, Silvia. 2014. "Measuring the Costs of Short-Termism." 12 *Journal of Financial Stability*. 16–25.

Directive (EU) 2017/828 of the European Parliament and of the Council, of 17 May 2017, Amending Directive 2007/36/EC as Regards the Encouragement of Long-Term Shareholder Engagement (Effective as of 9 June 2017).

Donaldson, William H. 2005. Speech at 2005 CFA Institute Annual Conference. 8 May. http://www.sec.gov/news/speech/spch050805whd.htm.

Easterbrook, Frank H. and Fischel, Daniel R. 1981. "The Proper Role of a Target's Management in Responding to a Tender Offer." April. 94:6 *Harvard Law Review*. 1161–1204.

European Union Green Paper. 2011. "The EU Corporate Governance Framework." COM (2011)164. 5 April.

Farrar, John H. and Mayes, David G. (eds.). 2013. *Globalization, the Global Financial Crisis and the State*. Edward Elgar: Cheltenham.

Farrell, Sean. 2015. "The World's Biggest Accounting Scandals." 21 July. *The Guardian*. https://www.theguardian.com/business/2015/jul/21/the-worlds-biggest-accounting-scandals-toshiba-enron-olympus.

Fink, Larry. 2018. CEO Letter, BlackRock, Inc. January. https://www.blackrock.com/corporate/investor-relations/larry-fink-ceo-letter.

Gallagher, SEC Commissioner Daniel M. 2015. "Activism, Short-Termism, and the SEC: Remarks at the 21st Annual Stanford Directors' College." 23 June.

Gilson, Ronald J. and Black, Bernard S. 1999. *The Law and Finance of Corporate Acquisitions*. 2nd ed. Supp. 1999. The Foundation Press: New York.

Gilson, Ronald J. and Kraakman, Reinier. 2005. "Takeovers in the Boardroom: Burke Versus Schumpeter." August. 60:4 *The Business Lawyer*. 1419–1433.

Graham, John R., Cam, Harvey, and Shiva, Rajgopal. 2005. "The Economic Implications of Corporate Financial Reporting." December. 40 *Journal of Accounting and Economics*. 3–73.

Haldane, Andrew. 2015. "Who Owns a Company." Speech at the University of Edinburgh Corporate Finance Conference. 28 July. http://www.bankofengland.co.uk/publications/Pages/speeches/2015/833.aspx.

Haldane, Andrew and Davies, Richards. 2011. "The Short-Long." Speech at the 29th Société Universitaire Européene de Recherches Financières Colloquium: New Paradigms in Money and Finance? May. Brussels.

Healy, Paul M. and Palepu, Krishna G. 2003. "The Fall of Enron." Spring. 17:2 *Journal of Economic Perspectives*. 3–26.

"Implementation of the Kay Review: Progress Report." 2014. Department for Business Innovation & Skills. October.

Jacobs, Ben. 2015. "Hillary Clinton Decries Wall Street's 'Quarterly Capitalism' in Tax Reform Pitch." 24 July. *The Guardian*.

Jacobs, Justice Jack B. 2012. "Patient Capital: Can Delaware Corporate Law Help Revive It?" 68:4 *Washington and Lee Law Review*. 1645–1664.

Jacobs, Michael T. 1991. *Short Term America: The Causes and Cures of Our Business Myopia*. Harvard Business School Press: New York.

Jackson, Tony. 2009. "Short-Termism Made Institutions Vulnerable." 13 December. *Financial Times*.

Kay, John. 2012. 'The Kay Review of UK Equity Markets and Long-Term Decision Making." Final Report. July.

"The Kay Review of UK Equity Markets and Long-Term Decision Making: Government Response to the Committee's Third Report of Session 2013–14." 2014. Special Report of Session 2013–14, House of Commons. 22 October 2013.

Kraakman, Reinier, et al. 2009. *The Anatomy of Corporate Law: A Comparative and Functional Approach*. 2nd ed. Oxford University Press: Oxford, UK.

Krehmeyer, Dean, Orsagh, Matthew, and Schacht, Kurt N. 2006. "Breaking the Short-Term Cycle: Discussion and Recommendations on How Corporate Leaders, Asset Managers, Investors, and Analysts Can Refocus on Long-Term Value." CFA Centre for Financial Market Integrity/Business Roundtable Institute for Corporate Ethics. https://www.cfainstitute.org/-/media/documents/article/position-paper/breaking-the-short-term-cycle.ashx.

Lipton, Martin. 1979. "Takeover Bids in the Target Boardroom." November. 35 *The Business Lawyer*. 101–134.

McGee, Suzanne. 2016. "Long-Term Investors Are Taking on the Hedge Funds Over Short-Term Vision." 4 February. *The Guardian*.

Merced, Michael J. de la and Phillips, Matt. 2018. "Trump Asks S.E.C. to Study Quarterly Earnings Requirements for Public Firms." 17 August. *DealBook*. https://www.nytimes.com/2018/08/17/business/dealbook/trump-quarterly-earnings.html?rref=collection%2Fissuecollection%2Ftodays-new-york-times&action = click&contentCollection = todayspaper&region = rank&module=package&version=highlights&contentPlacement=5&pgtype=collection.

Moore, Marc T. and Walker-Arnott, Edward. 2014. "A Fresh Look at Stock Market Short-Termism." 41:3 *Journal of Law and Society*. 416–445.

Oyedele, Akin. 2017. "Here Is the Letter the World's Largest Investor, BlackRock CEO Larry Fink, Just Sent to CEOs Everywhere." 24 January. *Business Insider UK*. http://uk.businessinsider.com/blackrock-ceo-larry-fink-letter-to-ceos-2017-1?r=US&IR=T.

Pearlstein, Steven. 2009. "Wall Street's Mania for Short-Term Results Hurts Economy." 11 September. *Washington Post*. www.washingtonpost.com/wp-dyn/content/article/2009/09/10/AR2009091004224.html.

Porter, Michael E. 1992. "Capital Disadvantage: America's Failing Capital Investment System." *Harvard Business Review*. 65–82.

"Promoting Long-Term Wealth: Reshaping Corporate Governance." 2017. A Report by Tomorrow's Company for the All-Party Parliamentary Corporate Governance Group. January.

Salter, Malcolm S. 2012. "How Short-Termism Invites Corruption…And What to Do About It." 12 April. Harvard Business School. Working Paper 12-094.

Strine, Leo E., Jr. 2015. "Securing Our Nation's Economic Future: A Sensible, Nonpartisan Agenda to Increase Long-Term Investment and Job Creation in The United States." University of Pennsylvania Institute for Law & Economics Research Paper No. 15–41.

Rappaport, Alfred. 2011. *Saving Capitalism from Short-Termism: How to Build Long-Term Value and Take Back our Financial Future*. McGraw-Hill: New York.

Roe, Mark J. 2013. "Corporate Short-Termism—In the Boardroom and in the Courtroom." August. 68 *Business Lawyer*. 977–1006.

Tonello, Matteo. 2006. "Revisiting Stock Market Short-Termism." Corporate/Investor Summit Series. The Conference Board.

Tulay, Mark. 2017. "Why the World's Largest Asset Managers are Pushing Long-Term Thinking." 27 July. *GreenBiz*. https://www.greenbiz.com/article/why-worlds-largest-asset-managers-are-pushing-long-term-thinking.

Turner, Matt. 2016. "Here Is the Letter the World's Largest Investor, BlackRock CEO Larry Fink, Just Sent to CEOs Everywhere." 2 February. *Business Insider UK*. http://uk.businessinsider.com/blackrock-ceo-larry-fink-letter-to-sp-500-ceos-2016-2?r=US&IR=T.

Weldon, Duncan. 2015. "Is Short-Termism Wrecking the Economy." 30 July. *British Broadcasting Corporation*. http://www.bbc.co.uk/news/business-33718644.

White, Gary. 2013. "Prince Charles Urges Companies to End Short-Termism." 3 February. *The Telegraph*.

CHAPTER 4

What Has Been Done to Correct Short-Termism?

Before analyzing in detail what may actually be causing the stock market short-termism (SMST) problem, it is first useful to examine the public policy and financial industry reforms implemented to date that are meant to address the perceived SMST issue. Consequently, this chapter surveys reforms in all jurisdictions that have identified a SMST concern and assesses whether such reforms are 'hard' and 'soft' law, or financial industry initiatives. The review in this chapter is categorized into asset owner, intermediary and company manager reforms on the basis that each of these groups serves a distinct role within stock markets, and SMST allegations manifest differently in each role. Section A reviews the SMST reforms directed at correcting the SMST of asset owners. Section B focuses on the SMST of intermediaries, including asset managers affiliated with particular asset owners, and SMST-driven reforms addressing company managers are then reviewed in Sect. C.

The SMST reforms in this chapter are categorized into asset owner, intermediary and company manager reforms. However, there undoubtedly is cross-over between the categorizations. For instance, the United Kingdom (UK) Investor Forum[1] is discussed in Sect. A under asset

[1]As noted previously, this is a UK community interest group purporting to represent interests of the entire equity ownership chain in the UK formed in 2014 based on a recommendation in Kay (2012) (Kay Review).

K. M. Willey, *Stock Market Short-Termism*,
https://doi.org/10.1007/978-3-030-22903-0_4

owners, but also impacts intermediaries and company managers. SMST reformers, most notably UK Professor John Kay, have advocated a comprehensive approach to reform. As mentioned in the Kay Review, "[n]o single reform will provide the solution, but when implemented together, we believe our recommendations will help to deliver the improvements to equity markets necessary to support sustainable long-term value creation by British companies."[2] Given the overlap of SMST concerns in each category of market participant, a holistic approach may be most prudent for policymakers. However, the reforms have been delineated in this chapter to provide a thematic framework to identify the reforms and how they propose to correct SMST.

The results in this chapter demonstrate that minimal SMST-driven reform has actually been implemented and, of the implemented SMST reforms, most are 'soft' law or financial industry initiatives. Further, the survey results also provide evidence that of the implemented reforms, many are 'light' touch in that they are disclosure or 'comply or explain' based or contain an 'opt-out' mechanism. The complexity of the SMST problem and the inconclusive evidence on the harms of SMST may help explain why there has been so little implemented reform, despite significant discussion on the SMST issue and calls for reform. The basis for this complexity and indeterminate evidence is explored further in the following chapters, culminating in an attempt in Chapter 8 to examine if the implement reforms surveyed in this chapter are, at least conceptually, effective as measured against the most probable causes of the SMST concerns.

A. Asset Owner SMST Reforms

The following Sect. A considers the asset owner SMST reforms, which reforms are summarized in Appendix 'A' (Table 1). These SMST reforms relate to:

1. Measures favouring long-term share ownership,
2. Changes to taxation policy associated with the duration of share ownership,

[2] Kay (2012, 9).

3. Disclosure by listed companies,
4. Direct communication with shareholders,
5. Changes to stock-lending regulation,
6. Formation of a long-term index, and
7. Hedge funds.

Although the SMST reforms examined in this section may also impact intermediaries and company managers, such reforms are considered in this section on the basis that the primarily intention of such reforms appears to be to correct the SMST of asset owners. As mentioned in Chapter 2, the main concern raised is that asset owners, particularly those who hold shares of listed companies for short time periods, appear to exhibit a preference for short-term financial returns, which is detrimental and should be discouraged. Alternatively, another argument made is that long-term shareholding or 'patient' investing should be encouraged as long-term asset owners have, or should have, a vested interest in the long-term viability of listed companies.[3] Though there is much consideration of 'hard' law SMST-driven reform advancing these propositions, as demonstrated in the discussion below, few 'hard' law reforms have been enacted, and most implemented reform in this space is 'soft' law or financial industry initiatives.

1. *Measures Favouring Long-Term Share Ownership*

This section compiles the regulatory and financial industry reforms that encourage longer-term ownership of listed companies in an attempt to address SMST-concerns. The areas of reform considered are:

1. Additional voting rights and rewards for long-term shareholders,
2. Board nomination rights for long-term shareholders, and
3. Dual class structures.

[3] As will be explored in Chapter 5, the assumption that long-term asset owners are more interested in long-term value than short-term shareholders may be problematic as evidence suggests long-term asset owners may knowingly pursue short-term returns at the expense of sustainable longer-term value. See the discussion generally in Fried (2015) and Dent (2010).

Underlying these measures is the rationale that longer-term shareholders are vested in the long-term financial sustainability of the listed company. Further, some asset owners—for example, high-frequency traders—may hold their shares for substantially less time than other longer-term asset owners. These short-term shareholders may be incentivized to push for short-term share price maximization or financial returns, which may provide short-term benefits at the expense of the longer-term viability of the listed company.[4]

a. Additional Voting Rights and Rewards for Long-Term Shareholders

Long-term asset owners, who may be more committed to long-term corporate financial sustainability, should, it has been argued, receive a voting advantage or other incentives based on duration of their share ownership.[5] Such advantage could be 'Loyalty' or 'L-Shares' with greater voting rights, or rights to receive additional securities/dividends after a time period.[6] L-Shares would reward long-term shareholders, and potentially discourage short-term share trading.

There has been much discussion on L-Shares,[7] and with respect to increased voting rights based on duration of share ownership, the 'one shareholder, one vote' corporate democracy principle has been questioned by SMST reformers.[8] Generally accepted by corporate law scholars as the basis for efficient distribution of corporate voting rights, the principle is that each unit of ownership has the same voting power in an organization.[9] The suggestion made by SMST reformers is that actually all shareholders are not equal, and that long-term shareholders should be afforded enhanced voting rights in order to ensure that the long-term interests of the listed company are furthered. Despite this extensive ongoing discussion, the only enacted 'hard' law reforms based on SMST concerns has been the Florange Law[10] enacted in France.

[4] Dallas (2012, 297).

[5] Quimby (2013, 389).

[6] Ibid.

[7] For example, see Delvoie and Clotten (2015) and Quimby (2013).

[8] See Quimby (2013).

[9] See synopsis in Hayden and Bodie (2008).

[10] LOI n° 2014-384 du 29 mars 2014 visant à reconquérir l'économie réelle (1) NOR: EFIX1322399L enacted in April 2014 (Florange Law).

The Florange Law reverses the prior position in France and provides that shares held in registered form for at least two years in French listed companies are automatically afforded double voting rights, unless the listed company's articles are expressly amended by two-thirds of the shareholders to provide otherwise. The stated purpose of the Florange Law is to promote long-termism, as evidenced by the title of the amendments, '*Mesures En Faveur De L'actionnariat De Long Terme*'[11]—'Measures to Protect Long-Term Ownership', and it aims to counter short-termism by encouraging more loyalty between investors and companies.[12]

The Florange Law has been criticized as protectionist.[13] The assertion has been made that the French State and large trade unions, which together exercise significant voting positions in French listed companies,[14] gain additional control of French listed companies at the expense of non-French minority shareholders.[15] The timing of such changes may also be particularly fortuitous for such French shareholders, as they look to raise cash by selling shares in domestic companies while still retaining voting influence.[16] Though it is a 'hard' law change, the Florange Law does provide an 'opt out' if shareholder approval is obtained.

French law has long permitted French listed companies to voluntarily offer L-Shares with bonus dividends to their shareholders who have held shares in registered form for at least two years in order to encourage long-term shareholdings.[17] These bonus dividends are limited to 0.5% of the listed company's capital, and a maximum of 10% of the regular dividend.[18] This structure is not unique to France. The Netherlands, for example, also has listed companies which grant multiple voting rights to

[11] Ibid., Article 5.

[12] Shareholder Rights (2015).

[13] Johnson (2015).

[14] Trade unions exercise these interests through voting employee share schemes.

[15] Johnson (2015).

[16] Shareholder Rights (2015).

[17] See Delvoie and Clottens (2015, 20) where the authors discuss the introduction of legislation on loyalty dividends in 1994. As an example, L'Oréal France offers Loyalty Shares to registered shareholders who hold shares for two years. Online: http://www.loreal-finance.com/eng/registered-shares-loyalty-bonus.

[18] "Other Services—France: Loyalty Bonus Shares" (September 9, 2016) Clearstream. Online: http://www.clearstream.com/clearstream-en/products-and-services/market-coverage/europe-t2s/france/other-services---france/61430.

certain categories of shareholders.[19] At the European Union (EU) level, loyalty shares were considered at the start of the process to amend the EU Shareholder Rights Directive.[20] However, as the amendments took shape, the EU opted against including any guidance on loyalty shares.[21] These types of L-Shares with either bonus dividends or extra voting rights do not appear to materially be in use elsewhere, other than in fairly limited circumstances in Europe.[22]

Use of these L-Shares is also entirely optional, and, other than in respect of the Florange Law, SMST does not appear to have significantly factored into the previous legislative motivation in France for facilitating such types of L-Share structures. However, the impetus by listed companies for using such structures appears to relate to rewarding loyalty and maintaining a stable shareholder basis,[23] which coincides with the intended use of such shares to address SMST concerns discussed above. Consequently, L-Shares are included in the analysis in this chapter as an implemented—albeit on a limited scale—financial industry-driven voluntary SMST-reform.

Increased voting rights for long-term shareholders were temporarily introduced in Italy. However, a campaign against this legislation by independent directors got such support that the legislation was not extended past its sunset clause of 31 January 2015.[24] In the UK, increased voting

[19] See Delvoie and Clottens (2015, 21), where the authors confirm that such structure has been used since 2006, but there is no specifically legal basis for—or prohibition against—doing so.

[20] Directive (EU) 2017/828 of the European Parliament and of the Council, of 17 May 2017, amending Directive 2007/36/EC as regards the encouragement of long-term shareholder engagement (effective as of 9 June 2017).

[21] Delvoie and Clottens (2015, 23).

[22] Conaghan et al. (2017).

[23] For example, Ferrari N. V., a Netherlands company, indicates in the terms and conditions of its special voting shares that the purpose of its loyalty voting program is to reward the long-term ownership of common shares and promote stability of the company's shareholder base. Online: http://corporate.ferrari.com/sites/ferrari15ipo/files/dms-20012424-v1-index_13_-_ferrari_terms_and_conditions_special_voting_.pdf.

[24] Temporary legislative amendments in July 2014 allowed Italian listed companies to modify their statutes via a simple shareholder majority vote to introduce double voting rights to shareholders owning shared for two years (Law Decree No. 91 of 24 June 2014, converted into law by Law No. 116 of 11 August 2014 amended the Legislative Decree No. 58 of 24 February 1998).

based solely on length of ownership was considered but rejected in the Kay Review as impractical to implement and unlikely to achieve the desired ameliorative effect on SMST.[25] The UK Government endorsed Kay's conclusion, and observed that UK company law was sufficient flexible to allow companies to reward long-term shareholders.[26] As noted above, at the EU level, Sergio Cofferati, rapporteur for the Committee on Legal Affairs of the European Parliament, proposed an amendment to the EU Amended Shareholder Rights Directive[27] giving shareholders holding shares for two years or more benefits including additional voting rights.[28] However, such provisions were not included in the final amendments to the EU Amended Shareholder Rights Directive. Therefore, only the Florange Law and the use of L-Shares as SMST reforms.

b. Board Nomination Rights for Long-Term Shareholders

Additional board nomination rights—i.e. the ability to propose candidates to be elected as directors—based on length of share ownership were briefly introduced in the United States (US) by the US Securities and Exchange Commission (SEC) Proxy Access Rule (SEC Proxy Access Rule)[29] as authorized under the Dodd-Frank Act.[30] As discussed in Chapter 3,[31] the intention of the Dodd-Frank Act was to improve accountability and transparency, end 'too big to fail' and bailouts by taxpayers and implement stronger consumer protection regulations in the wake of the global financial crisis (GFC).

Arguably, however, at least a few of the changes implemented in the Dodd-Frank Act also meant to mitigate some of the harmful effects of short-termism in equity markets. It is difficult to precisely isolate SMST-driven reforms from the sweeping body of reforms in the legislation. However, the set of reforms in the Dodd-Frank Act which are said to

[25] Kay (2012, 63).

[26] Implementation (2014, 51).

[27] Directive (EU) 2017/828 of the European Parliament and of the Council, of 17 May 2017, amending Directive 2007/36/EC as regards the encouragement of long-term shareholder engagement (effective as of 9 June 2017) (EU Amended Shareholder Rights Directive).

[28] Jones (2015).

[29] SEC Rule 14a-11.

[30] Pub. L. 111–203, H.R. 4173 (Dodd-Frank Act).

[31] See Chapter 3, Sect. D.1.

be meant to address the SMST issue are those contained in Title IX—Investor Protections and Improvements to the Regulation of Securities of the Dodd-Frank Act. These include Subtitle A—Increasing Investor Protection, Subtitle E—Accountability and Executive Compensation, and Subtitle G—Strengthening Corporate Governance. Indeed, it is this set of reforms that are cited by commentators who have considered whether the Dodd-Frank Act addressed SMST.[32]

The SEC Proxy Access Rule mandated that US public companies must include shareholder director nominees in proxy materials under certain circumstances, which mostly significantly included that the shareholder nominating the board candidate must hold at least 3% of the voting power of a company's securities for at least three years.[33] The SEC's rationale for imposing this condition was short-termism concerns. Specifically, the SEC expressly stated in the paper on the proposed rule that "… long-term shareholders are more likely to have interests that are better aligned with other shareholders and are less likely to use the rule solely for short-term gain."[34]

The SEC Proxy Access Rule was, however, vacated by the US Court of Appeals for the District of Columbia Circuit in July 2011 on the grounds that the rule was "arbitrary and capricious."[35] The US Court ruled that the SEC "inconsistently and opportunistically framed the costs and benefits of the rule; failed adequately to quantify the certain costs or to explain why those costs could not be quantified; neglected to support its predictive judgments; contradicted itself; and failed to respond to substantial problems raised by commentators."[36] Of particular interest, one of the criticisms leveled at the SEC Proxy Access Rule was that it actually may have increased short-termism, as the short-term interests of certain shareholders who hold shares for three years or more would be given a stronger platform into a listed company.[37]

[32] Dallas (2012) and Thomas et al. (2010).

[33] Kastiel (2015).

[34] SEC, Proposed Rule Paper, Facilitating Shareholder Director Nominations, 2009, https://www.sec.gov/rules/proposed/2009/33-9046.pdf, at 50.

[35] *Business Roundtable and Chamber of Commerce of the United States of America v Securities and Exchange Commission* 647 F.3d 1144 (2011).

[36] Ibid., paras 1148–1149.

[37] See Kastiel (2015), which comprehensively summarizes the arguments for and against proxy access.

Though the Proxy Access Rule was vacated by the US courts, the practice of granting board nomination rights based on duration of share ownership continued. Specifically, the constitutional documents of many US listed companies—e.g. bylaws—, typically contain a provision allowing shareholders to include their director nominees in the company's proxy materials sent to all shareholders, provided that the nominating shareholder has held their shares for three years and holds at least 3% of the voting rights.[38] The story of mandatory proxy access rules in the US demonstrates the complexity of imposing regulation intended to combat SMST concerns. The continued use of the 3%/3-year thresholds in practice also highlights the need for a deeper understanding of what is actually causing the SMST problems, and how regulatory and financial industry measures can effectively deal with this issue.

c. Dual Class Structures

It is also worth mentioning dual class share structures, as a discussion of this structure has emerged in the context of SMST reform. For example, a recommendation by the Roosevelt Institute to end short-termism was to encourage alternative share structures such as loyalty shares, which recommendation specifically included furthering dual class structures.[39] Dual class share structures are intended to preserve control by providing certain long-term shareholders—namely founders and other insiders—with increased voting rights over other shareholders who are not related to the business of the company. In a dual class share structure, two or more classes of shares are issued, one of which is issued to founders/executives and provides more voting rights than the public shares, and the other class is issued to the general public with significantly less voting rights than the founder shares.[40] Using this method, Google insiders, for example, hold Class B shares which vote 10:1 to the publicly held shares, giving insiders 64% of the voting power of Google.[41]

[38] Ibid.

[39] Konczal et al. (2015, 5).

[40] 'Dual Class Stock' Investopedia. Online: http://www.investopedia.com/terms/d/dualclassstock.asp.

[41] Emspak (2017).

Dual class structures have long been legally permitted on stock exchanges in some jurisdictions, including Canada and the US, and have been cited as a potential solution to the SMST problem.[42] Precisely, it is argued that "[a] dual-class share structure can allow a management team to ignore the short-termism often seen in financial markets."[43] However, even in the jurisdictions where these dual class structures are permitted to be listed for trading, their value as a SMST corrective measure has been questioned on the basis that the founders may abuse their increased voting rights and act in their own interests rather than the interests of all shareholders.[44] The debate on dual class structures is considered further in Chapter 8.[45]

Despite this debate, Singapore recently made changes to its corporate law to permit dual class shares, and the Singapore Stock Exchange (SGX) has allowed trading of such securities on its secondary market, citing correction to SMST concerns.[46] Suggesting that this change may be more of a marketing move to attract business to reinvigorate the listless SGX rather than a genuine SMST-corrective measure, primary listings of dual class structures are still under consideration.[47] Possibly as a result of the discussion on the merits of this structure as a remedy to SMST, other than the example of Singapore discussed above, listing restrictions on dual class shares with increased voting have not been amended outside of the jurisdictions where they are already in place in response to SMST concerns.

2. *'Carrot and Stick'—Taxation*

Proposals to change taxation policy to ameliorate issues of short-termism would necessitate 'hard' law reforms to applicable taxing legislation. Using taxation policy to discourage perceived 'excessive' share trading[48]

[42] For example, see Quimby (2013), and the recommendations in Konczal et al. (2015, 5).

[43] Modesto (2016).

[44] See, for example, "Dual Class Share Structures: The Cost of Control," 21 July 2011. *The Economist* and the Commonsense Corporate Governance Principles 2016. Online: http://www.governanceprinciples.org/ which state that "[d]ual class voting is not a best practice."

[45] See Chapter 8, Sect. A.1.c

[46] Choo (2016).

[47] Lee (2017).

[48] What constitutes 'excessive' trading is not conclusively defined but appears to encompass HFT.

and encourage longer-term ownership is of considerable interest to SMST reformers, and the proposed reforms aimed at using taxation to correct the SMST issue are discussed below. The 'carrot' is a reduction of the capital gains taxation rate meant to encourage longer-term shareholding, and the 'stick' is the introduction of a financial transaction tax (FTT)—e.g. a Tobin tax[49]—as is proposed in the EU[50]—, meant to discourage excessive trading. Admittedly, FTTs are directed at the parties trading shares, which are primarily intermediaries. However, as costs of FTTs flow through to asset owners, such SMST-driven reforms are considered here. Though 'hard' law taxation reforms have been considered, none have yet been implemented.

a. Capital Gains Rate Changes

Changes to the capital gains tax rates on distributions have been proposed as a remedy for SMST. In particular, reducing the capital gains rate on dividends paid to shareholders of listed companies who have held their shares for a significant period of time is seen as beneficial. The thinking is that asset owners—via their asset managers—should be encouraged to hold onto their shares as the pressure on company managers to prop up share prices in the short-term comes from a focus on short-term trading by asset managers and asset owners.[51] Though not clearly articulated by the proponents of a capital gains tax change, the reasoning appears to be that asset owners—via asset managers—are locked into their shareholdings for longer periods of time. Therefore, they may also be less likely to sell their shares based on negative short-term results of the listed company. This locked in scenario takes the pressure off company managers to engage in short-term earnings manipulation needed to keep share prices high. Long-term shareholders should, theoretically at least, be more concerned about ensuring that listed companies are focused on long term value generation rather than

[49]Tax suggested in 1970s by economist and Nobel laureate, James Tobin, to impose a modest tax on all short-term financial transactions.

[50]"EU Proposal for a Council Directive implementing enhanced cooperation in the area of financial transaction tax", COM (2013) 71, Brussels (EU FTT Proposal).

[51]Dallas (2012, 348) and Aspen Institute (2009).

responding to short-term actions of management. A change to capital gains tax was considered in the Kay Review,[52] but the most developed discussion in this area has been in the US.

US taxpayers are currently taxed on capital gains, namely net profits earned on the sale of shares. There is already an incentive in the US capital gains system encouraging longer-term shareholding. Capital gains on shares held for less than a year are taxed as ordinary income, and shares held for longer than a year are taxed at a lower rate.[53] There have been calls for capital gains policy in the US to be changed to further encourage longer-term shareholding. The Aspen Report 2009 recommended revising US capital gains taxation and removing limitations on capital loss deductibility for very long-term holdings, currently capped at US$3000 per year.[54] Short-termism driven reform to capital gains taxation was reiterated by Delaware Supreme Court Chief Justice Leo E. Strine.[55] Chief Justice Strine suggested the "oxymoronic definition of a long-term gain – which is now one year – should be changed to something more worthy of the term, such as four or five years."[56] Capital gains taxation policy change to correct the perceived SMST-issue was also a policy position of former Democratic Presidential nominee, Hillary Clinton.

Stating the need to encourage investors to focus on long-term growth and abandon a culture of short-term speculation, Senator Clinton proposed capital gains changes in her 2016 Presidential campaign. These

[52] Respondents in the Kay Review consultation process did suggest long-term investors receive taxation concessions. However, this was rejected by Kay on the basis of irrelevance as it was determined most UK shareholders do not pay capital gains tax, as most UK taxpayers are able to take advantage of exemptions or structure their shareholdings to avoid such taxation (see Kay 2012, 62 and 84). Sir George Cox, in an independent review by Sir George Cox commissioned by the Labour Party Cox Review (26 February 2013), "Overcoming Short-termism within British Business: The key to sustained economic growth", suggested a change to the capital gains tax rate (from 50 to 10% over 10 years) to incentivize longer-term shareholding.

[53] US Internal Revenue Code, 26 U.S.C. § 1. The current rates on long-term shareholdings have been the same since 2003, except the two lowest income brackets were reduced to 0% in 2008 as part of Obama's platform to encourage investment in small business and assist struggling families (Obama-Bidden Plan 2008).

[54] Aspen Institute (2009, 3) (Aspen Report 2009).

[55] Chief Justice Strine's comments on this topic are significant given Delaware's prominence as a corporate domicile for most US companies.

[56] Strine (2015, 8–9).

included taxing capital gains on a six-year sliding scale and doubling the period of time gains are taxed at the top rate of 39.6%.[57] President Trump initiated a major overhaul of the US tax system, which was enacted effective for tax years after 31 December 2017.[58] Capital gains proposals encouraging long-term shareholding may re-emerge during further efforts at tax reform in the US. However, as noted in Chapter 3,[59] this is unlikely as President Trump's focus appears to instead be on reducing corporate tax rates rather than providing tax incentives to reduce SMST. Consequently, despite this discussion, there has of yet been no capital gains taxation reforms post-GFC in the jurisdictions surveyed designed to correct the SMST problem.

b. Trading Taxes

Variations of an FTT, essentially a modest tax on all short-term financial transactions including the purchase and sale of shares, as a SMST corrective measure have received attention post-GFC. However, no such reforms have yet been implemented. It has been suggested that an FTT on trades of securities may diminish the perceived harmful effects of SMST by reducing excessive trading,[60] and encouraging longer-term investing.[61] Theoretically, the cost of an FTT may make asset managers and asset owners think twice about selling shares, and instead focus on investments seeking long-term growth and sustainable earnings. The idea is that these longer-term shareholders will, indirectly by not selling their shares in response to negative short-term results, apply less pressure on company managers to keep the short-term share price high, as they are more concerned about long-term cash generating potential.

[57] Jacobs (2015).

[58] H.R.1—An Act to provide for reconciliation pursuant to titles II and V of the concurrent resolution on the budget for fiscal year 2018.

[59] See Chapter 3, Sect. D.1.

[60] As noted above, excessive trading is associated with HFT, and the short-termism concerns of HFT have been articulated as the costs of such trades which erode ultimate saver value (Aspen Institute, 2) and a negative trend in equity markets favoring trading over trust relationships (Kay 2012, 39).

[61] See the discussion in Strine (2015, 6–12).

An FTT has been called for in the US for years,[62] and was recently taken up by the Aspen Institute,[63] and supported by Chief Justice Strine.[64] In her presidential campaign, Hillary Clinton also mentioned a US transaction tax on HFT (high frequency trading), which essentially involves using sophisticated technological tools to rapidly trade securities, although specifics were not provided.[65] Despite this ongoing discussion there have not been any regulatory proposals for an FTT in the US. In the UK, an FTT was not addressed in the Kay Review, possibly as the UK already has a stamp duty on financial transactions—though most intermediaries are exempt.[66] The UK Government considered an FTT in its response to the Kay Review, as there was some support for such tax in the consultation process.[67] However, the UK Government determined not to explore such a tax further, arguing that for an FTT to be meaningful it would need to be implemented globally or the entities taxed would just relocate to non-taxing jurisdictions.[68]

An FTT has been proposed by the European Commission to, amongst other things, discourage financial transactions which do not contribute to the efficiency of financial markets or the real economy, or may contribute to a future crisis.[69] Although short-termism reform has not been clearly articulated as a reason for the EU FTT Proposal, SMST concerns arguably can generally been seen in the rationale provided for the EU FTT Proposal, as the short-termism problem may be seen to impact market efficiency. The EU FFT Proposal is to charge financial institutions a tax of 0.1% against the exchange of securities if one of the financial institutions in a transaction resides in an EU Member State. The EU FTT Proposal is currently stalled—and was strongly resisted by the UK[70]—but

[62] Ibid., 7–8, where Chief Justice Strine discusses the imposition of a less than 1% tax on any securities or derivative trade.

[63] Aspen Institute (2009, 3), which called for an excise tax but did not offer specifics.

[64] Strine (2015, 7–8).

[65] "Wall Street Reform", The Office of Hillary Rodham Clinton. Online: https://www.hillaryclinton.com/issues/wall-street/.

[66] Schedule 13, UK Finance Act 1999.

[67] Kay Review Government Response (2014, 44).

[68] Ibid., 17.

[69] EU Proposal for a Council Directive implementing enhanced cooperation in the area of financial transaction tax', COM (2013) 71, Brussels (EU FTT Proposal).

[70] "Financial Transactions Tax: UK launches legal challenge." *BBC News* (20 April 2013).

received conceptual support from 10 EU Members[71] and apparently has the support of 64% of the EU citizens.[72] The imposition of the EU FTT Proposal may now gain some momentum given that the UK, a vocal opponent of an EU FTT, is in the process of leaving the EU. However, despite much discussion, a short-termism driven FTT has to date not been implemented in any of the jurisdictions surveyed.

3. *Disclosure Reforms—Less Is More?*

Disclosure of information by market participants, particularly on the operations of listed companies and asset managers actions with respect to investment in such listed companies, plays a crucial role in the SMST discussion, and has seen some 'hard' law reform. These disclosure reforms impact asset owners, intermediaries and company managers, but are discussed below as the primary purpose of these reforms appears to be assisting asset owners—often via asset managers who may actually make the investment decisions based on the parameters set by asset owners—make prudent investment decisions. A concern raised is that stock markets are inundated with rapidly disseminated information, much of which is "simply noise."[73]

The specific SMST issue raised is that this 'noise' allegedly makes it difficult for asset owners—often via asset managers—to discern the information needed to properly assess if a company is meeting its long-term objectives.[74] Additionally, it has been suggested that the timing of information dissemination may exacerbate SMST concerns. Company managers may feel pressured to constantly generate short-term results in order to produce fresh 'news' to satisfy a perceived need in the market for corporate 'progress', which concept has been referred to as 'informational centricity'.[75] Consequently, reforms discussed below are divided into two categories: (1) timing, and (2) quality. Timing of disclosure, mainly on mandatory quarterly reporting, is considered first as this is a significant area of discussion for SMST-reformers.

[71] Maurice (2015).

[72] Speech of EU Commissioner Šemeta (4 February 2014). Online: http://europa.eu/rapid/press-release_SPEECH-14-92_en.htm?locale=en.

[73] Kay (2012, 73).

[74] Ibid., and Dallas (2012).

[75] See argument by Moore and Walker-Arnott (2014), that the informational centricity of modern markets pressures company managers to generate 'fresh' news demonstrating perceived business 'progress'.

a. Timing of Material Listed Company Disclosure

A key touch point in the SMST discussion is the apparent obsession with quarterly reporting in certain markets, particularly the US.[76] Mandatory quarterly reporting has long been a requirement of companies listed on US stock exchanges but is a more recent development in the UK and EU generally.[77] Similarly, other jurisdictions with developed equity markets—for example, Singapore and Hong Kong—fairly recently introduced mandatory quarterly reporting.[78] The concern with quarterly reporting is that asset owners and intermediaries may be 'impatient'. They may unduly focus on and react to the results of the most recent quarter—by selling shares and thereby negatively impacting the share price—without clearly understanding how such earnings fluctuations fit into a specific corporate long-term growth strategy. This response in turn increases pressure on company managers to take corporate actions that produce positive short-term results at the expense of long-term success—for example, deferring research and development investment opportunities.[79]

To reduce the perceived pressures for short-term decision-making arising from excessive—e.g. quarterly—reporting of financial performance, Kay recommended that UK mandatory quarterly reporting—i.e. interim management statements—be removed.[80] The UK Government agreed, observing that rigid quarterly reporting may promote an excessive short-term focus and impose an unnecessary regulatory burden without providing useful or meaningful information for asset owners.[81] Consequently, the UK Government was supportive of EU efforts to

[76] Pearlstein (2009).

[77] Ernstberger et al. (2015).

[78] Introduced in Singapore Listing Rules (2002)—see "Singapore Exchange Amends Listing Rules", *Mondovisione* (20 January 2002). Online: http://www.mondovisione.com/media-and-resources/news/singapore-exchange-amends-listing-rules—and Hong Kong Listing Rules (2011)—see "HKEx Proposes Mandatory Quarterly Reporting by Main Board Listed Companies from 2011 Year-End and Other HKEx Initiatives" *Charltons* (January 2009). Online: https://www.charltonslaw.com/hkex-proposes-mandatory-quarterly-reporting-by-main-board-listed-companies-from-2011-year-end-and-other-hkex-initiatives/.

[79] See the review in Ernstberger et al. (2015, 6–10).

[80] Kay (2012, 13).

[81] Implementation (2014, 19).

amend the EU Transparency Directive removing mandatory requirements for quarterly reporting,[82] which 'hard' law changes took effect in November 2013. This reform was adopted as UK 'hard' law effective as of November 2014, a year ahead of when such amendments would have applied to all EU member states.[83]

The EU's stated rationale for removal of the mandatory quarterly reporting requirement was to reduce short-term pressure on companies and give asset owners an incentive to adopt a longer-term vision.[84] Agreeing with this rationale, Legal & General, a vocal financial industry advocate for the removal of quarterly reporting, dropped quarterly reporting in 2015 citing short-termism concerns. Instead, Legal & General stated that it would provide 'timely and frequent updates' as well as full-year and half-year reports.[85] Although the EU removal of mandatory quarterly reporting is a 'hard' law reform, the measures adopted by EU member states are optional and listed companies can elect to continue with quarterly reporting. As it is optional, the reform may have a diminished effect in practice as many EU companies are also listed in the US or have US shareholders who expect quarterly reporting. Therefore, such companies may be subject to legal—or in the case of non-SEC reporting companies with US shareholders—market pressures to report quarterly. Evidencing this issue, in the UK, the vast majority of listed companies have continued with quarterly reporting.[86]

There is an indication that this market pressure may be changing. The UK Investment Association (UKIA),[87] an influential representative body for UK fund managers, recently published an action plan which was very critical of quarterly reporting. Citing short-termism concerns, the UKIA, said that it wishes "to see companies move away from such short-term

[82] Directive 2013/50/EU (EU Transparency Directive).

[83] UK Financial Services and Markets Act (Transparency) Regulations 2014 giving authority to the FCA to remove the requirement from the Disclosure and Transparency Rules in the FCA Handbook. https://www.handbook.fca.org.uk/.

[84] UK Financial Services and Markets Act (Transparency) Regulations 2014, Recital (4).

[85] Wallace (2015).

[86] Moore and Petrin (2017, 127).

[87] See the UK Investment Association. Online: www.theinvestmentassociation.org.

reporting and guidance in favour of long-term metrics."[88] EU/UK reforms have bolstered ongoing discussion in the US.[89] Most recently, President Trump has called for the SEC to consider moving from a quarterly to a six-month reporting period.[90] The SEC, however, continues to require quarterly reporting, and no changes are proposed though the SEC has acknowledged the discussion.[91] EU reforms have also prompted further discussion globally, with the SGX recently revisiting the issue of mandatory quarterly reporting.[92]

b. Quality and Content of Market Disclosure

Reforms around timing and mandatory quarterly reporting cannot be viewed in isolation from calls for 'better' long-term focused disclosure. SMST reformers argue that it is not only timing creating the supposed SMST concern but also the content of disclosure, which they suggest is too short-term focused.[93] Improvements to reporting propose to reduce short-termism by focusing on two principal elements: (1) connecting corporate actions with long-term strategy and less on short-term—e.g. quarterly—earnings results; and (2) emphasizing corporate social responsibility (CSR) and environmental, social and corporate governance (ESG) factors in addition to financial measures of the performance of a listed company. These CSR and ESG factors, theoretically at least, represent inherently longer-term interests than short-term earnings, although this connection to the SMST issue is tenuous.[94]

[88] See The Investment Association, 'Supporting UK Productivity with Long-Term Investment: The Investment Association's Productivity Action Plan' (March 2016), 16. Online: https://www.theinvestmentassociation.org/assets/files/press/2017/20170901-productivityactionplan.pdf, as referenced in Moore and Petrin (2017, 127).

[89] See comments by Lipton (2015) where Mr. Lipton suggests that the SEC remove mandatory quarterly reporting based on short-termism concerns, and by Pozen and Roe (2015), where the authors argue against eliminating quarterly reporting on the grounds that it would reduce corporate transparency.

[90] Merced and Phillips (2018).

[91] Higgins, Keith F, "International Developments—Past, Present and Future", SEC Keynote Address at PLI (21 January 2016).

[92] "Singapore Exchange Reviewing Mandatory Quarterly Reporting", Singapore Business Review (11 January 2016).

[93] Dallas (2012, 324).

[94] Ibid.

Of the jurisdictions surveyed, 'hard' law disclosure SMST-driven reforms have only been made in the UK and the EU. In the UK, Kay coupled his recommendation on quarterly reporting in the Kay Review with a recommendation that high, quality, succinct narrative reporting should be encouraged.[95] The UK Government supported this recommendation, and 'hard' law regulations to this effect were implemented on 1 October 2013.[96]

These UK regulations removed some disclosure requirements completely, and also required all UK listed companies—other than some small and medium-sized entities—to produce a separate strategic report as part of a restructured annual report. The strategic report must include not only financial performance indicators, but also key performance indicators including information relating to environmental and employee matters. The goal of such amendments was to make reporting clearer and more relevant, thereby encouraging more engagement with companies on the creation of long-term sustainable value.[97] 'Soft' law guidance on the strategic report has also been offered in the UK by the Financial Reporting Council (FRC).[98]

The EU has also implemented 'hard' and 'soft' law SMST-motivated reforms around improved disclosure. Particularly, it made a 'soft' law recommendation on the quality of corporate governance reporting, noting that high quality disclosure facilitates better investment decisions and well run-companies are more likely to be competitive and sustainable in the long-run.[99] This recommendation provided guidance to EU listed companies to assist them report on compliance with relevant governance codes or explain why they do not. The EU also adopted a 'hard' law directive aimed at improving non-financial—i.e. CSR/ESG—disclosure by large companies, a stated purpose of which was to combine long-term profitability with social justice and environmental protection.[100]

[95] Kay (2012, 13).

[96] The Companies Act 2006 (Strategic Report and Directors' Report) Regulations 2013.

[97] Implementation (2014, 20).

[98] Financial Reporting Council, Guidance on the Strategic Report (June 2014).

[99] EU Recommendation 2014/208/EU.

[100] Directive 2014/95/EU, which was in place in EU Member States by December 2016.

In the US, disclosure reforms based on SMST concerns were suggested in the Aspen Report 2009. Though detailed proposals were not provided, the Aspen Report 2009 called "for greater transparency in investor disclosures [which] can also play an important role in helping corporations maintain a long-term orientation."[101] This was echoed by Chief Justice Strine when he asserted, though also no specifics were provided, that promoting long-term US competitiveness required first improving the quality of information provided to investors.[102] Despite these calls for reform, SMST driven-reforms to the quality of disclosure of US listed companies have not yet been proposed by the SEC.

A non-jurisdiction specific short-termism disclosure-related reform has been proposed by the International Integrated Reporting Council (IIRC). IIRC is a global coalition of regulators, investors, companies, standard setters, accounting professionals and non-government organizations (NGOs), which is in the process of examining many aspects of global financial and non-financial corporate reporting. IIRC is developing an integrated reporting framework, the goal of which is to incorporate qualitative and quantitative factors into a concise report designed to encourage companies to better communicate their long-term value creation.[103] This SMST reform by IIRC is a voluntary financial industry initiative. However, as set out above, reforms directed at quality of disclosure has seen some 'hard' and 'soft' law short-termism driven reform.

4. *Direct Communication/Engagement*

SMST-reformers suggest that channels between asset owners and company managers should be strengthened and they should communicate and engage directly.[104] This differs from the disclosure referred to in Sect. A.3 above, in which information is provided to the market as a whole. With communication—also termed engagement—individual asset owners or managers, or groups thereof—interact privately and directly with the listed company or companies in which they hold an investment. Theoretically, this facilitates engagement by long-term asset owners, who

[101] Aspen Institute (2009, 5).

[102] Strine (2015).

[103] Integrated Reporting. Online: http://integratedreporting.org.

[104] For example, see the Kay (2012), Recommendation 5.

may have a greater interest in long-term growth than short-term shareholders, which premise is questionable as discussed further in Chapter 6 in the context of the relevance of investor timeframes.[105] Most reform in this area is limited to UK financial industry initiatives. However, the EU has proposed a short-termism driven 'hard' law reform facilitating direct communication.

The EU Amended Shareholder Rights Directive attempts to reduce the role of intermediaries in the equity ownership chain by better connecting listed companies directly with asset owners, and in doing so encourage greater engagement with listed companies by asset owners. The argument made is that asset owner involvement is necessary as failure to engage has negative consequences for the long-term performance of both listed companies and investors.[106]

Article 3a of the EU Amended Shareholder Rights Directive provides that EU Member States shall ensure that listed companies have the right to identify their shareholders and requires that that EU Members must ensure that intermediaries provide listed companies with information on shareholder identity. Further, Article 3b of the EU Amended Shareholder Rights Directive provides that listed companies, which do not communicate directly with their shareholders, must make available all information related to such shares on the listed company's website or, if instructions are given by the shareholder, through an intermediary, which must transmit the information to the shareholder without undue delay.

In the Kay Review, Kay also advocated for greater communication between asset owners and company managers to counter the SMST issue. Specifically, he recommended that companies should consult with their long-term asset owners over major board of director appointments in order to give such 'serious' investors an advantage over traders.[107] Kay's recommendation assumed, potentially problematically, that such asset owners are interested in the long-term growth of the listed company. Assuming they are interested in long-term growth, the UK Government also noted significant market and regulatory impediments

[105] See Chapter 6, Sect. A.3.

[106] EU Amended Shareholder Rights Directive, Whereas Clause (15).

[107] Kay (2012), Recommendation 5.

to such engagement, including competition among asset owners/intermediaries and insider trading restrictions. Insider trading regulation, for example the UK Market Abuse Regulation,[108] may act to limit engagement by asset owners. If an asset owner engages with a listed company and in doing receives 'inside information', the asset owner would be subject to sanctions if it trades its shares while in possession of such insider information. Consequently, asset owners may be reluctant to engage with company managers out of concerns about limitations on the asset owners' ability to freely trade their investment.

Given these serious impediments, rather than require engagement, the UK Government pointed to the financial industry initiative of the UK Investor Forum[109] as an appropriate venue, and the 'Good Practice Statement for Company' Directors' as the method to develop good practice. It also commissioned the FRC to investigate further as part of its general review of UK governance which is ongoing.[110] Specific proposals on company engagement with 'serious' investors on general operations have not yet been recommended and were not included in the Green Paper on Corporate Governance Reform 2016.[111]

Based on Kay's recommendation, the UK Investor Forum was established in 2014. The UK Investor Forum was meant to address concerns raised in the Kay Review. These concerns were that asset owner and company manager engagement focused disproportionately on corporate governance, causing a vacuum in respect of companies' strategies for long-term, sustainable competitive advantage. Also, Kay was concerned about impediments to engagement arising from increased international ownership and fragmented shareholding, and perceived regulatory barriers inhibiting collective engagement.[112] The UK Investor Forum is a community interest company with a board of directors appointed to represent the interests of the entire investment chain.[113] It is discussed here as its key objective is communication with asset owners. However, it has significance for intermediaries and company managers.

108 EU Market Abuse Regulation (596/2014).

109 The UK Investor Forum. https://www.investorforum.org.uk/ (UK Investors Forum).

110 Implementation (2014, 17).

111 Corporate Governance Reform Green Paper. November 2016. UK Government Department for Business, Energy & Industrial Strategy.

112 Kay (2012, 9–51).

113 The Investor Forum. Online: www.investorforum.org.uk.

With the aim of building partnerships between asset owners and intermediaries and companies in which they invest, the UK Investor Forum established forums to advise the financial industry and promote collective engagement. Membership in the UK Investor Forum is open to all investors in, and professional asset owners and managers of, UK-listed companies, but participation is entirely voluntary. There has been some interest as 31 investors participated in 2017, and 16 collective engagements were conducted during 2015–2016 and 14 collective engagements were conducted during 2015–2016.[114] However, other than this initiative and Articles 3a and 3b of the EU Amended Shareholder Rights Directive, there are no SMST reforms facilitating direct communication in the jurisdictions surveyed.

5. *Stock-Lending*

As discussed below, 'stock-lending' has been raised in the context of SMST-driven reform. With stock-lending, shares are 'lent' to a borrower. The 'lent' shares may then be used by the borrower in securities transactions, including short sales of such shares. The lending party, often an asset manager, receives consideration for the lending which may or may not be rebated to the asset owner. The precise SMST issue associated with stock-lending has not clearly been, but the key concern appears to be that stock-lending separates asset owners from effective control of their shares as ownership and voting control is transferred temporarily to the borrowers who, particularly if securities are borrowed to support a short-sale, are not interested in the long-term viability of the company.[115]

Kay accepted that the practice of stock-lending may serve a valid function in capital markets. He was, however, concerned about the transparency of stock-lending relationships.[116] Kay argued that asset owners should know if their shares are being lent, and be able to exercise

[114] Investor Forum—Collective Engagement Review 2017–2015. Online: https://www.investorforum.org.uk/review.

[115] See the definition of 'securities lending' at https://www.investopedia.com/terms/s/securitieslending.asp and the discussion of this concept termed 'empty voting', in Ali et al. (2014), and the issues with securities lending discussed in Croce et al. (2011, 8).

[116] Kay (2012, 31).

greater judgment over when or if it is appropriate to do so.[117] Thus, Kay recommended that all income from stock-lending be disclosed and rebated to investors.[118] The UK Government preferred disclosure over a strict requirement to rebate income to asset owners, meaning that asset managers may retain stock-lending fees if they disclose they are doing so to asset owners.[119]

The UK Government noted that disclosure of stock-lending is now part of asset manager guidance and referenced the UCITS Directive,[120] a directive regulating EU collective investment schemes. Adopted in July 2014, the UCITS Directive has been transitioned into 'hard' law in EU Member States.[121] The UCITS Directive goes further than UK guidance and, as proposed by Kay, makes a 'hard' law change requiring that investors in EU Undertakings for Collective Investment in Transferable Securities (EU UCITS) receive all income from stock-lending net of operational costs. This is the only 'hard' law reform on stock-lending in the jurisdictions surveyed, which reform is motivated at least in part by short-termism concerns. However, it may be that the primary motivator with this reform was concerns over intermediaries taking advantage of asset owners. Further, this reform is limited to EU UCITS, which comprise a notable part but not all of EU capital markets.[122]

6. *LTVC Index*

SMST reformers assert that it is difficult for asset owners interested in longer-term investing to adequately assess if a listed company is effectively generating sustainable longer-term corporate value.[123] The LTVC

[117] Ibid.

[118] Ibid., Recommendation 10.

[119] Implementation (2014, 40).

[120] ESMA Guidelines for competent authorities and UCITS management companies on ETFs and other UCITS issues, ESMA/2012/832EN (UCITS Directive).

[121] For example, the Financial Services (Collective Investment Schemes) Act 2011 Financial Services (Collective Investment Schemes) (Amendment) Regulations 2016 in the UK.

[122] Managing almost €6 trillion in assets, UCITS account for approximately 75% of collective investments by small investors in Europe (EC Statement, 15 April 2014). Online: http://europa.eu/rapid/press-release_STATEMENT-14-121_en.htm.

[123] Barton and Wiseman (2014).

Index is a recent financial industry initiative that claims to fill this void by signaling long-term focused listed companies to asset owners. The listed companies selected to be on the LTVC Index are supposedly more likely to maintain a competitive advantage and, thus, sustain longer-term corporate value.

The LTVC Index was developed by Canada Pension Plan Investment Board (CPPIB) and asset manager RobecoSAM and was launched on 21 January 2016.[124] The LTVC comprises about 250 companies identified through a Dow Jones proprietary system to take a long-term view, which also have a sustained history of financial quality. To craft the LTVC Index, Dow Jones relied on both quantitative and qualitative data. Qualitative data was generated with an Economic Dimension Score compiled by RobecoSAM. The Economic Dimension Score scored companies based on a wide-range of primarily corporate governance criteria. Quantitative data was largely derived from a firm's return on equity, balance sheet accruals ratio and leverage ratio.[125]

The LTCV Index has received considerable attention and six global institutional investors have expressed support. Interestingly, three have not yet decided to invest funds in tracking the LTVC Index, stating they have in house strategies for investing.[126] The LTCV Index merits further attention once it has an operating history to determine if in fact it is a useful tool to correct the SMST issue or, instead, if it is merely a clever marketing gimmick.

7. *Hedge Funds*

As a means of addressing the SMST of specific market participants, namely activist hedge funds, US Senators Tammy Baldwin and Jeff Merkley introduced draft bipartisan legislation in 2017 (Brokaw Act).[127]

[124] "S&P Long-Term Value Creation Global Index Launched by S&P Dow Jones Indices." *Dow Jones Institutional News* (21 January 2016).

[125] "Introducing the S&P LTVC Global Index." S&P Dow Jones Indices, McGraw Hill Financial (January 2016). Online: file:///C:/Users/ASW/Downloads/introducing-the-sp-ltvc-global-index.pdf.

[126] "Schemes Support New S&P Index but Do Not Invest." *Global Money Management* (22 January 2016).

[127] S.1744—115th Congress (2017–2018).

The term 'hedge fund' derives from trading techniques used by fund managers to hedge against market losses by going 'long' if they foresee a market rise, and 'short' if they anticipate a drop.[128] The term has been extended to mean a certain type of alternative investment structures only available to sophisticated investors that use pooled funds and often employs a hedging strategy and an aggressive approach to unlocking market opportunities. Examples of activist hedge funds include Pershing Square Capital Management, Third Point and ValueAct Capital Partners. Senators Baldwin and Merkley argue that activist hedge funds are "leading the short-termism charge"[129] as "they abuse lax securities laws to gain large stakes in public companies."[130] With these large stakes, the Senators argue, "they make demands to benefit themselves at the expense of the company's long-term interests."[131] Such demands commonly "are for more debt, stock buybacks, reduced research and development (R&D), cost-cutting, layoffs, and general reduction any investment in long-term growth."[132]

To address this issue, the Brokaw Act proposes to shorten disclosure times for the formation of associations by hedge funds—i.e. 'wolf packs',[133] amends the definition of 'person or group' to capture alleged 'wolf packs', and requires derivative disclosure to end any secretive shorting of a position by hedge funds.[134] The Brokaw Act has been introduced but not yet passed committee stage in the US Senate.[135] Further, it is not clear if hedge funds actually contribute to the SMST issue, which is explored further in Chapter 6.[136]

[128] Gad (2018).

[129] Summary of the Brokaw Act, 'The Problem of Short-Termism & Activist Hedge Funds. Online: https://www.baldwin.senate.gov/imo/media/doc/3.7.16%20-%20Brokaw%20Act%201.pdf (Brokaw Act Summary), 1.

[130] Ibid.

[131] Ibid.

[132] Ibid.

[133] These are groups of activist investors who work in unison to gain control over the boards of listed companies. See the discussion in Lu (2016).

[134] Brokaw Act Summary.

[135] See the status of S.1744—Brokaw Act, 115th Congress (2017–2018). Online: www.congress.gov.

[136] See Chapter 6, Sect. A.1.

The analysis in this section demonstrates that there have been some implemented reforms to correct the perceived issue of asset owner SMST, but reform efforts have been modest given the level of discussion. Of the enacted 'hard' law reforms, the Florange Law and EU Transparency Directive have 'opt-out' mechanisms The only 'hard' law reforms prescribing certain action are UK and EU reforms to disclosure reporting and the communication reforms in Articles 3a and 3b of the EU Amended Shareholder Rights Directive, and reforms to the UCITS Directive on stock-lending, which are limited to EU UCITS. The remaining asset owner SMST-driven reforms are 'soft' law or financial industry initiatives.

B. Intermediary SMST Reforms—'Other People's Money'

Given the complexity of the equity ownership chain and the corresponding disconnect created between asset owners and listed companies as discussed in Chapter 2, SMST reformers have scrutinized the role played by intermediaries.[137] This scrutiny is warranted as intermediaries—primarily asset managers—have become the dominant players in the investment chain.[138] Acting on behalf of institutional investors—by far the largest group of investors in many modern equity markets—asset managers "play a key role in exercising the attributes of share ownership most relevant to company decision making: the right to vote and the right to buy or sell a given share."[139] Similar to asset owner SMST reforms, intermediary SMST-driven reforms intend to replace a short-term approach with more prudent long-term investing. Specifically, intermediary reforms aim to: (1) better align the interests of intermediaries with the long-term interests of asset owners, thereby encouraging more responsible long-term management of investments; and/or (2) reduce the role of intermediaries, who allegedly may be overly focused on short-term returns.

[137] Johnston and Morrow (2014).

[138] Kay (2012, 11 and 32).

[139] Ibid., 11.

This section focuses first on reforms receiving the most attention, namely, (1) stewardship and disclosure, (2) duty to further long-term interests, and (3) asset manager remuneration. It then looks at reforms receiving less attention, which are reforms directed at reducing the influence of intermediaries such as voting restrictions and direct shareholding.[140] Finally, reforms for a special case of intermediaries—proxy advisors—are considered. Intermediary SMST reforms are summarized in Appendix 'A' (Table 2). As evidenced below, most implemented reform in this space is 'soft' law or financial industry initiatives.

1. *Stewardship and Disclosure*

An area garnering significant attention from reformers is setting guiding principles of desired behaviour for market participants, and publicly disclosing adherence to such guidelines and on long-term strategy generally. Guiding principles are specifically meant to encourage greater accountability, mainly by asset managers, on how investments should be responsibly managed to provide sustainable long-term returns for asset owners. Of note in this respect are Kay's recommendations focusing on 'stewardship', a concept based primarily on respect for those persons whose funds are invested and managed, and trust in those persons by whom the funds are invested or managed.[141]

To counter short-termism, Kay recommended promoting stewardship. This was to be achieved by: (1) improving the UK Stewardship Code[142]; (2) adopting good practice statements for intermediaries, as well as asset owners and company managers; and (3) creating the UK Investor Forum.[143] Though Kay advocated broadening the existing concept of stewardship, he did not offer much in the way of specifics. The UK Government endorsed the good practice statements in the Kay Review, however, and, as discussed in Sect. A.4 of this chapter, encouraged the establishment of the UK Investor Forum to facilitate collective engagement in the equity ownership chain of UK listed companies.

[140] HeinOnline/Factiva search indicates the terms 'stewardship/guiding principles', 'duty of care/fiduciary duty' and 'remuneration' are cited most frequently of intermediary reforms identified in Appendix 'A' (Table 2) in the context of short-termism.

[141] Kay (2012, 12).

[142] https://www.frc.org.uk/investors/uk-stewardship-code (UK Stewardship Code).

[143] Kay (2012, 12).

The UK Government further claimed that 'soft' law amendments to the UK Stewardship Code in 2012 remedied short-termism concerns that were raised in the Kay Review.[144] The UK Stewardship Code was released by the FRC in 2010, and contained guidelines directed at institutional investors meant to improve the governance of UK listed companies. It was updated in 2012 to clarify that stewardship goes beyond merely monitoring compliance with the UK Corporate Governance Code. The updated UK Stewardship Code provided for asset managers and asset owners, albeit on a 'comply or explain' basis, to engage with board of directors on the company's strategy to deliver sustainable long-term returns.[145] Only UK asset managers are legally required to comply with the UK Stewardship Code, or explain why they do not.[146] As of May 2018, 77 asset managers have signed up to the UK Stewardship Code.[147] Voluntary compliance has been significant and as at May 2018, 94 asset owners and 12 service providers have also signed up to the UK Stewardship Code.[148]

Many other jurisdictions have followed the UK's lead with respect to stewardship, or independently developed similar codes for stewardship by asset managers and asset owners. For example, Japan adopted a non-binding, comply or explain Stewardship Code in 2014, modeled largely after the UK Stewardship Code, which code was revised in 2017. This Japanese Stewardship Code included requirements for asset managers and asset owners to engage with board of directors on the company's strategy to deliver sustainable long-term returns.[149] As at 5 April 2018, 227 signatories—including 162 asset managers—had adopted the Japanese Stewardship Code.[150] The concept of stewardship by asset

[144] Implementation (2014, 11).

[145] Ibid.

[146] UK Stewardship Code, 4, principle 4.

[147] https://www.frc.org.uk/investors/uk-stewardship-code/uk-stewardship-code-statements.

[148] Ibid.

[149] Principles for Responsible Institutional Investors, Japan's Stewardship Code (26 February 2013).

[150] Japanese Financial Services Authority, "Stewardship Code; 227 institutional investors have signed up to the Principles for Responsible Institutional Investors as of April 5, 2018." Online: https://www.fsa.go.jp/en/refer/councils/stewardship/20160315.html.

owners and asset managers has gained traction worldwide. As at 31 March 2018, a total of 19 jurisdictions, including the UK and Japan as discussed above, have adopted stewardship codes, all of which have been adopted after 2010.[151] The EU Amended Shareholder Rights Directive also has provisions which contain elements found in stewardship codes.

Similar to requirements contained in many stewardship codes, Article 3h of the EU Amended Shareholder Rights Directive provides that EU Member States must ensure that institutional investors publicly disclose how investment strategy is aligned to their liabilities and contributes to medium and long-term performance of their assets, and, if asset managers are engaged, they must publicly disclose the main elements of this arrangement. Additionally, Article 3i of the EU Amended Shareholder Rights Directive provides that EU Member States must ensure that asset managers disclose, on an annual basis, to the institutional investor with which they have entered into the arrangements referred to in Article 3h how their investment strategy and implementation thereof complies with that arrangement and contributes to the medium to long-term performance of the assets of the institutional investor or of the fund. With Article 3i, the disclosing party must comply or explain why it did not. Though these reforms are 'hard' law changes, they employ a 'comply or explain' model, or in the case of Article 3h, a disclosure model, rather than providing prescriptive requirements to which asset owners and asset managers must comply.

Despite the prevalence of stewardship codes and the accompanying disclosure of asset manager and asset owner investment strategy, many questions have been raised around the effectiveness of these stewardship codes in encouraging engagement focused on long-term performance, and on whether buy-in to these stewardship codes has been meaningful. When the UK Stewardship Code was first introduced, Professor Brian Cheffins argued that due to the sustained fragmentation of share ownership occurring over the past 20 years in the UK, the UK Stewardship Code was unlikely to foster substantially greater shareholder involvement in UK corporate governance.[152] Further, on the fifth anniversary of the implementation of the UK Stewardship Code, Simon Wong of

[151] 'Global Stewardship Codes', Minerva Analytics (20 March 2017). Online: https://www.manifest.co.uk/portfolio/global-stewardship-codes/.

[152] Cheffins (2010).

the Northwestern University School of Law examined stewardship codes implemented globally and argued that "[t]hey are largely devoid of substance."[153] Speaking directly to the UK Stewardship Code, Wong said that it "has generally failed to address the root causes of poor shareholder stewardship, opting instead to focus on process and mechanics."[154] Demonstrating that compliance may be aesthetic rather than substantive, survey evidence in Japan suggests that although the stewardship concept is largely supported by signatories, little actually changed in practice in Japan.[155] Buy-in from UK asset managers may also be questioned, as they arguably may just have adopted the long-term principles but do little different in practice.[156]

In an attempt to address issues around compliance, the FRC implemented a tiering system for signatories to the UK Stewardship Code in 2016.[157] Based on an assessment of their reporting in relation to the principles of the UK Stewardship Code, the FRC publicly ranked signatories into Tier 1, Tier 2 and Tier 3, with a Tier 3 ranking indicating that substantive improvements were required.[158] In August 2017 approximately 20 signatories to the UK Stewardship Code—half of those initially placed in Tier 3—who had not improved their compliance and achieved Tier 2 status were removed from the list of signatories.[159]

The UK Government also pointed to financial industry initiatives meant to correct short-termism through stewardship in response to Kay's recommendations in the Kay Review.[160] These financial industry

[153] Wong (2015).

[154] Ibid.

[155] Chen (2015, 13).

[156] For example, the FRC indicated reporting by UK Stewardship Code signatories demonstrated many are not following through with their stewardship commitments (FRC Developments in Corporate Governance and Stewardship (January 2016). Online: https://www.frc.org.uk/getattachment/ca1d9909-7e32-4894-b2a7-b971b4406130/Developments-in-Corporate-Governance-and-Stewardship-2016.pdf, at 3).

[157] Financial Reporting Council, 'Tiering of Signatories to the Stewardship' (14 November 2016). Online: https://www.frc.org.uk/news/november-2016/tiering-of-signatories-to-the-stewardship-code.

[158] Ibid.

[159] 'UK Stewardship Code: And Then There Were Two (Tiers)' *Minerva Analytics* (6 August 2017). Online: https://www.manifest.co.uk/uk-stewardship-code-frc-removes-requiring-improvement-category/.

[160] Implementation (2014, 11).

initiatives included a new Stewardship Disclosure Framework developed by the National Association of Pension Funds (NAPF), a trade organization for those involved with workplace pensions. This NAPF Stewardship Disclosure Framework encourages asset managers of pension funds to clearly articulate their stewardship approaches to clients.[161] The NAPF Stewardship Disclosure Framework aims to provide greater transparency on stewardship policies and activities of asset managers who are signatories to the UK Stewardship Code in a centralized public format.[162]

Financial industry initiatives outside of the UK have also attempted to guide the behaviour of market participants away from short-termism. For example, Dominic Barton, global head of McKinsey & Company (McKinsey) has been a prominent advocate for finance industry driven initiatives. He claims the financial industry must correct the issue or change will be legislated upon it.[163] Together with the CPPIB, McKinsey founded the online platform 'Focusing Capital on the Long Term' (FCLT) in 2013, meant to develop practical structures, metrics, and approaches for longer-term behaviour in the investment and business worlds.[164]

FCLT brings together asset managers—e.g. State Street Global Advisors and Wellington Management—, asset owners—e.g. NZ Superannuation Fund, Ontario Teachers' Pension Plan, etc.—, and service providers, to help enhance long-term corporate value creation. As noted, the purpose of this platform is to develop practical structures, metrics, and approaches for longer-term behaviours in the investment and business worlds.[165] FCLT aims to do so by bringing together financial industry participants to discuss reform and by increasing public awareness. It also summarizes other voluntary initiatives for reducing SMST on its website. These initiatives include the Principles for Responsible Investment (PRI).[166] PRI is a voluntary set of principles

[161] Ibid.

[162] Stewardship Disclosure Framework. Online: http://www.plsa.co.uk/PolicyandResearch/Corporate-Governance/Stewardship/Stewardship-disclosure-framework.aspx.

[163] Ibid.

[164] http://www.fclt.org.

[165] Ibid.

[166] Principles for Responsible Investment. Online: http://www.unpri.org/.

for intermediaries established in partnership with the United Nations Environmental Program (UNEP) Financial Initiative and the United Nations (UN) Global Compact meant to provide a standard for asset managers to act in the long-term interests of beneficiaries and incorporate environmental, social and governance issues into investment practices. As of 2017, PRI had over 1200 signatories from over 50 countries representing approximately US$59 trillion under management.[167]

Although there has been a degree of financial industry-driven reform encouraging market participants—particularly asset managers—to take a longer-term perspective, as demonstrated above, reform in this space has been largely voluntary. Even regulatory reforms, such as the UK Stewardship Code application to UK asset managers, and Article 3h of the EU Amended Shareholder Rights Directive regarding disclosure of investment strategy are on a 'comply or explain' basis. Consequently, the ability of these initiatives to encourage company managers of listed companies to take a longer-term perspective depends largely on the interest and goodwill of the market participants, which to date has not been rigorously tested. However, more tangible 'hard' law reforms proposals have been suggested to target perceived intermediary SMST, including imposing a duty to further long-term interests.

2. *A Duty to Further Long-Term Interests?*

Citing SMST concerns, SMST-focused reformers have called for certain intermediaries, namely asset managers who manage shares on behalf of asset owners, to have a legal duty to further the long-term interests of asset owners.[168] Currently, the standard of care and duties owed by asset managers to their asset owner clients varies greatly depending on the governing jurisdiction and contractual arrangements between the parties.[169] SMST reformers assert that intermediaries, as holders of other people's money, should have an obligation to make decisions furthering the long-term interest of the asset owners rather than maximizing

[167] Principles for Responsible Investment Annual Report 2017. Online: https://www.unpri.org/download?ac=3976.

[168] Aspen Institute (2009, 5) and Dallas (2012, 364).

[169] See Busch and DeMott (2012) summarizing duties and standards of care owed to a client by asset managers in a number of jurisdictions, including the EU, UK and US.

short-term profit.[170] The inherent difficulty in this proposition is that asset owners may also want short-term profits. Consequently, intermediaries may not be properly fulfilling their agency role if they instead focus on purported asset owner long-term interests. Further, asset managers could conceivably be in breach of their legal duties if a long-term investment was made and such investments simply performed poorly.

A large part of this conversation on short-termism and intermediaries has been around 'fiduciary' duties. The meaning of this term varies from jurisdiction to jurisdiction, but 'fiduciary' relationships are generally presumed to have common characteristics and attract a core set of legal duties, most notably a duty of loyalty.[171] In the Aspen Report 2009, as echoed by Chief Justice Strine, there was a call for a 'fiduciary' duty to better align the interests of financial intermediaries and their clients.[172] No specifics were provided in the Aspen Report 2009 on if this would be legal duty and how it would apply. The Dodd-Frank Act, however, went further and gave authority was given to the Investor Advisory Committee established pursuant to the Dodd-Frank Act to consider a fiduciary duty for brokers and dealers, which duty would be more stringent than what was currently in place and parallel the high standard of conduct that was applicable to investment advisors.[173]

The US Investment Advisory Committee reviewed and recommended that the fiduciary duties on investment advisors be applied to brokers and dealers when they provide personalized investment advice to retail investors.[174] Despite this recommendation, the fiduciary standard has not yet been uniformly extended to the activities of brokers and dealers, and an exemption to the fiduciary standard continues to apply when the advice provided to retail clients is incidental to the conduct of their business and no special compensation is received. Consequently, in the US there has been no extension of fiduciary duties based on SMST-concerns.

[170] Dallas (2012, 364).

[171] See discussion in Miller (2013).

[172] Aspen Institute (2009, 5).

[173] Dodd-Frank Act, Title IX, Section 913 (g).

[174] Recommendation of the Investor Advisory Committee: Broker-Dealer Fiduciary Duty (November 2013). Online: http://www.sec.gov/spotlight/investor-advisory-committee-2012/fiduciary-duty-recommendation-2013.pdf, as discussed in 'SEC's Investor Advisory Committee Recommends Framework for Uniform Fiduciary Duty Governing Broker-Dealers and Investment Advisors' Morgan Lewis (11 December 2013). Online: https://www.morganlewis.com/pubs/secs-investor-advisory-committee.

A discussion on 'fiduciary' duties was also incorporated into the Kay Review. A 'fiduciary' is defined in UK law as "someone who has undertaken to act for and on behalf of another in a particular matter in circumstances which give rise to a relationship of trust and confidence."[175] In the Kay Review, Kay concluded that some intermediaries serving as fiduciaries are interpreting their duties too narrowly, specifically as meaning that they must maximize short-term financial returns for their investors. This concern, coupled with a broader goal of extending fiduciary duties to all relationships in the investment chain, resulted in Kay making two recommendations. He recommended that: (1) EU/UK regulators apply fiduciary standards to all relationships involving discretion over the investment of others, or advice on investments; and (2) the UK Law Commission review the legal concept of fiduciary duty as applied to investment.[176] Based on these recommendations, the UK Government commissioned a report from the UK Law Commission.

The UK Law Commission was asked to explain the nature of fiduciary and other duties to act in the best interests of savers, and to describe how these duties apply to investment intermediaries.[177] Notably, it was not called on to address the practicality of imposing a legal fiduciary duty on all market intermediaries or to suggest legislative reform. Instead, the report presented by the UK Law Commission was explanatory, and primarily clarified the duties of trustees in the funded pension context. In its report, the UK Law Commission suggested tweaks to existing regulation and offered guidance on how fiduciary duties should be applied. Ultimately, it only concluded that pension fund trustees are not precluded from considering long-term interests and ESG factors. On fiduciary duties for non-pension trustee intermediaries, the UK Law Commission did not recommend a formal review but shifted the issue to the EU/international level by recommending the UK Government "review the current operation of the system of intermediated shareholding, with a view to taking the lead in negotiating solutions at a European or international level."[178]

[175] *Mothew (t/a Stapley & Co) v Bristol & West Building Society* [1996] EWCA Civ 533.

[176] Kay (2012, 13).

[177] 'Fiduciary Duties of Investment Intermediaries', UK Law Commission (4 June 2014) Law Com No 350. Online: http://www.lawcom.gov.uk/app/uploads/2015/03/lc350_fiduciary_duties.pdf.

[178] Ibid.

Up until the recent UK referendum on leaving the EU, discussions with the EU were ongoing. However, the UK Government moved away from calling intermediary duties 'fiduciary', observing the term has a specific meaning in law and equity. It instead described these as 'minimum standards.' The UK Government articulated principles to guide such standards, namely that all market participants should act in good faith, in the best long-term interests of their clients and beneficiaries, and in line with generally prevailing standards of decent behaviour.[179] These principles have not been enacted in legislative form. However, the UK Government asked the Financial Services Authority[180] and its successor organization, the FCA, to look into setting standards.

The FCA claimed that these standards played into discussion at the EU level on amendments to the Market in Financial Instruments Directive (MiFID II).[181] However, there is no evidence of amendments to MiFID II supporting this assertion, and the focus of reform was on market harmonization, international competition and investor protection.[182] Consequently, despite much discussion, there have been no reforms to standards of care or duties owed by intermediaries based on SMST concerns.

3. *Asset Manager Remuneration*

SMST reformers have suggested the current structure of asset manager remuneration raises short-termism concerns. However, despite much discussion, the only 'hard' law reform to date has been with respect to EU UCITS. The concern raised by Kay and also in the Aspen Report 2009 is that asset managers are not incentivized towards long-term investing as compensation is based on quarterly assessments of performance of assets under management. The Aspen Report 2009 suggested that there should be regulation to base compensation of long-term oriented funds

[179] Implementation (2014, 33).

[180] FSA was abolished when the Financial Services Act 2012 came into force on April 1, 2013.

[181] Markets in Financial Instruments Directive (2014/65/EU) and Markets in Financial Instruments Regulation (Regulation 600/2014) approved by the EC on 13 May 2014 (effective 2018), providing harmonized regulation for EU investment services.

[182] MiFID II Commission Press Release (14 January 2014).

on the fund's long-term performance.[183] Kay suggested that pay should not be related to short-term performance of the fund or asset management firm.[184] Instead, a long-term performance incentive should be provided via an interest in the fund to be held at least until the manager is no longer responsible for that fund. Further, Kay recommended that asset manager remuneration be structured to align the interests of asset managers with client interests and timescales.[185]

The UK Government agreed in principle with Kay, but its redress efforts focused on voluntary guidance rather than 'hard' or 'soft' law. It endorsed Kay's 'Good Practice Statement for Asset Managers', which included principles of remuneration. It also pointed to the NAPF Framework, as further discussed in Sect. B.1 above, and additional financial industry initiatives, including the Investment Management Association (IMA) guidance on disclosure of fund charges, as steps in the right direction.[186] The stated purpose of these initiatives was to increase transparency on remuneration thereby promoting long-term success of UK business.

At the EU level, the UCITS Directive does take some 'hard' law steps towards better aligning incentives of asset managers with long-term interests of investors. However, these rules only relate to EU UCITS, which cover a significant portion but not all of Europe's asset management firms. Specifically, the EU UCITS rules provide that:

1. Guaranteed variable remuneration—e.g., guaranteed bonus of ×% of returns—is only to be paid in exceptional circumstances;
2. Remuneration policies must be reviewed yearly and should be consistent with effective risk management;
3. A substantial portion of remuneration must be paid in EU UCITS units and deferred for a reasonable period of time; and
4. Staff cannot use personal hedging strategies or insurance in remuneration.

[183] Aspen Institute (2009, 5 and 9)

[184] Kay (2012), Recommendation 16.

[185] Ibid.

[186] Implementation (2014, 37–39).

4. *Voting Restrictions/Process*

SMST reformers have focused on intermediary voting—the process whereby intermediaries vote shares on behalf of asset owners at general meetings of listed companies—on behalf of asset owners as a means to correct short-termism. They argue that shares should be voted, and if intermediaries exercise voting rights they should do so in accordance with the asset owner interests. Theoretically at least, this action results in the long-term interests of asset owners being advanced as asset owners, assuming they have a long-term focus to investments, supposedly should take a longer view of investment than intermediaries.[187] In the UK, changes to the UK Stewardship Code placed a requirement on intermediaries to disclose voting policies and to make use of voting power, and explain why if they did not.[188] Similarly, in the EU, Article 3c of the EU Amended Shareholder Rights Directive includes provision meant to ensure intermediaries facilitate the exercise of asset owner rights, including voting rights, or explain why they do not.[189]

Whereas UK/EU measures only attempt to facilitate the voting process to correct short-termism, Swiss reforms actually restrict voting by intermediaries, which reforms were based on the idea asset owners will, or should, be more vested in the long-term viability of a company than intermediaries. These reforms came out of a 2013 referendum on the proposals in the 2008 Minder Initiative[190] to amend the Swiss Federal Constitution limiting excessive executive pay and intermediary voting, which passed by 67.9%. The stated aim of the Swiss law was to protect the economy, private property and shareholders and ensure sustainable management of businesses. Thomas Minder, the businessman-turned-politician behind the campaign, also stated that the proposals were aimed at ending a culture of short-termism and rewards for company managers of badly-run companies rather than just capping salaries.[191]

[187] Johnston and Morrow (2014, 29).

[188] UK Stewardship Code, 9, principle 6.

[189] EU Amended Shareholder Rights Directive, Article 3c.

[190] Thomas Minder initiative in English, 'Maurice's Musings' (1 March 2013) (Minder Initiative).

[191] "Swiss vote for tough curbs on executive pay." *Aljazeera* (3 March 2013).

As a result of this referendum, the Swiss Constitution now prohibits all proxy voting by an intermediary or by a depositary in respect of any Swiss public companies listed on stock exchanges in Switzerland or abroad.[192] Also, pension funds must vote in the interests of the beneficiaries and publicly disclose how they voted. These Swiss measures arguably are intended to counter short-termism by removing voting rights for intermediaries. This is supposedly meant to limit the rights of intermediaries and encourage voting by asset owners, which may motivate such shareholders—who may have a greater interest in the long-term viability of a listed company—to be involved in governance. This may have the opposite effect in practice; however, as the proxy voting process is intended to facilitate greater involvement in corporate governance by asset owners. Shareholders may opt out of the system if they are not able to use proxy voting. Violation of the law may result in imprisonment for up to three years and a fine of six years remuneration. However, no SMST-driven reforms to voting other than as discussed above have been implemented.

5. *Direct Shareholding*

Direct shareholding has been raised in the context of SMST reform. Kay recommended exploring a cost effective means for individuals to hold shares directly on an electronic register.[193] The rationale for this recommendation was that individual asset owners, particularly retail shareholders, may be able to engage more effectively with a company if they hold listed shares directly rather than via intermediaries.[194] The SMST concern was not clearly articulated by Kay, but appears to be that asset owners who hold shares directly may retain their shares for longer, and therefore may be more interested in the long-term value of the company.

Currently, to be able to effectively trade on a market, listed shares are held in electronic book entry form through a central depositary—e.g. CREST in the UK and Cede & Co in the US. In the UK, electronic

[192] Swiss Federal Constitution, Article 93(3)(a), which provides shareholders may vote remotely online, but may not be represented by a governing officer of the company or a custodian bank.

[193] Kay (2012), Recommendation 17, 13.

[194] Ibid., 84–85.

ownership is currently limited to members of the central system—i.e. to brokers—although for a cost nominee accounts may be set up for asset owners and brokers may sponsor individual membership.[195] The UK Government has stated it remains committed to facilitating individual holdings via EU initiatives in this area.[196] A key issue with the argument that facilitating direct retail holding will reduce perceived SMST concerns, is that in practice brokers are mere market functionaries. Rather than making investment decisions, brokers follow instructions, and moving this function directly to retain investors or asset owners generally, would not correct the SMST issue, but could hurt market liquidity.

As a result of discussions at the EU level, EU regulations[197] were enacted in September 2014. Specifically, the CSD Regulation aims to increase safety and efficiency of securities settlement and settlement infrastructures in the EU by providing that the immobilization and dematerialization—i.e. how shares are taken off book entry and recorded directly on a register—should not imply any loss of rights for the holders of securities and should be achieved in a way that ensures security holders can verify their rights. Arguably, the CSD Regulation could combat short-termism by facilitating direct ownership, but short-termism has not been cited as a reason for the reform. Also, the CSD Regulation does not take effect until 1 January 2023 for new securities, and 1 January 2025 for all securities, and it may also now not apply to the UK given the UK's exit from the EU. Consequently, no short-termism reforms facilitating direct shareholding have been implemented.

6. *Metrics and Models*

A wide variety of metrics are used by financial analysts—often engaged by asset managers—to measure a listed company's performance and populate valuation models. In the UK, the main factors used by financial analysts to develop a forecast or recommendation are cash flows, current share price relative to fundamental value, competitive advantage, balance

[195] For how this process works in the UK see "Investing: How to Hold Shares", London Stock Exchange website. Online: http://www.londonstockexchange.com/traders-and-brokers/private-investors/private-investors/about-share/how-hold-shares/how-hold-shares.htm.

[196] Implementation (2014, 52).

[197] Regulation (EU) No 909/2014 'On securities settlement and on Central Securities Depositories' (CSD Regulation).

sheet strength, and earnings outlook.[198] Behind each of these factors are common measures of performance that include earnings per share (EPS), free cash flow and net asset value, which feed into related valuation models used by financial analysts.[199] These models are ultimately used to measure the performance of investments and in deciding whether to buy or sell shares of a listed company.[200] As discussed further below, the concern raised is that increased reliance on these metrics and models by asset managers and, consequently, by asset owners may raise SMST concerns as financial analysts tend to base results on short-term frames and specific criteria, which may not accurately account for long-term growth.

Of the jurisdictions surveyed, only the UK has a developed discussion of models and metrics in the context of short-termism. The short-termism concerns raised by these complex metrics and models were discussed in the Kay Review. Kay observed that market complexity, and the corresponding growth of intermediation, have resulted in increased reliance on metrics and models developed by asset managers that tend to base results on short-term frames and specific criteria, which may not accurately account for long-term growth.[201] These types of structures may be unsuited to investors with a longer-term investment horizon, and could also be problematic if used as the basis for asset manager remuneration. Accordingly, Kay recommended that the UK Government commission a review of how these metrics and models are used in the investment chain focusing on how they measure long-term investments,[202] and also that regulators avoid the implicit or explicit prescription of a specific model in valuation or risk assessment and instead encourage the exercise of informed judgment by asset managers.[203]

In response, the UK Government commissioned a research project on models and metrics in the investment chain, which made a number of recommendations largely mirroring the Kay Review conclusions.[204] This research project concluded that metrics and models do rely heavily

[198] BIS Research Paper No. 190, 'Metrics and models used to assess company and investment performance' (October 2014) (BIS Paper No. 190), 68.

[199] Ibid.

[200] Ibid.

[201] Kay (2012, 75–76).

[202] Ibid., Recommendation 13.

[203] Ibid., Recommendation 14.

[204] BIS Paper 190.

on qualitative, and not only quantitative factors, as inputs often rely on qualitative judgments. Thus trust-based relationships, informed dialogue and the exercise of judgment are crucial. For metrics and models to better facilitate effective long-term investment decision-making, the UK research project concluded that there needs to be less reliance on intermediaries—and specifically, advocated for: (1) improved dialogue between companies and investors about future earnings and dividends; (2) improved information relayed to companies about changes in equity positions so as not to provoke a short-term reaction.[205] Speaking directly on accountability by asset managers to investors, the UK research project called for: (1) long-term objectives and stewardship to be embedded into the asset manager selection process; and (2) for asset manager reports accounting for investor time-lines.[206] Each of these proposed corrections are not directly related to changes in the metrics and models currently used, but instead require reforms to corporate governance generally, which would then as a result improve the inputs into such metrics and models.

7. *Proxy Advisors*

Proxy advisors, also called proxy voting agencies and shareholder voting research providers, are not directly in the equity ownership chain. However, as discussed in Chapter 2,[207] proxy advisors play an important role in the exercise of shareholder voting rights. Specifically, for a fee paid by users, proxy advisors such as Institutional Shareholder Services (ISS) and Glass Lewis & Co., LLC conduct research and make voting suggestions on proposals—e.g. board appointments, 'say on pay', and ESG matters—put forward at listed company meetings.

It is unclear exactly how the proxy advisory process contains issues relevant to short-termism, as proxy advisors appear not to be a priori short-termist—and if proxy advisors do not have a short-term bias, adherence to their recommendations may counter the short-termism of asset owners and asset managers. However, as there is considerable

[205] Ibid.

[206] Ibid.

[207] See Chapter 2, Sect. B.2.

reliance on proxy advice by asset owners/managers,[208] it has been argued that the proxy advisory process should be more transparent and freer from conflicts so that asset owners/managers can prudently manage investments.

Further, asset managers and asset owners may use proxy advisors, but they should ensure that they monitor the validity of the voting recommendation and assess whether such recommendation accords with their own investment parameters. Chief Justice Strine, has argued that proxy advisors do not have enough qualified persons to provide a genuine recommendation for every vote.[209] Consequently, Chief Justice Strine recommended that institutional investors should not rely upon proxy advisory recommendations that did not reflect the investment horizon and investing strategy of their investors, and in particular, index funds should not rely upon proxy advisory firms that did not provide index fund specific voting recommendations.[210] Despite these recommendations, the SEC has not proposed any short-termism reforms to the proxy advisory process. The SEC did, however, provide guidance generally confirming that the onus lies on asset managers to properly manage their proxy advice.[211] In the UK, the Kay Review did not specifically address the role of proxy advisors in the context of SMST reform. However, the role of proxy advisors was considered by the EC.

The EU Amended Shareholder Rights Directive proposed 'hard' law changes to the regulation of proxy advisors. The aim of these reforms was to ensure the reliability and quality of proxy advisors advice, thereby contributing to a longer-term perspective of shareholders and ensuring better operating conditions for EU listed companies.[212] The changes require proxy advisors to adopt and adhere to a code of conduct or explain why they do not.[213] This code of conduct is meant to ensure that research and voting recommendations are accurate and reliable and are

[208] Tonello (2006).

[209] Strine (2015, 26).

[210] Ibid., 43–44.

[211] SEC Staff Legal Bulletin No. 20 'Proxy Voting: Proxy Voting Responsibilities of Investment Advisers and Availability of Exemptions from the Proxy Rules for Proxy Advisory Firms' (30 June 2014).

[212] EU Amended Shareholder Rights Directive, Explanatory Memorandum, 2.

[213] Ibid., Article 3j.

developed in the client's sole interest. With more reliable voting recommendations, asset owners/managers should, at least theoretically, be able to more prudently manage investments for the long-term. Other than in the EU, however, there are no short-termism reforms to the proxy advisory process in the jurisdictions surveyed.

This section demonstrates that there have been some implemented reform efforts meant to correct perceived intermediary SMST. However, most of such reform has been 'soft' law—e.g. UK Stewardship Code—or voluntary measures setting guiding principles. Of the enacted 'hard' law reform, only the Minder Initiative limiting intermediary voting and the UCITS Directive regulating intermediary remuneration have prescriptive requirements. Articles 3h and 3i of the EU Amended Shareholder Rights Directive relate instead to public disclosure of investment strategies and the other reforms in the EU Amended Shareholder Rights Directive, namely Article 3c on the intermediary voting process and Article 3j on the proxy advisory process, are also 'light' touch as they are on a 'comply or explain' basis.

C. Company Manager SMST Reforms

Short-termism reforms also address 'managerial myopia', or company manager bias towards immediate results, as reformers suggest that market pressures and individual interests in short-term financial returns may negatively influence company manager behaviour.[214] Consequently, this section looks at reforms to executive remuneration, which claim to be based, at least in part, on short-termism concerns. Best practice suggestions aimed at reducing company manager short-termism are then considered. Finally, short-termism in the context of mergers and acquisitions (M&A) is reviewed, as company manager short-termism has been raised as a concern in M&A activity. Reforms are summarized in Appendix 'A' (Table 3). Although there are some implemented 'hard' law company manager reforms, as demonstrated in this section, reforms are limited to EU and UK remuneration reporting.

[214] See Dallas (2012, 270) and Moore and Petrin (2017, 128) summarizing the biases and market pressures contributing to company manager short-termism.

1. *Executive Remuneration*

As acknowledged by Kay in the Kay Review, executive remuneration is a subject of much controversy and attention in its own right, and not only in the context of short-termism.[215] The bigger questions asked are if high levels of executive pay in listed companies are just or appropriate, and whether executive pay levels adequately align with listed company performance. Kay limited his analysis to whether the structure of executive remuneration in UK listed companies contributed to, or detracted from, good long-term decision-making. Similarly, this section only considers efforts to reform executive remuneration based on SMST concerns. The main SMST concern raised by reformers is that executive remuneration resulting from short-term performance and unrestricted equity—i.e. equity with no 'vesting' restrictions', precisely requirements that shares be held for a period of time before they may be sold[216]—results in short-sighted decisions at the cost of longer-term economic performance.[217] The UK response to such concerns is considered first given the detailed discussion in the Kay Review, and the resulting 'hard' law changes.

In his review, Kay focused on the main elements of long-term compensation plans set by remuneration committees of listed companies, namely executive incentive schemes and bonuses. His key concern was that the customary three-year timeframe of such long-term plans was too short given that the decision-making of UK CEO's may have a much longer impact.[218] Consequently, Kay recommended that UK companies should structure executive remuneration to relate incentives to sustainable long-term business performance, and that share-based long-term incentives should only be provided in the form of shares held at least until after the executive has retired from the business.[219]

The UK Government did not implement the specifics of Kay's recommendations. It did agree, however, with his general recommendation to better link executive pay with long-term performance, but observed

[215] Kay (2012, 77–79).

[216] See the definition of 'vesting' at https://www.investopedia.com/terms/v/vesting.asp.

[217] Bolton et al. (2006).

[218] Kay (2012, 78–79).

[219] Ibid., Recommendation 15.

that this connection was best achieved through promoting good corporate practice rather than mandated a specific remuneration structure.[220] Particularly, the UK Government referred to reporting requirements aimed at correcting short-termism governance in regulations enacted in October 2013 applicable to UK listed company executive remuneration.[221] These UK Remuneration Regulations also contain a 'say on pay' provision, giving shareholders a binding say on executive pay policy. This builds on the UK's previous robust listed company remuneration regulatory regime, which included an advisory vote on pay.[222] However, the change to a binding 'say on pay' does not appear to be motivated by short-termism concerns—arguably because if investors are short-term focused, a 'say-on-pay' could foster SMST—but rather are intended to address concerns about excessive remuneration and also more generally on better linking executive compensation to corporate performance.[223]

The UK Remuneration Regulations did require a new form of remuneration report to be presented to shareholders annually setting out each director's pay for the previous financial year, and how such pay is linked to performance.[224] Such disclosure is not unique to the UK 'say on pay' structure. Detailed remuneration disclosure has long been a requirement for listed companies, and has been required under the US Securities Exchange Act of 1934 since its inception in 1934.[225] Changes to 'say on pay' regimes in other jurisdictions now routinely link remuneration disclosure with performance.[226] However, the UK Remuneration

[220] Implementation (2014, 42).

[221] UK Enterprise and Regulatory Reform Act 2013 and The Large and Medium-sized Companies and Groups (Accounts and Reports) (Amendment) Regulations 2013 (UK Remuneration Regulations).

[222] Introduced for UK listed companies in 2000 and included in UK Companies Act, 2006 §439.

[223] Implementation (2014, 42).

[224] UK Large and Medium-sized Companies and Groups (Accounts and Reports) (Amendment) Regulations 2013 (2013 UK Regulations), Schedule 8.

[225] Frydman and Saks (2010, 2103).

[226] Organisation for Economic Co-operation and Development (OECD), Corporate Governance Factbook (2015, 96–97).

Regulations go further than the reporting requirements in other jurisdictions[227] and previous UK requirements.[228] The UK Remuneration Regulations expressly provide that UK listed companies must disclose how each component of the remuneration package supports short and long-term strategic objectives of the listed company.[229] Though it does not have mandatory 'say on pay' legislation, Singapore amended its 'soft' law Code of Corporate Governance in 2012 to require disclosure in the remuneration report on how remuneration is linked to the short-term and long-term performance of SGX listed companies.[230]

In the EU, Article 9a of the EU Amended Shareholder Rights Directive requires that EU Members ensure that listed companies in their jurisdictions establish a remuneration policy to be adhered to in the payment of executives and submitted to a shareholder vote at least once every three years.[231] The remuneration policy must be in line with the company's long-term interests, and management must explain how the policy contributes to long-term interests and sustainability.[232] Article 9b of the EU Amended Shareholder Rights Directive also requires that a remuneration report be produced and voted on by shareholders, which vote may be binding or advisory as set by the EU Member State. This remuneration report must also specify how remuneration is linked to the company's long-term performance.[233]

[227] A survey of jurisdictions with robust executive remuneration requirements as evidenced by the adoption of binding or advisory 'say on pay' requirements—including US, UK, EU, Switzerland, Netherlands, Sweden, Germany, France, Norway, and Australia—indicates disclosure is centered on reporting types of compensation and the relationship to performance generally. Although some 'soft' law governance codes—e.g. Norway and Australia—provide executive compensation should not lead to 'short-termism', specific reporting on how pay links to short and long-term strategy to the extent contained in the Remuneration Regulations is not provided.

[228] UK Large and Medium-sized Companies and Groups (Accounts and Reports) Regulations 2008, the predecessor legislation to the Remuneration Regulations, did not require reporting on the link between pay and short and long-term strategy.

[229] 2013 UK Regulations, Schedule 8, item 26(a).

[230] Singapore Code of Corporate Governance 2012, Principle 1. Guideline 5.2 and 8.1.

[231] EU Amended Shareholder Rights Directive, Article 9a.

[232] Ibid., Article 9a(2) and (3).

[233] Ibid., Article 9b.

Prior to UK/EU initiatives, the Swiss considered executive pay. The Minder Initiative, discussed earlier on voting rights of intermediaries in Sect. B of this chapter, also addressed the issue of perceived excessive executive compensation. Although the primary motivation was curbing excessive executive pay, short-termism concerns appeared to have factored into the motivation for the proposed reforms.[234] The Minder Initiative resulted in 'hard' law changes to the Swiss Federal Constitution resulting in reforms to executive compensation of Swiss listed companies—both in Switzerland and abroad.[235]

Curbing excessive pay was undoubtedly a key driver, and the Swiss reforms went somewhat beyond a 'say on pay' as found in other jurisdictions by requiring separate voting by boards/committees on pay packages and limiting certain types of payments. However, it is not at all clearly discernible how these reforms are meant to counter short-termism. Consequently, these Swiss reforms are not considered an implemented 'hard' law short-termism remuneration reform.

Similarly, there have been discussions in the US on the issue of short-termism in executive compensation.[236] The Dodd-Frank Act, Title IX, Subtitle E—Accountability and Executive Compensation, introduced changes into the US regime. These changes introduced a requirement into the US Securities Exchange Act of 1934 that shareholders have a 'say-on-pay' vote at least every three years.[237] There is no discussion by the SEC, or the newly established Investor Advisory Committee, linking these 'say-on-pay' requirements to SMST-driven reform. However, in addition to a 'say-on-pay', Title IX, Subtitle E—Accountability and Executive Compensation of the Dodd-Frank Act also provided for the SEC to make amendments to the disclosure of executive compensation arrangements.

The Aspen Institute also engaged in the discussion on SMST and executive remuneration, arguing that the focus of US reforms on narrow performance metrics and disclosure increases incentives for short-term behaviour.[238] This position is consistent with earlier principles developed

[234] Thomas Minder initiative in English, 'Maurice's Musings' (1 March 2013).

[235] Swiss Federal Constitution, Article 95, Paragraph 3.

[236] Thanassoulis (2012).

[237] Dodd-Frank Act, Title IX, Subtitle E, Section 951.

[238] The Aspen Institute, "Pay vs. Performance Disclosure—Comments on Proposed Regulations." (2015). Online: https://www.sec.gov/comments/s7-07-15/s70715-54.pdf.

by the Aspen Institute urging companies to better align compensation of executives with long-term value creation.[239] Building on this position, Chief Justice Strine observed that "[b]ecause executive compensation should be designed to provide top executives with appropriate incentives to manage well and create sustainable increases in corporate value, it seems counterintuitive and counterproductive that compensation arrangements should run on annual terms, with constant tinkering and changing of key provisions."[240] He suggested it is more sensible to have compensation committees set employment contracts for a reasonable length of time to assess their contribution to management and 'say on pay' votes held every third/fourth year rather than annually.

Building on this discussion, in implementing changes to executive disclosure in 2015, the SEC noted that some compensation plans may cause executives to focus overly on short-term performance to the detriment of long-term performance. Consequently, in August 2015 the SEC enhanced disclosure requirements, requiring US listed corporations to disclose in 2018 registration statements and annual 10-K filings the relationship between executive compensation actually paid for five years and corporate financial performance, specifically the total shareholder return of the listed corporation and its peer group.[241] As discussed, in Chapter 8,[242] there are questions as to whether these US executive compensation disclosure reforms, as with performance disclosure elsewhere, conceptually actually address SMST concerns. However, as demonstrated above, actual 'hard' law implemented short-termism driven reforms to executive compensation have been moderate, and are limited to UK, US and EU reforms related to remuneration reporting.

[239] Aspen Institute (2009, 6).

[240] Strine (2015, 26).

[241] Implemented in August 2015 by an amendment to US securities regulation on executive compensation required as part of the Dodd-Frank reforms—SEC, 'Pay Versus Performance', Proposed Rule proposing amendments to Item 402 of Regulation S-K to implement Section 14(i) of the Securities Exchange Act of 1934.

[242] See Chapter 8, Sect. B.3.a.

2. *Best Practices*

SMST reformers have advocated for company managers to be given improved direction on how best to manage listed companies for the long-term.[243] Although there are various voluntary reforms addressing best practices for company managers to achieve long-term objectives, no 'hard' or 'soft' law SMST reforms have yet been implemented.

In the UK, Kay observed that company managers are stewards of company assets and business operations. In accordance with the UK Companies Act, Kay asserted that the directors' duties are to the company and not its share price, and companies should aim to develop relationships with investors rather than with 'the market'. In furtherance, the Kay Review offered a 'Good Practice Statement for Company Directors' building on directors' duties under the UK Companies Act and highlighting their role in long-term value creation.[244] This statement also asserted that company managers should not allow expectations of market reaction to particular short-term performance to influence company strategy. Endorsed by the UK Government,[245] this statement is meant to work in tandem with reforms to UK executive remuneration discussed above. However, the statement has not been legislatively enacted, and there is no indication the UK Government intends to do so.

The UK did include additional considerations on the duties of directors in Section 172 of the UK Companies Act adopted in 2006.[246] Specifically, Section 172 of the UK Companies Act sets out the duty of directors to promote the success of the company, which is to act in good faith in the way that is most likely to promote the success of the company for the benefit of its members as a whole. Section 172 goes on to enumerate a non-exhaustive list of factors that the directors should have regard to when fulfilling such duty, including, notably, "the likely consequences of any decision in the long-term."[247] These expanded duties may have implications for SMST reform and are discussed further in Chapter 6.[248] However, the broader language in Section 172

[243] See summary in Dallas (2012, 355–357).

[244] Kay (2012, 58).

[245] Implementation (2014, 42)

[246] UK Companies Act 2006, Chapter 46 (UK Companies Act)

[247] Ibid., Section 172(1)(a).

[248] See Chapter 6, Sect. B.1.a.

encompassing long-term interests appears to have been adopted as a result of codifying duties based on equitable and common law rules rather than any specific SMST concerns.[249] Therefore, Section 172 is not included in the table of SMST reforms.

In addition to the discussion on duties, there is a plethora of financial industry-driven initiatives on executive standard setting, and best practices for company managers also exist to voluntarily guide behaviour towards long-term sustainability.[250] Larry Fink, CEO of BlackRock Inc. (BlackRock), has for three years running put out a call to action to company managers of S&P 500 and large EU companies. Mr. Fink has expressed concerns about stock market short-termism, and called for:

1. Excess cash not to be returned to shareholders at the expense of value-creating investments;
2. CEOs to clearly lay out a strategic framework for long-term value creation to shareholders annually; and
3. ESG issues to be focused on by asset managers and handled well by companies.[251]

Governance and professional organizations are also avid supporters of initiatives promoting company manager long-termism.[252] For example, see the Institute of Directors (IOD). Submission to the Kay Review (18 November 2011), Institute of Corporate Governance (Brazil), 'Sustainability Guide for Companies', Australian IOD, 'Curbing excessive short-termism: A guide for boards of public companies' (April 2013), New Zealand IOD, 'The Four Pillars of Governance Best Practice' (2012), and King Report on Governance for South Africa

[249] UK Companies Act 2006, Explanatory Notes, Note 299.

[250] For example, 'Tomorrow's Company, Future of Finance' (long-term global effort led by CFA Institute focused on building long-term sustainable value), and 'Generation Foundation' (non-profit foundation focused on promoting sustainable capitalism).

[251] Turner (2016), Oyedele (2017), and Fink (2018).

[252] See Institute of Directors (UK), Submission to the Kay Review (18 November 2011), Brazilian Institute of Corporate Governance, 'Sustainability Guide for Companies' (2008), Institute of Directors (Australia), 'Curbing Excessive Short-Termism: A Guide for Boards of Public Companies' (April 2013), Institute of Directors (New Zealand), 'The Four Pillars of Governance Best Practice' (2012), and King Report on Governance for South Africa (2009).

(2009). However, these are all voluntary initiatives, and, as stated above, there are no implemented 'hard' or 'soft' law short-termism reforms in this area.

3. *M&A*

As discussed in Chapter 3,[253] short-termism in the context of M&A activity featured prominently in the discussion in the US during the takeover boom of the 1970/1980s.[254] Since the GFC, however, there has not been any significant SMST-driven reform or reform proposals to M&A regulation, other than in the UK. In the UK, the Kay Review identified hyper-activity by company managers focused on M&A activity at the expense of developing fundamental operational capabilities of the business as a characteristic of short-termism in capital markets. Kay also observed that short-term incentives have led to some takeovers of listed companies which are not in the public interest or the long-term interests of investors.[255] Consequently, Kay recommended that the scale and effectiveness of UK merger activity be kept under careful review.[256]

The UK Government accepted Kay's recommendation, and identified that changes to the UK Takeover Code enacted in 2011 to further protect targets, and subsequent revisions requiring offerors to disclose post-offer intentions, were a step-change towards ensuring that UK M&A activity was motivated by long-term considerations.[257] It also reported that the UK Competition and Markets Authority, established in 2013 to promote competition for the benefit of consumers within and outside the UK, had a clear objective of long-termism built into its strategy. The UK Government stated that the UK approach to foreign takeovers was reviewed and deemed appropriate.[258] No further notable M&A short-termism reforms have been made or proposed by policymakers in the jurisdictions surveyed.

Despite much discussion, Sect. C of this chapter demonstrates that there has been minimal 'hard' law reform attempting to correct alleged managerial myopia. SMST-driven reform in this space has been limited to enhanced

[253] See Chapter 3, Sect. 3 A.

[254] See discussion in Roe (2013, 979).

[255] Kay (2012, 10).

[256] Ibid., 13.

[257] Kay Implementation (2014, 47).

[258] Ibid., 49.

US, EU and UK reporting requirements on how executive compensation links to long-term strategy. All other implemented company manager short-termism reforms appear to be voluntary financial industry initiatives.

As shown in this chapter, SMST rhetoric appears to be weaving its way into the fabric of listed company corporate governance. As demonstrated by this analysis, policymakers—particularly in the UK and EU—have framed some post-GFC stock market reforms around short-termism. Further, they have been actively sculpting long-term objectives into some—albeit minimal—substantive regulatory change. To date, however, the SEC has been a harder sell, although there are some strong voices pushing for SMST-driven reform in the US. Despite the significant level of discussion and numerous proposals, the actual output of short-termism reform in all jurisdictions surveyed has been relatively modest.

Of the implemented 'hard' law reforms shown in Appendix 'B' (Table 4), most reforms are disclosure based or on a 'comply or explain' basis—e.g. Articles 3c, 3h, 3i and 3j of the EU Amended Shareholder Rights Directive—or provide an 'opt out'—e.g. Florange Law and EU Transparency Directive. Voting restrictions in the Minder Initiative, the EU UCITS Directive—which only applies to EU UCITS—, and US/UK/EU reporting requirements on long-term strategy and remuneration in Articles 9a and 9b and the shareholder communication requirements in Articles 3a and 3b of the EU Amended Shareholder Rights Directive are the only 'hard' law reforms with non-optional requirements. Consequently, prescriptive 'hard' law reform mandating behaviour has been modest. There are some implemented 'soft' law reforms, particularly in UK and the EU, and voluntary financial industry initiatives than prescriptive 'hard' law reform. Regardless, the total output of SMST-driven reform has been modest contrasted with the short-termism discussion.

As implemented reform to date has been minimal, the question remains what if anything should be done to correct SMST. The review in this chapter provides a useful benchmark summarizing what has been done to date. This benchmark may be used to measure what further actions are required, if any, to address the perceived SMST issue. This analysis also demonstrates that SMST is on the radar of policymakers, and is driving some reform, albeit at a more moderate pace than the extensive reform proposals suggest. Recent empirical studies have bolstered the case for SMST reform.[259] However, there continues to be a

[259] Cremers et al. (2019).

lively discussion in academia and the popular press on whether there is a SMST issue at all, and if so, what is causing SMST and if the SMST problem is actually harmful.

There is a strong possibility that those persons advocating that SMST is a real and harmful problem have not yet convincingly presented their case, which may explain why implemented regulatory and financial industry reform has been minimal and relatively 'light' touch to date. Consequently, the following chapters consider in further detail if there is in fact a harmful SMST problem, and if so, what is causing it. This analysis cumulates in Chapter 8 with an assessment of the conceptual effectiveness of the implemented reforms based on the most probable causes of SMST.

References

Ali, Paul, Ramsay, Ian, and Saunders, Benjamin. 2014. "Securities Lending, Empty Voting and Corporate Governance." May. CIFR Working Paper 023/2014.

Aspen Institute. 2009. "Overcoming Short-Termism: A Call for a More Responsible Approach to Investment and Business Management." 9 September.

Barton, Dominic and Wiseman, Mark. 2014. "Focusing Capital on the Long Term." January–February. *Harvard Business Review*. 44–51.

Bolton, P., Scheinkman, J., and Xiong, W. 2006. "Executive Compensation and Short-Termist Behavior in Speculative Markets." 73:3 *The Review of Economic Studies*. 577–610.

Busch, D. and DeMott, D. 2012. *Liability of Asset Managers*. Oxford University Press: Oxford, UK.

Cheffins, Brian. 2010. "The Stewardship Code's Achilles Heel." November. 73:6 *The Modern Law Review*. 1004–1025.

Chen, Quin. 2015. "Japan Stewardship Code—What Investors Think (So Far)." May/June. 8:2 *IPREO Newsletter*. http://1igflvrxbfpltom39pcvl-jnx.wpengine.netdna-cdn.com/wp-content/uploads/2015/10/BetterIR_May_2015.pdf#page=13.

Choo, Rachel. 2016. "Dual-Class Share Structure in Singapore." 22 December. *Duan Morris & Selvam LLP*. https://www.duanemorris.com/articles/dual-class_share_structure_in_singapore_1216.html.

Conaghan, Thomas P., Lesur, Lionel, Reighard, Lindsay, and Leroy, Loius. 2017. "Worldwide: Rewarding Long-Term Shareholders: European and US Loyalty Share Programmes." 18 September. *Mondaq* http://www.mondaq.com/unitedstates/x/629580/Shareholders/Rewarding+LongTerm+Shareholders+European+And+US+Loyalty+Share+Programmes.

Cremers, K. J. Martijn, Pareek, Ankur, and Sautner, Zacharias. 2019. "Short-Term Investors, Long-Term Investments, and Firm Value: Evidence from Russell 2000 Index Inclusions." 26 March. https://ssrn.com/abstract=2720248.

Croce, Raffaele D., Stewart Fiona, and Yermo, Juan. 2011. "Promoting Longer-Term Investment by Institutional Investors: Selected Issues and Policies." 2011:1 *OECD Journal: Financial Market Trends*.

Dallas, Lynne L. 2012. "Short-Termism, the Financial Crisis, and Corporate Governance" 2011–2012. 37:2 *The Journal of Corporation Law* 265–364.

Delvoie, Jergen and Clotten, Carl. 2015. "Accountability and Short-Termism: Some Notes on Loyalty Shares." 9:1. *Law and Financial Markets Review*. 19–28.

Dent, George. 2010. "Essential Unity of Shareholders and the Myth of Investor Short-Termism." 35:1 *Delaware Journal of Corporate Law*. 97–150.

Emspak, Jesse. 2017. "GOOG or GOOGL: Which Stock Do You Buy? (GOOG, GOOGL)." 6 June. *Investopedia*. http://www.investopedia.com/articles/markets/052215/goog-or-googl-which-google-should-you-buy.asp.

Ernstberger, Jürgen, Link, Benedikt, Stich, Michael, and Vogler, Oliver. 2015. "The Real Effects of Mandatory Quarterly Reporting." 15 April. SSRN Working Paper.

Fink, Larry. 2018. CEO Letter, BlackRock, Inc. January. https://www.blackrock.com/corporate/investor-relations/larry-fink-ceo-letter.

Fried, Jesse M. 2015. "The Uneasy Case for Favoring Long-Term Shareholders." 124 *The Yale Law Journal*. 1554–1628.

Frydman, Carola and Saks, Raven E. 2010. "Executive Compensation: A New View from a Long-Term Perspective, 1936–2005." 23:5 *Review of Financial Studies*. 2099–2138.

Gad, Sham. 2018. "What Are Hedge Funds." 20 February. *Investopedia*. https://www.investopedia.com/articles/investing/102113/what-are-hedge-funds.asp.

Hayden, G. M. and Bodie, M. T. 2008. "One Share, One Vote and the False Promise of Shareholder Homogeneity." 30:2 *Cardozo Law Review*. 445–505.

"Implementation of the Kay Review: Progress Report." 2014. Department for Business Innovation & Skills. October.

Jacobs, Ben. 2015. "Hillary Clinton Decries Wall Street's 'Quarterly Capitalism' in Tax Reform Pitch." 24 July. *The Guardian*.

Johnson, Steve. 2015. "Protectionist' French Law Alarms Investors." 22 February. *Financial Times*.

Johnston, Andrew and Morrow, Paige. 2014. "Commentary on the Shareholder Rights Directive." University of Oslo Faculty of Law Research Paper No. 2014-41.

Jones, Huw. 2015. "Deep Splits Among EU Lawmakers Over Shareholder Rights Reforms." 20 January. *Reuters*.

Kay, John. 2012. "The Kay Review of UK Equity Markets and Long-Term Decision Making." Final Report. July.

"The Kay Review of UK Equity Markets and Long-Term Decision Making: Government Response to the Committee's Third Report of Session 2013–14." 2014. Special Report of Session 2013–14, House of Commons. 22 October 2013.

Kastiel, Kobi. 2–15. "Proxy Access, SEC Uncertainty and Related Issues in 2015." February 24. *Harvard Law School Forum on Corporate Governance and Financial Regulation*. https://corpgov.law.harvard.edu/2015/02/24/proxy-access-sec-uncertainty-and-related-issues-in-2015/.

Konczal, Mike, Mason, J. W., and Page-Hoongrajok, Amanda. 2015. "Ending Short-Termism: An Investment Agenda for Growth." 6 November. *The Roosevelt Institute*.

Lee, Marissa. 2017. "SGX Says 'Still Evaluating' Feedback on Dual-Class Shares." 22 September. *The Straights Times*. http://www.straitstimes.com/business/sgx-says-still-evaluating-feedback-on-dual-class-shares.

Lipton, Martin. 2015. "Legal & General Calls for End to Quarterly Reporting." 19 August. *Harvard Law School Forum on Corporate Governance and Financial Regulation*. https://corpgov.law.harvard.edu/2015/08/19/legal-general-calls-for-end-to-quarterly-reporting/.

Lu, Carmen X. W. 2016. "Unpacking Wolf Packs." 125:3 *The Yale Law Journal*. 560–795.

Maurice, Eric. 2015. "EU Financial Transaction Tax on Life Support." 8 December. *EU Observer*. https://euobserver.com/economic/131435.

Merced, Michael J. de la and Phillips, Matt. 2018. "Trump Asks S.E.C. to Study Quarterly Earnings Requirements for Public Firms." 17 August. *DealBook*. https://www.nytimes.com/2018/08/17/business/dealbook/trump-quarterly-earnings.html?rref=collection%2Fissuecollection%2Ftodays-new-york-times&action=click&contentCollection=todayspaper&region=rank&module=package&version=highlights&contentPlacement=5&pgtype=collection.

Miller, P. 2013. "Justifying Fiduciary Duties." 58:4 *McGill Law Journal*. 969–1023.

Modesto, Ryan. 2016. "The Case for Investing in Companies with Dual-Class Shares." 18 April. *Globe and Mail*. https://beta.theglobeandmail.com/globe-investor/investment-ideas/research-reports/the-case-for-investing-in-companies-with-dual-classshares/article29638161/?ref=http://www.theglobeandmail.com.

Moore, Marc T. and Petrin, Martin. 2017. *Corporate Governance: Law, Regulation and Theory*. Palgrave Corporate & Financial Law: London, UK.

Moore, Marc T. and Walker-Arnott, Edward. 2014. "A Fresh Look at Stock Market Short-Termism." 41:3 *Journal of Law and Society*. 416–445.

OECD. Corporate Governance Factbook. 2015.

Oyedele, Akin. 2017. "Here Is the Letter the World's Largest Investor, BlackRock CEO Larry Fink, Just Sent to CEOs Everywhere." 24 January. *Business Insider UK*. http://uk.businessinsider.com/blackrock-ceo-larry-fink-letter-to-ceos-2017-1?r=US&IR=T.

Pearlstein, Steven. 2009. "Wall Street's Mania for Short-Term Results Hurts Economy." 11 September. *Washington Post*. www.washingtonpost.com/wp-dyn/content/article/2009/09/10/AR2009091004224.html.

Pozen, R. and Roe, Mark. 2015. "Attacks on Quarterly Earnings Fall Short." 9 October. The *Wall Street Journal*.

Quimby, P. Alexander. 2013. "Addressing Corporate Short-Termism Through Loyalty Shares." 40:2 *Florida State University Law Review*. 389–414.

Roe, Mark J. 2013. "Corporate Short-Termism—In the Boardroom and in the Courtroom." August 2013. 68. *Business Lawyer* 977–1006.

"Shareholder Rights in Europe: Short-Term or Short-Changed." 2015. 2 May. *The Economist*.

Strine, Leo E., Jr. 2015. "Securing Our Nation's Economic Future: A Sensible, Nonpartisan Agenda to Increase Long-Term Investment and Job Creation in The United States." University of Pennsylvania Institute for Law & Economics Research Paper No. 15–41.

Thanassoulis, J. 2012. "Industry Structure, Executive Pay and Short-Termism." 59:2 *Management Science*.

Thomas, Lizanne, Profusek, Robert A., and Ganske, Lyle G. 2010. "Dodd-Frank: Short-Title, Short-Termism." July. *Jones Day Publications*. http://www.jonesday.com/dodd-frank/#_ftn1.

Tonello, Matteo. 2006. "Revisiting Stock Market Short-Termism." Corporate/Investor Summit Series. The Conference Board.

Turner, Matt. 2016. "Here Is the Letter the World's Largest Investor, BlackRock CEO Larry Fink, Just Sent to CEOs Everywhere." 2 February. *Business Insider UK*. http://uk.businessinsider.com/blackrock-ceo-larry-fink-letter-to-sp-500-ceos-2016-2?r=US&IR=T.

Wallace, Tim. 2015. "Legal and General Scraps Quarterly Reporting." 11 December. *Telegraph*.

Wong, Simon. 2015. "Is Institutional Investor Stewardship Still Elusive?" 24 September. *Harvard Law School Forum on Corporate Governance and Financial Regulation*. https://corpgov.law.harvard.edu/2015/09/24/is-institutional-investor-stewardship-still-elusive-2/.

CHAPTER 5

Is There a Short-Termism Problem at All?

Chapter 4 concluded that despite extensive discussion, not many reforms have been implemented to correct the stock market short-termism (SMST) problem. Further, of the SMST-driven regulatory reforms that have been implemented, most are 'light' touch as the majority of these reforms are 'comply or explain' or disclosure based, or 'soft' law or voluntary non-legal initiatives rather than prescriptive 'hard' law reforms. In order to determine whether there is in fact a problem justifying even this limited public policy response to the SMST issue and if any further reforms are necessary to correct SMST, this chapter wades into the debate—primarily happening within financial and legal scholarship—on if there is a SMST problem at all, and, if so, what may be causing the SMST issue.

First considered is the evidence presented supporting the argument that there is a SMST problem. After assessing the strength of this evidence and accepting that there is a basis for concern, this chapter then considers how SMST may be evident in share pricing, as share prices are an important communication mechanism between listed companies and the market. In particular, this chapter assesses how there can be a SMST problem at all if share prices, as mainstream economic theory suggests, are a decent measure of the risk-adjusted future returns of a listed company. To do so, the efficient capital market hypothesis (ECMH) is considered, which hypothesis essentially holds that markets are informationally efficient, meaning that share prices reflect all publicly available information.

K. M. Willey, *Stock Market Short-Termism*,
https://doi.org/10.1007/978-3-030-22903-0_5

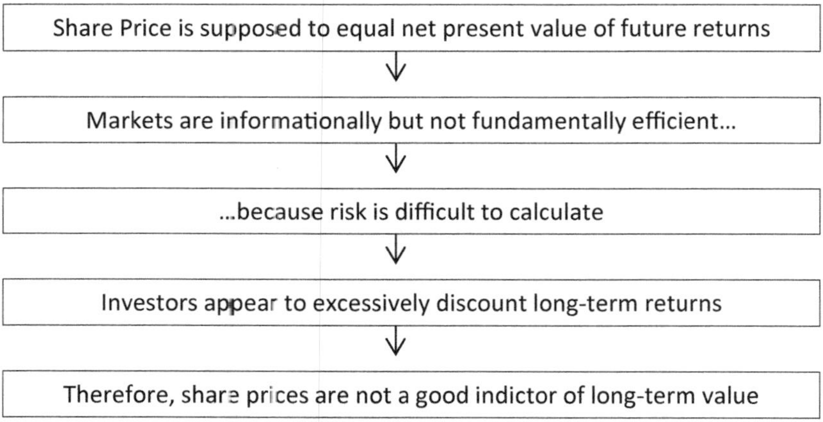

Fig. 1 SMST and share pricing

Accepting that capital markets are generally *informationally* efficient, this chapter then examines whether capital markets are also *fundamentally* efficient—meaning that share prices are a decent measure of the underlying long-term value of the firm. In doing so, a complex part of share pricing is analyzed, specifically the discount rates applied to future returns by investors and the interaction with investor bias. The hypothesis that short-termism in share pricing is evident in excessive discount rates applied by investors is explored. Building on this intuitive concept that immediate rewards are worth more than uncertain long-term rewards using economic and financial research, this chapter concludes—as summarized in the arguments set out in Fig. 1—that the evidence is suggestive that SMST is occurring, and it is in large part due to the excessive discounting of future returns by investors. This excessive discounting, and the resulting impact on share prices, is known to company managers and, accordingly, there is a strong incentive to prioritize short-term financial results. Consequently, this chapter questions if share prices are a decent measure of the long-term value of listed companies.

A. Evidence of the SMST Problem

Before turning to an analysis of short-termism in share pricing, this section reviews and assesses the strength of the evidence presented on whether there is a short-termism problem. The depth of survey evidence conducted on market participants, which consistently indicates a SMST problem, is first considered. After acknowledging the weaknesses of the survey methodology as a precise tool to measure the SMST problem, analysis of a systemic short-termism bias in capital markets is considered. Quantitative evidence in support of the existence of a SMST problem is also then assessed. As quantitative evidence is thin on the ground, other forms of evidence which use proxies to extrapolate the existence of a SMST problem are considered. Though none of the evidence provided on its own conclusively confirms the existence of a SMST problem, the consistent survey results of market participants, analysis of investor bias, the evidence of increasing excessive discounting of long-term cash flows, and the proxies used to measure short-termism, present if not a compelling, at least a suggestive, picture that there is a SMST problem worth addressing.

1. Survey Evidence

There is an abundance of survey evidence consistently confirming that company managers feel pressured to provide short-term returns and that they take positive actions to do so. Survey evidence has been summarized by Davies et al. (2014),[1] and notably includes detailed surveys of United States (US) listed company executives conducted by researchers Graham et al. which found that: (1) managers would reject a positive-net present value (NPV) project if that positive-NPV lowered earnings below quarterly consensus expectations; (2) over 75% of the sample would give up economic value in order to smooth earnings; and (3) managers said that these actions in (1) and (2) were driven by the desire to satisfy investors.[2]

These results have been repeatedly confirmed. For example, McKinsey & Company (McKinsey) and the Canadian Pension Plan (CPP) conducted an international survey of over 1000 corporate directors and chief executive officers (CEOs) in 2013. In this survey, 63% of the respondents indicated the pressure on their senior executives to demonstrate strong short-term financial performance had increased in the past five years, and 79% of the respondents said they felt the most pressure to demonstrate strong financial performance over a time period of less

[1] Davies et al. (2014, 16).

[2] See Graham et al. (2005), updated in Graham et al. (2006).

than two years.[3] More recently, in 2016, the National Association of Corporate Directors in the US found that of the more than 600 public company directors and governance professionals surveyed, 75% indicated that short-term pressures were undermining management's focus on long-term strategic objectives and value creation.[4] However compelling this evidence is, survey evidence may be seen to have at least three identifiable inherent issues.

First, the responses to survey questions by company managers could be untruthful or self-serving—surveys are essentially human data and thus are fallible.[5] For example, company managers may attribute blame for their short-term actions unduly on asset owners or asset managers in order to encourage reforms that provide themselves with greater discretion to manage the affairs of listed companies. This criticism may be true, but there is no documented assessment that the survey evidence gathered on SMST is untruthful or self-serving—rather, much of this evidence has been done anonymously thereby reducing the incentives to be untruthful or self-serving. A second issue with survey evidence is that surveys indicate that managers feel pressured to produce short-term results, but this does not evidence that they are in fact doing so. Consequently, survey evidence should ideally be supported by other—e.g. quantitative—evidence demonstrating that SMST is in reality occurring in the market. Such quantitative evidence of SMST is considered in Sect. A.2 below.

Finally, a third criticism may be that even if company managers are prioritizing short-term financial returns and engaging in real earnings management—as discussed in Chapter 6[6]—, such short-termist actions do not necessarily equate to societal harm. Evidence of the societal

[3] CPP Investment Board (2013, 6) and as referenced in Barton and Wiseman (2014, 46).

[4] Results of the 2016/2017 NACD Public Company Governance Survey as referenced in "More Than Half of Public Company Boards Recognize the Effects of Short-Termism," 5 December 2016. *NACD Press Release*. Online: https://www.cnbc.com/2016/12/05/globe-newswire-more-than-half-of-public-company-boards-recognize-the-effects-of-short-termism.html.

[5] See Rapley (2017) criticizing economic research on the basis that it is not scientific and relies on human data. The author observes that "[u]nlike people, subatomic particles don't lie on opinion surveys or change their minds about things."

[6] See Chapter 6, Sect. B.2.

harms of SMST is considered further in Chapter 7. However, even if the evidence does not yet definitively indicate a harmful SMST problem, as suggested by Roger Martin, Academic Director of the Martin Prosperity Institute, weight should be put on the negative behaviours of individuals rather than the outputs, as eventually short-termist behaviours will impact outputs.[7] Thus, if company managers say they are behaving in a short-termist manner in response to perceived or actual pressure from investors for short-term financial results, this behaviour by company managers could eventually translate into societal harm. Consequently, survey results are suggestive, if not compelling, evidence of a SMST problem.

2. *Short-Term Bias—A Systemic Issue?*

A popular assertion post-global financial crisis (GFC) is that short-termism is a systemic problem—i.e. the blame lies with the structure of the market itself, and a short-term bias of all market participants. For example, the Aspen Institute declared that short-termism is a 'system-wide' problem,[8] and the Kay Review[9] referred to the 'systemic nature'[10] of the short-termism problems identified. Lynne Dallas also argued that the problem is caused by the "short-term focus of corporate managers, asset managers, investors, and analysts."[11] An explanation of how exactly short-termism is 'systemic' has not been offered by such claimants, but the assumption may be drawn that short-termism is a behaviour exhibited by all participants in equity capital markets.

This idea of short-termism as a behavioural characteristic[12] or a social phenomenon[13] has been explored further by academics. Defining the

[7] Martin (2015, 5).

[8] Aspen Institute (2009, 3).

[9] Kay (2012) (Kay Review).

[10] Kay (2012, 9).

[11] Dallas (2012, 268).

[12] Ibid., 310–316, in which Dallas reviews various cognitive biases she argues play a role in encouraging short-termism.

[13] Moore and Walker-Arnott (2014, 418), at which the authors describe stock market short-termism as a "very real and multi-faceted behavioral and cultural paradigm encompassing the attitudes and practices of investors, financial professionals, and investee company managers."

issue in such a broad manner has the effect of removing blame from any one set of market participants, which may be in line with the large philosophical questions on the purpose of capital markets emerging post-GFC.[14] A systemic bias may be a neat way of explaining the issue, and if such a bias is shown it could be useful in formulating policy responses.

Although biases may be widespread, many commentators have focused instead on two central aspects to the short-termism problem, namely asset owner short-termism and managerial short-termism, also termed managerial myopia.[15] As will be discussed further in Chapter 6[16] managerial myopia appears to be the flip side of asset owner short-termism—investor irrationality—rather than a standalone problematic behaviour. The rationality of investors has been challenged, most notably in the field of behavioural economics. Numerous factors have been identified which impact the rationality of investor behaviour, including over confidence, biased judgments, herd mentality and loss aversion.[17] However, it has been argued that these irrationalities, in terms of individual equity buying and selling decisions, cancel each other out.[18] Further, the argument has also been made that if there are investor irrationalities in the market these are dealt with by internal market corrective measures.[19]

There are compelling arguments that counter the position that markets are self-correcting. Most significantly, certain biases—for example, a tendency to under-value long-term returns and over-value short-term returns—, as discussed in the context of excessive discounting below, may be so pervasive that they do not cancel each other out.[20]

[14] For example, Mazzucato (2016).

[15] See the summary of investor short-termism and managerial short-termism provided in Moore and Walker-Arnott (2014, 423–432) and in Moore and Petrin (2017, 124–132).

[16] See Chapter 6, Sect. E.

[17] Malkiel (2016, 231).

[18] See Malkiel (2016, 230) where Malkiel claims that traditional economists can wriggle out of the challenge that investors are irrational by "declaring that the trades of irrational investors will be random and therefore cancel each other out without affecting prices."

[19] Ibid., where Malkiel states that "even if investors are irrational in a similar way, efficient-market theory believers assert that smart rational traders will correct mispricings."

[20] See the discussion in Moore and Walker-Arnott (2014, 420–421) and Moore and Petrin (2017, 121–123).

Further, corrective measures such as price arbitrage opportunities may not be readily available in practice.[21] Consequently, although some individual investor irrationality in terms of equity buying and selling may be effectively washed out in the market, and market mechanisms generally facilitate information efficiency, share prices may still be fundamentally inefficient if pervasive biases, such as excessive discounting of long-term returns, are present. However, the difficulty is in empirically demonstrating the pervasiveness of this investor irrationality.

3. *Quantitative Evidence of SMST*

Although survey evidence and behavioral economics analysis of investor biases may be suggestive of a SMST problem, hard evidence demonstrating that there is a SMST problem is lacking, and, arguably, may never be convincingly provided given the nature of the problem. Moore and Petrin compare the issue to global warming, stating that "for every commentator who regards it [short-termism] as one of the most serious and pressing problems facing the corporate and financial world today, there would appear to be another commentator equally keen to deny that there is even a material 'problem' as such at all."[22] Roger Martin has suggested that the existence and consequences of short-termism are fundamentally unknowable because there is no control group.[23] Although he comes down on the side of the debate saying that there is a SMST problem, demonstrating this inherent evidentiary issue, Martin said "we can't compare the performance of America with short-termism to that of America devoid of short-termism – or even prove beyond a doubt that short-termism exists in the first place."[24] Perhaps for this reason, there have been relatively few attempts to capture the potential costs of SMST in quantitative terms.

[21] Moore and Walker-Arnott (2014, 421–423) where the authors argue that the arbitragers may themselves by susceptible to the bias, they may have rational motives to continue acting with the prevailing market trends, and it may be costly to assess and act on such opportunities which may negate any gains.

[22] Moore and Petrin (2017, 119).

[23] Martin (2015, 3).

[24] Ibid.

One area where there has been some quantitative analysis is around excessive discounting of future cash flows using company level equity price data. Further details on how excessive discounting actually evidences a SMST concern are discussed further in this chapter in Sect. B.2.a below. In brief, a line of financial analysis originating with the work of David Miles in 1993 measures expected cash flows against equity prices and finds some evidence of excessive discounting—meaning that investors are under-valuing the long-term and prioritizing short-term financial returns.[25]

Miles research has been applied to a range of countries and time frames with broadly similar conclusions.[26] Of note is the research by Ian Dobbs in 2009, where Dobbs focused on the 'value loss' that can occur as a result of company managers focusing on short-termism decision criteria in determining whether to proceed with an investment.[27] Dobbs concluded that there is a value loss, but that this value loss is relatively minimal. This result is consistent with the conclusions of Richard Davies of the Economist and Andrew Haldane of the Bank of England and others. In 2011, Davies et al. provided an analytical framework and generated empirical estimates of the potential costs of SMST.

To provide evidence that excessive discounting by investors is happening in the real world, Davies et al. tested a data set of 624 listed companies that were listed on the United Kingdom (UK) FTSE and US S&P indices over the period 1980–2009, which listed companies spanned a broad range of industries.[28] Consistent with previous research, Davies et al.'s results showed that the discount rates used by investors—in other words the hurdle rates on whether an investment is worth making—are typically set higher than the firm's cost of capital. Such rates often being set at 5% or more above conventional estimates of the cost of capital. The results showed a statistically significant incidence of short-termism in the 1995–2004 time period. Consistent with Dobbs earlier research, Davies et al.'s research indicates that there is evidence of short-termism during this 1995–2004 time period. Although the short-termism

[25] Miles (1993).

[26] Cuthbertson et al. (1997), Black and Fraser (2002), Allen (1996), Adler (2000), and Meier and Tarhan (2006).

[27] Dobbs (2009).

[28] Ibid., 19.

measured in the results provided by Davies et al. during the 1995–2004 time period appears to be minimal,[29] the results could be significant given how such short-termism works in the discounting of future returns as discussed further in Sect. B.2.a. Using their results, Davies et al. provided a rough estimate that "the elimination of short-termism would then result in a level of output around 20% higher than would otherwise be the case."[30]

Davies et al.'s research does have some additional notable limitations. The data set used by Davies et al. is limited to US and the UK firms, and does not include other jurisdictions, notably firms in the European Union (EU). Also, the time period surveyed by Davies et al. is prior to the GFC, and to show evidence of an ongoing problem the results should be updated to include data post-GFC. Further, the reason that there was evidence of excessive discounting during the 1995–2004 period may be a correction by investors from losses suffered during the 1985–1994 time period. However, subsequent research demonstrates that 1995–2004 was not merely a correction to the previous time period, and that excessive discounting has continued.

Davies et al.'s research was corroborated in a more recent 2016 study by Rachelle Sampson and Yuan Shin of the University of Maryland. Sampson and Shi's study was designed to measure market discounting at the firm level in order to capture how much stock markets discount future dividends and values of US public firms, using a data set from 1980 to 2013.[31] Using a similar methodology as Davies et al., Sampson and Shi produced results broadly consistent with Davies et al., and also showed that the trend of increasing SMST has continued in the 10-year period beyond the most recent sample considered in Davies et al.[32] These results suggest that the 1995–2004 period was not a temporary market correction, but instead that SMST is a substantive ongoing concern.

Sampson and Shi's research adds to the intuitive argument, bolstered by survey evidence and understanding of investor biases discussed above in Sects. A.1 and A.2, respectively, that investors excessively discount

[29] See Table 5 summarizing these results in Davies et al. (2014, 21).

[30] Ibid., 25.

[31] Sampson and Shi (2016, 2018).

[32] Sampson and Shi (2016, 16).

future returns. This section demonstrates that there is quantitative evidence of a SMST problem. The empirical results may only have provided minimal evidence of short-termism; however, the impacts of short-termism may be much greater. Nonetheless, this has yet to be empirically tested. Further, empirical testing that extends Davies et al.'s results is currently only limited to Sampson and Shi's study. Consequently, thought it may not be compelling enough on a standalone basis, this quantitative evidence can be used to support the survey results and analysis of bias to justify 'hard' law SMST-driven industry reforms.

4. *Using Proxies to Measure SMST*

The lack of conclusive quantitative evidence on the existence of a SMST problem should not lead to the conclusion that there is no issue. As asserted above, it is probable that this research is inconclusive because it is difficult to compare the performance of an equity market with short-termism to that of an equity market without short-termism. Recognizing this difficulty, a number of proxies have been used to test for short-termism. Types of proxies used to evidence short-termism include the number of patent applications for listed and non-listed companies demonstrating that listed companies are less innovative,[33] and evidence of cuts to research and development after a listed company fails to meet the previous year's earnings expectations.[34]

More significantly, research by Asker et al.[35] tested a panel of US companies and found that firms whose share price—and by implication, the firm's investors—was very sensitive to earnings announcements tended to forgo valuable investment opportunities. They concluded that firms that were held privately invested significantly more in investment opportunities than similar public firms and were more responsive to investment opportunities, and their tests of periods when firms moved from private to public ownership confirmed these results. Addressing these results, Davies et al. argued that "[t]he inference is that private firms do not face the same earnings-driven pressure to scrimp on investment as

[33] Bernstein (2012).

[34] Bushee (1998).

[35] Asker et al. (2011, 2015).

publicly quoted firms."[36] Davies et al. also conducted their own analysis and concluded that "UK private firms tend to plough back between 4 and 8 times more of their profits into their business over time than publicly held firms."[37] Admittedly, these conclusions are only inferences with respect to short-termism, and privately companies may just be better managed, or require more capital for investment. Using a proxy to measure short-termism is an imprecise science and could be argued to be comparing apples to oranges.

Nonetheless, when these proxy tests are layered onto the considerable survey evidence of market participants, the analysis of wide-spread investor bias, and the quantitative evidence of at least a minimal amount of ongoing excessive discounting of long-term returns, there is an indication of a short-termism bias in equity markets. For the purpose of the analysis in this book, I accept that there is a viable basis to the claims that there is a SMST problem. Ultimately, however, policymakers and the financial industry will need to reach their own conclusions on whether the plausible proposition that there is a SMST problem provides a sufficient basis for reform. Alternatively, they may want to consider whether there are issues meriting a public policy intervention that are currently couched in SMST rhetoric, but instead may be best examined independently of SMST concerns.

B. Share Pricing and SMST

Accepting that there is suggestive evidence of a SMST problem, further analysis of the share pricing of listed companies is required. The share price of a listed company, being the current price at which a share is bought or sold based on supply and demand, is an important communication mechanism among stock market participants.[38] Share prices are generally seen to equate to an estimate of the risk adjusted present value of future financial returns of a listed company.[39] The question may then

[36] Davies et al. (2014, 17).

[37] Ibid., 25.

[38] Little (2016).

[39] Articulations of this concept abound, but it is perhaps best summarized by noted US economist Malkiel Burton, in Malkiel (2016, 31–33), where he sets out the logic of this 'firm-foundation theory'.

genuinely be asked, "if share prices fairly reflect expected future returns of a listed company how can there be a short-termism problem?"

Let us take the 2017 Snapchat initial public offering (IPO) as an example to illustrate this point. Snapchat's shares sold at US$17.00 per share in its March 2017 IPO, giving the company a total valuation of US$23.8 billion.[40] Snapchat has not yet booked a profit,[41] so the market was basing this share price entirely off of the future cash generating potential of the company. Consequently, if the market expected Snapchat to return future cash distributions to investors equal to the risk-adjusted present value of such returns—e.g. US$23.8 billion pro-rated per share—, how can the market be short-termist—i.e. overvaluing short-term returns and undervaluing future returns? Rather, from the high prices in the Snapchat example, the market appears capable, if in fact not overly exuberant, of pricing long term returns.[42] Therefore, any claims that stock markets are short-termist as discussed in Sect. A above need to first address whether share prices are an accurate measure of the future cash generating potential of a listed company.

1. *Efficient Capital Market Hypothesis*

Whether share prices accurately reflect a listed company's long-term cash generating potential is usually considered in the context of economic and financial theory, most notably by means of the efficient capital markets hypothesis.[43] The faith placed in the ECMH has been questioned. Specifically, it has been argued that the ECMH is "a poor basis for either regulation or investment",[44] and that such faith in the ECMH

[40] Farrell and Krouse (2017).

[41] Berger (2017).

[42] See Roe (2013, 980) where Roe observes that "there is much evidence that stock market sectors are often enough overvaluing the long term, most obviously in the intermittent bubbles in technology and other new industries."

[43] There has been extensive consideration of the ECMH. See the discussion in Armour and Cheffins (2016, 765–770). However, the ECMH was first clearly articulated and popularized by Eugene Fama in 1965. See Fama (1965, 55), where Fama notes that previous discussion of random walk theory was limited to technical academic journals, and his intention was to briefly and simply describe the theory and the issues it raises concerning the work of market analysts.

[44] Kay (2012, 10).

ECMH Form	Information in Share Price
Weak	Only information on past prices
Semi-Strong	All publicly available information
Strong	All information (including insider)

Fig. 2 ECMH forms

contributed to, or caused, the GFC.[45] There may be merit to this argument, and analysis of the ECMH has come a long way since Harvard economist Michael Jensen wrote in 1978 that "there is no other proposition in economics which has more solid empirical evidence supporting it than the Efficient Market Hypothesis."[46] In the decades since the 1970s, the ECHM has been vigorously tested and critiqued.[47] Although the ECMH has been questioned post-GFC, securities regulation and market practice, particularly in the US, the UK and the EU, continues to be influenced by ECMH-related principles of disclosure.[48] The pervasiveness of the ECMH, and its inherent conclusion that information is reflected in share pricing, necessitates consideration of SMST in this context.[49]

The ECMH asserts that stock markets are 'informationally efficient' as share prices respond to information relevant to the future returns of the listed company, and competitive forces in stock markets rapidly digest this information. Consequently, according to ECMH theorists there is no way to earn excess profits by using this information—i.e. you cannot consistently beat the market.[50] Strong, semi-strong and weak forms of the ECMH have been identified, as set out in Fig. 2, and each of these

[45] See the summary in Malkiel (2016, 284).

[46] Jensen (1978).

[47] For example, see Business Insider (2010) and Schwager (2012).

[48] See Prüm (2013) and *Halliburton Co. v. Erica P. John Fund, Inc.* 573 U.S.—, 134 S. Ct. 2398, 2414 (2014), in which the US Supreme Court held affirmed that markets are generally efficient.

[49] Commenting on the high-quality body of research in this area, Shiller also observes that "whether or not we ultimately agree with it, we must take the efficient markets theory seriously" (Shiller 2015, 195) and also see Moore and Walker-Arnott (2014, 419).

[50] Fama (1965, 56).

forms of the ECMH addresses the type of information included in share prices.[51]

The weak form of the ECMH says that ***all information on past prices*** is included in current share prices, and thus you cannot predict future share prices by analyzing past prices, commonly known as technical analysis—i.e. future share prices are a 'random walk' unrelated to past trends.[52] The semi-strong form of the ECMH asserts that share prices reflect ***all publicly available*** information, which includes information on past prices, and all current information disclosed to the market by listed companies.[53] There is considerable support for the semi-strong form of the ECMH being a reasonably accurate description of market structure.[54] The strong-form of the ECMH goes a step further and asserts that share prices reflect all ***knowable information***, which includes private or insider information.[55] This strong version of the ECMH is questioned, however, on the basis that it shown to be possible to gain from using inside information.[56] Assuming for the sake of argument that the ECMH in its semi-strong form is the most accurate existing description of market conditions, share prices would then generally reflect all publicly available information.

2. *SMST, Fundamental Efficiency and Asset Pricing*

If share prices are by and large informationally efficient, then how can there be a short-termism problem? It is important to note here that the ECMH refers to 'informational' not 'fundamental' efficiency. In other words, the ECMH does not necessarily mean that share prices are an accurate assessment of the cash generating potential of a listed company.

[51] Empirical work testing each of these forms was summarized in Fama (1970).

[52] See the discussion in Armour and Cheffins (2016, 766), Malkiel (2016, 183), and Welch (2014, 306).

[53] Ibid.

[54] For example, see Malkiel (2016, 184), where Makiel notes the support for index investing.

[55] See the discussion in Armour and Cheffins (2016, 766), Malkiel (2016, 182–183), and Welch (2014, 306).

[56] See Malkiel (2016, 183), where Malkiel notes that the strong form of the ECMH is an "obvious overstatement" as "[i]t does not admit the possibility of gaining from inside information" and Fama (1991, 1575), where Fama states that "the extreme version of the market efficiency hypothesis [being the strong form] is surely false."

Rather, the ECMH only asserts that share prices are informationally efficient, in other words that they reflect all available information.[57] The theory is, however, that if share prices reflect all available information, then a listed company's share price will "plausibly be the best available estimate of the value of the business as it is being run"[58] or at least "a good estimate of its intrinsic value."[59] In addition to the availability of information though, an assessment of the risk adjusted future returns of a listed company both on a firm specific and a market-wide basis is also required to be made by an investor based on such available information in order for the share price to be a measure of fundamental or intrinsic value of a listed company.[60] Further, the ECMH is based on a number of assumptions which merit further analysis, including most significantly that all market participants are acting rationally.[61]

a. Testing for Excessive Discounting

An assessment of such fundamental value of a listed company requires risk to be accurately measured by investors. This risk discounting by investors is largely intuitive—in other words, the promise of a dollar next year is worth less than a dollar now—as reflected in the old adage, a bird in the hand is worth two in the bush. However, economic theory provides a range of analytical tools that are used by investors to calculate risk via an appropriate discount rate.[62] The most well-known of these mechanisms is the capital-asset pricing model (CAPM) developed by Stanford professor William Sharpe and late financial specialists John Lintner and Fischer Black.[63] The basic premise of the CAPM is that when making an investment, investors need to be compensated for the time value of their money as well as the specific risk related to such investment.[64] Despite the use of often complex mechanisms such as the CAPM, it is not clear what an appropriate rate of return should be when assessing future

[57] Armour and Cheffins (2016, 766).

[58] Ibid., 767.

[59] Fama (1965, 56).

[60] This follows logically from the discussion above that share prices are an assessment of the risk adjusted future returns of a listed company.

[61] Fama (1965, 56) where Fama refers to "large numbers of rational, profit-maximizers."

[62] See the discussion in Malkiel (2016, 209–228).

[63] Ibid., 209, 213–219 and Welch (2014, 218–236).

[64] Investopedia. Online: http://www.investopedia.com/terms/c/capm.asp.

returns of listed companies, and it is notoriously difficult to test asset pricing models.[65] It is here that attention has been focused by economic and financial experts considering whether there is a SMST problem—or more particularly, a bias in assessing risk adjusted returns causing company managers to maximize short-term financial results.

As discussed in Sect. A.3 above, in 2011 Davies et al. provided an analytical framework demonstrating how if an investor increases the discount rate of future returns even modestly, the NPV of the investment is significantly impacted. This economic formula is provided in Davies et al. and essentially holds that NPV equals the sum of each year of expected returns multiplied by a factor for excessive discounting and divided by the rate of return minus the initial investment.

In the formula set out by Davies et al.,[66] the authors use a hypothetical scenario of an investment of $60, which is riskless and has a dividend rate of $10 each 10-year period, and a terminal value of $0. With a discount rate of 9%, the investment's cash flows are $65 today, providing an NPV of $5, meaning the investment is worth making. If future dividends are discounted too heavily ($x = 0.95$, i.e. a 5% discount) dividends are now worth $52 and the NPV is −$8 rather than $5. With a negative NPV, the project is not a worthwhile investment.[67] The formula developed by Davies et al. brings vigor to our intuitive understanding that investors in many circumstances prefer to be paid dividends and see increases in share prices today and adds to this understanding that even small changes to the discount rates will significantly impact an investor's assessment on whether a particular investment is worthwhile. To provide evidence that this discounting by investors is happening in the real world, Davies et al. tested a data set of 624 listed companies that were listed on the UK FTSE and US S&P indices over the period 1980–2009, which listed companies spanned a broad range of industries.[68]

The financial model developed by Davies et al. to demonstrate SMST is complex, but the basic premise is that they have measured each firm's returns against the expected rate of return using a CAPM model and generated a myopia coefficient of x for each firm—and industry sector.

[65] Welch (2014, 332).

[66] See formula (6) in Davies et al. (2014, 18).

[67] Ibid., 18.

[68] Ibid., 19.

The null hypothesis—no short-termism—implied that $x = 1$, and any numbers under 1 indicated myopia. Davies et al.'s primary research results were replicated to show a significant incidence of short-termism in US and UK stocks in the 1995–2004 time period studied. Their results showed overall evidence of myopia, and that myopia was most evident in the later period of the time sampled, namely 1995–2004. Extrapolating from these results, Davies et al. also showed that in the UK and US at least, cash flows five years ahead are discounted at rates more appropriate for eight or more years ahead, 10-year cash flows are valued as if 16 or more years ahead and cash flows more than 30 years ahead are scarcely valued at all.[69] Consequently, market discount rates—i.e. hurdle rates—are generally too high meaning payback periods are too short.

As discussed in Sects. A.1 and A.3 Davies et al.'s conclusions build on earlier research in this area and the results were corroborated in a 2016 study by Sampson and Shin. Admittedly, this quantitative evidence of excessive discounting is minimal, and only indicates a minor short-termism issue. However, when combined with the total body of evidence discussed in Sect. A of this chapter, the research of Davies et al. and Sampson and Shi add to the intuitive argument that investors excessively discount future returns. As will be explored further in Chapter 6[70] company managers are aware of this excessive discounting of future returns and given that company managers seek to maximize the value of the listed company—in other words, keep share prices high—managers prioritize near-term cash flows such as dividends and positive short-term earnings over longer-term returns.[71]

b. SMST as Rational Constraint on Management

The perceived excessive discounting by asset owners and asset managers above what would reasonably be expected for future returns may just be "a crude way of adjusting for excessive optimism concerning project managers' cash flow forecasts, for scarcity of managerial talent, or because of financing/liquidity constraints, whether market or

[69] Haldane and Davies (2011, 1).

[70] See Chapter 6, Sects. B.1 and B.2.

[71] Davies et al. (2014, 16).

self-imposed."[72] This line of analysis that SMST is a reasonable means whereby investors accept some loss of value of their investment in exchange for constraining the behaviour of company managers emerged in the 1980s in the response to the alleged short-termism of hostile takeovers. As discussed in Chapter 3,[73] Martin Lipton argued that the short-termism inherent in hostile takeovers was harmful,[74] and US law professors, Frank Easterbrook and Daniel Fischel countered that such hostile takeovers were a necessary discipline tool on the excesses of management.[75] Similar claims have been made more recently that SMST is by and large an acceptable check on management action. Specifically, Professor Richard Thakor has developed a theory that the owners of the firm pursue short-termism in project choice in order to limit managerial rent-seeking behaviour.[76]

It is certainly reasonable that discount rates will be high given the myriad of uncertainties associated with the future operations of companies, which in addition to macro-economic factors such as political instability, reflect the increased agency costs inherent in the complex modern equity ownership chain.[77] Consequently, calling for measurable short-term returns is an option to reduce these agency costs. Undoubtedly, a higher degree of risk for investment in listed companies verses non-listed companies will always be prevalent in stock market investing. The evidence is suggestive that there is some value loss occurring given the uncertainties around future returns.

[72] See the summary of research in Dobbs (2009, 118).

[73] See Chapter 3, Sect. A.

[74] Lipton (1979, 104).

[75] Easterbrook and Fischel (1981, 1184).

[76] See Thakor (2016). Also, Professors Barzuza and Talley observe this long-standing tension between the rational short-termism of asset owners and the long-termism of company managers (Barzuza and Talley 2016, 1).

[77] 'Agency problems' are said to arise because of conflicts of interest among corporate constituencies, whereby the financial interest of one party—the 'principal'—is dependent on the actions taken by another party—the 'agent'. The core difficulty in the agency relationship is that the principal has handed control over to an agent, who often has better information than the principal about the relevant facts. The agent has an incentive to act opportunistically or he or she could be lazy or incompetent, and the principal must engage in costly monitoring to reduce the agent's opportunistic behaviour. As described in Kraakman et al. (2009, 35–36).

However, the question then should be on what can be done to reduce these apparently excessively high discount rates, which arguably go beyond merely accurately accounting for future risks, to make longer-term investments of listed companies more palatable to asset owners and asset managers. In other words, how can policy makers and the financial industry improve share pricing, so that it better reflects long-term value? Before looking further at reform proposals in the context of this analysis, it is necessary to first address some questions raised by those critical of the existence of a SMST problem—in particular, how stock markets can be short-termist when investors also appear to be very capable of assessing the future value of listed companies?

C. Arguments Against SMST in Share Pricing

Several noteworthy arguments have been raised to counter the assertion that there is a SMST bias evident in share pricing. The most compelling of these arguments is that rather than being short-termist, stock markets often appear very adept at assessing long-term value. Additionally, there are long periods of market booms suggesting market valuation fundamentals are strong. Each of these arguments is considered in further detail below.

1. Markets Appear to Overvalue the Long-Term

If we accept that there is a short-termism problem causing investors to under value long-term cash generating potential and, consequently, over-value short-term financial returns, how do we explain scenarios like Snapchat—with their high IPO share prices on largely uncertain future returns? Professor Mark Roe, critical of whether there is a SMST problem, explains this issue by saying that stock markets are obviously short-termist, but they are also long-termist—i.e. they under shoot and over shoot.[78] Others counter this position by arguing that such unfounded high prices are the result of company managers overselling the value of future projects, or unduly and excessively investing in

[78] Roe (2013, 980) and also see Favaro (2014).

current research and development in projects with uncertain long-term returns, in order to increase current share prices.[79]

Based on this line of reasoning, management of SnapChat would be acting myopically if they inflated the value of future growth potential or over-invested resources pre-IPO in Snapchat's research and development (R&D) to unduly maximize current share prices. The merit to this argument in questionable. If overinvesting in R&D positively impacted share prices, more company managers would take advantages of this result. An alternative, and perhaps strong retort, is the impact of the 'founder effect', namely the presence of a founder as a significant shareholder or CEO, on the excessive discounting bias of investors.

a. The 'Founder Effect'

It is possible that the stock of certain types of listed technology companies, such as Snapchat, are less susceptible to excessive discounting of future value due to their investor structure, which typically, but not always, includes a controlling founder shareholder,[80] or the market reputation of their founding management, such as Facebook. This 'founder effect' may mean that investors apply less of a discount when assessing future value, if the founder has a significant stake in the company, and/or continues in a CEO role. The discount rate could be reduced because the investors genuinely have faith in the founders' vision or ability to deliver future results.

Alternately, or perhaps in combination with such faith, the reduced discount rate may reflect that the founders with their large shareholdings or their CEO position have a much greater vested interest in the success of the listed company than would be the case otherwise. These founders could act to reduce the agency concerns associated with an investment in the listed company, thereby reducing the discounting of future returns. The existence of founders, and perhaps the resulting cult built around the management of certain listed companies such as Facebook, could go some way to ameliorating the effects of SMST in certain circumstances. The impact of such control and whether this structure is a viable method

[79] Dallas and Barry (2016, 559), and Bebchuk and Stole (1993, 720).

[80] For example, Evan Spiegal and Bobby Murphy, the co-founders of Snapchat, have retained a total of 43.6% of the voting shares post-IPO. Online: http://mashable.com/2017/03/02/snap-ipo-evan-spiegel/#QSN7boWwh5qo.

of SMST reform are considered further in Chapter 8.[81] Connected to this 'founder effect' is the concept of 'unicorns'.

b. 'Unicorns'

The idea of 'unicorns' was first articulated by Aileen Lee, founder of Cowboy Ventures. Lee analyzed US-based software companies backed by private or public market investors started since 2003.[82] She determined that only 0.07% of start-ups ever reached a valuation of US$1 billion or greater—thus deeming them as rare as the mythical creatures, unicorns.[83] Rather than being rare mythical creatures, such market 'unicorns' are now prevalent in many markets and include big names such as AirBnB and SpaceX. CB Insights has formed a Global Unicorn Club and identified 235 'unicorn' companies that have made a venture capital backed exit since 2009 for a total valuation of US$812 billion.[84] These 'unicorns' tend to have high IPO prices when they are listed—perhaps based on investor fears of missing out on the next Facebook, together with the 'founder effect' discussed above. Supporting this analysis, Bill Gurley of Benchmark Capital observes that "late-stage investors, desperately afraid of missing out on acquiring shareholding positions in possible 'unicorn' companies, have essentially abandoned their traditional risk analysis."[85] This investor approach to 'unicorns' could help explain why even though SMST appears to be occurring, there are pockets of high valued share prices in certain sectors.

c. Castles-in-the-Air

Yet another hypothesis for high shares prices over uncertain future revenue streams could be that this over-valuing of future returns is a result of 'castle-in-the-air' investing. The 'castle-in-the-air' theory, best articulated by noted economist John Maynard Keynes, holds that "professional investors prefer to devote their energies not to estimating intrinsic values, but rather to analyzing how the crowd of investors is likely to behave in the future and how during periods of optimism then tend to build

[81] See Chapter 8, Sect. A.1.c.

[82] Lee (2013).

[83] Ibid.

[84] The Global Unicorn Club, CB Insights. Online: https://www.cbinsights.com/research-unicorn-companies.

[85] Gurley (2015).

their hopes into castles in the air."[86] Rather than a realistic assessment of future value, the high IPO share prices of Snapchat, and other companies like it, may be the result of just such crowd optimism, which prices are driven higher as investors try to time the market and take advantage of the optimism of others. Accepting that a certain degree of crowd optimism in new offerings is to be expected and cannot be effectively tempered, the reforms efforts assessed in Chapters 4 and 8 primarily focus on SMST reform in the context of the ongoing operations of listed companies.

2. *SMST in a Market Boom*

A corollary question in this line of argument is how there can be short-termism, when the market as a whole is in a steady period of increasing prices—i.e. a market boom. Nobel-prize winning economist, Robert J. Shiller, considers investor behaviour against the backdrop of market-wide booms and busts in the US in his book *Irrational Exuberance*.[87] He observes that high stock market share price levels in boom periods do not "represent the consensus judgment of experts who have carefully weighed the long-term evidence."[88] Rather, Shiller argues "the market was high [at the peaks in 2000, 2007 and 2014] because of the combined effect of indifferent thinking by millions of people, very few of whom have felt the need to perform careful research on long-term investment value, and who are motivated substantially by their own emotions, random attentions, and perceptions of conventional wisdom."[89]

Shiller attributes boom periods to indifference as well as investors' personal motivations. It is outside the scope of this book to wade too much further into the debate on the causes of such stock market booms. However, based on the analysis in this chapter of the excessive—albeit perhaps partially reasonable—discounting of future returns by investors in widely held listed companies, I assert that it is not just indifferent thinking by such investors that drives up share prices during boom periods. Rather it is also active management on the part of listed companies

[86] Malkiel (2016, 33).

[87] Shiller (2015).

[88] Ibid., 225.

[89] Ibid.

to keep share prices high in response to the market's preference for short-term returns that impacts such stock market movements, which upswings are not based on fundamental value and eventually see a correction. How company managers respond to the short-term preferences of asset managers and asset owners and why company managers do so is explored further in Chapter 6.

The purpose of this chapter has been to consider whether there is a SMST problem, and as a corollary to this analysis, whether share pricing is an accurate representation of the long-term value of listed companies. The research examined provides suggestive evidence of a SMST problem, and also a sufficient basis to question the merit of share prices as an indicator of long-term value of listed companies. The evidence presented in this chapter suggests that at least in the US and the UK there appears to be an actual or perceived excessive discounting of long-term returns by investors, and a corresponding undue focus on the short-term financial returns of listed companies by company managers. The conclusions reached in this chapter suggest that SMST-driven reform efforts should focus on efforts to reduce this discounting so that share pricing better reflects long-term value or to completely cut off the SMST transmission mechanisms. However, before reviewing the SMST-driven reforms set out in chapter on this basis, it is first necessary to look further at the transmission mechanisms which transfer this SMST from investors into listed companies, and also to assess whether such SMST is actually harmful.

References

Adler, R. 2000. "Strategic Investment Decision Appraisal Techniques: The Old and the New." 43 *Business Horizons*. 15–22.

Allen, D. 1996. "High Hurdles." 74:9 *Management Accounting*. 24.

Armour, John and Cheffins, Brian. 2016. "Stock Market Prices and the Market for Corporate Control." 3 *University of Illinois Law Review*. 761–820.

Asker, John, Farre-Mensa, Joan, and Ljungqvist, Alexander. 2011. "Comparing the Investment Behavior of Public and Private Firms." NBER Working Paper No. 17394.

Asker, John, Farre-Mensa, Joan, and Ljungqvist, Alexander. 2015. "Corporate Investment and Stock Market Listing: A Puzzle?" 28:2 *Review of Financial Studies*. 342–390.

Aspen Institute. 2009. "Overcoming Short-Termism: A Call for a More Responsible Approach to Investment and Business Management." 9 September.

Barton, Dominic and Wiseman, Mark. 2014. "Focusing Capital on the Long Term." January–February. *Harvard Business Review*. 44–51.

Barzuza, Michael and Talley, Eric. 2016. "Short-Termism and Long-Termism." 15 February. Virginia Law and Economics Research Paper No. 2; UC Berkeley Public Law Research Paper No. 2731814; Columbia Public Law Research Paper No. 14-503; Columbia Law and Economics Working Paper No. 526. http://dx.doi.org/10.2139/ssrn.2731814.

Bebchuk, Lucian and Stole, L. A. 1993. "Do Short-Term Objectives Lead to Under-or Overinvestment in Long-Term Projects?" 48:2 *Journal of Finance*. 719–729.

Berger, R. 2017. "Snapchat IPO—Don't Confuse Popular with Profitable." 7 March. *Forbes*. https://www.forbes.com/sites/robertberger/2017/03/07/snapchat-ipo-dont-confuse-popular-with-profitable/.

Bernstein, S. 2012. "Does Going Public Affect Innovation?" Stanford Graduate School of Business. Working Paper.

Black, A. and Fraser, P. 2002. "Stock Market Short-Termism—An International Perspective." 12 *Journal of Multinational Financial Management*. 135–158.

Bushee, B. J. 1998. "The Influence of Institutional Investors on Myopic R&D Investment Behavior." 73:3 *The Accounting Review*. 305–333.

Business Insider. 2010. "What Warren Buffet Thinks of the Efficient Market Hypothesis." 1 December. http://www.businessinsider.com/warren-buffett-on-efficient-market-hypothesis-2010–12.

CPP Investment Board and McKinsey & Company: Global Survey Signals Short-Term Pressures on Business Leaders Are Mounting. 2013. CPP Investment Board and McKinsey & Company. 22 May. Press Release. http://www.marketwired.com/press-release/cpp-investment-board-mckinsey-company-global-survey-signals-short-term-pressures-on-1793872.htm.

Cuthbertson, K., Hayes, S., and Nitzsche, D. 1997. "The Behaviour of UK Stock Prices and Returns: Is the Market Efficient?" 107:443 *The Economic Journal*. 986–1008.

Dallas, Lynne L. 2012. "Short-Termism, the Financial Crisis, and Corporate Governance." 2011–2012. 37:2 *The Journal of Corporation Law*. 265–364.

Dallas, Lynne L. and Barry, Jordan. 2016. "Long-Term Shareholders and Time-Phased Voting." 40:2 *Delaware Journal of Corporate Law*. 541–646.

Davies, Richard, Haldane, Andrew G., Nielsen, Mette, and Pezzini, Silvia. 2014. "Measuring the Costs of Short-Termism." 12 *Journal of Financial Stability*. 16–25.

Dobbs, Ian M. 2009. "How Bad Can Short-Termism Be?—A Study of the Consequences of High Hurdle Discount Rates and Low Payback Thresholds." 20 *Management Accounting Research*. 117–128.

Easterbrook, Frank H. and Fischel, Daniel R. 1981. "The Proper Role of a Target's Management in Responding to a Tender Offer." April. 94:6 *Harvard Law Review*. 1161–1204.

Fama, Eugene F. 1965. "Random Walks in Stock Market Prices." 21:5 *Financial Analysts Journal*. 55–59.

Fama, Eugene F. 1970. "Efficient Capital Markets: A Review of Theory and Empirical Work." 25:2 *The Journal of Finance*. 383–417.

Fama, Eugene F. 1991. "Efficient Capital Markets: II." December. 46:5 *The Journal of Finance*. 1575–1617.

Farrell, M., Driebusch, C., and Krouse, S. 2017. "Snapchat Shares Surge 44% in Market Debut." 2 March. *Wall Street Journal*.

Favaro, Ken. 2014. "Long-Termism Is Just as Bad as Short-Termism." 25 September. *Harvard Business Review*. https://hbr.org/2014/09/long-termism-is-just-as-bad-as-short-termism.

Graham, John R., Cam, Harvey, and Shiva, Rajgopal. 2005. "The Economic Implications of Corporate Financial Reporting." December. 40 *Journal of Accounting and Economics*. 3–73.

Graham, John R., Cam, Harvey, and Shiva, Rajgopal. 2006. "Value Destruction and Financial Reporting Decisions." 62 *Financial Analysts Journal*. 27–39.

Gurley, Bill. 2015. "Investors Beware: Today's $100M+ Late-stage Private Rounds are Very Different from an IPO." 25 February. *Above the Crowd*. http://abovethecrowd.com/2015/02/25/investors-beware/.

Haldane, Andrew and Davies, Richards. 2011. "The Short-Long." Speech at the 29th Société Universitaire Européene de Recherches Financières Colloquium: New Paradigms in Money and Finance? May. Brussels.

Jensen, M. 1978. "Some Anomalous Evidence Regarding Market Efficiency." 6:2–3 *Journal of Financial Economics*. 95–101.

Kay, John. 2012. "The Kay Review of UK Equity Markets and Long-Term Decision Making." July. Final Report.

Kraakman, Reinier, et al. 2009. *The Anatomy of Corporate Law: A Comparative and Functional Approach*. 2nd ed. Oxford, UK: Oxford University Press.

Lee, Aileen. 2013. "Welcome to the Unicorn Club: Learning from Billion Dollar Start-ups." 2 November. *TechCrunch*. https://techcrunch.com/2013/11/02/welcome-to-the-unicorn-club/?guccounter=1.

Lipton, Martin. 1979. "Takeover Bids in the Target Boardroom." November. 35 *The Business Lawyer*. 101–134.

Little, K. 2016. "How Stock Prices Are Set." 10 August. *Financial Times*.

Malkiel, Burton. 2016. *A Random Walk Down Wall Street*. W. W. Norton: New York.

Martin, Roger. 2015. "Yes, Short-Termism Really Is a Problem." 9 October. *Harvard Business Review*. 2–7.

Mazzucato, Mariana. 2016. "Why Economic Recovery Requires Rethinking Capitalism." 15 November. *Institute for New Economic Thinking*. https://www.ineteconomics.org/perspectives/blog/why-economic-recovery-requires-rethinking-capitalism.

Meier, I. and Tarhan, V. 2006. "Corporate Investment Decision Practices and the Hurdle Rate Premium Puzzle." February. Working Paper. http://papers.ssrn.com/sol3/papers.cfm?abstractid=960161.

Miles, D. 1993. "Testing for Short Termism in the UK Stock Market." 104:421 *The Economic Journal*. 1379–1396.

Moore, Marc T. and Petrin, Martin. 2017. *Corporate Governance: Law, Regulation and Theory*. Palgrave Corporate and Financial Law: London, UK.

Moore, Marc T. and Walker-Arnott, Edward. 2014. "A Fresh Look at Stock Market Short-Termism." 41:3 *Journal of Law and Society*. 416–445.

Prüm, André. 2013. "The European Union Crisis Responses and the Efficient Capital Markets Hypothesis." 20:1 *Columbia Journal of European Law*. 1–29.

Rapley, John. 2017. "How Economics Became a Religion." 11 July. *The Guardian*.

Roe, Mark J. 2013. "Corporate Short-Termism—In the Boardroom and in the Courtroom." August. 68 *Business Lawyer*. 977–1006.

Sampson, Rachelle C. and Shi, Yuan. 2016. "Are US Firms and Markets Becoming More Short-Term Oriented? Evidence of Shifting Firm and Investor Time Horizons, 1980–2013." 27 July. http://ssrn.com/abstract=2837524.

Sampson, Rachelle C. and Shi, Yuan. 2018. "Are Investor Time Horizons Shortening?" 41:2 *Seattle University Law Review*. 543–550.

Schwager, Jack D. 2012. *Market Sense and Nonsense: How the Markets Really Work (and How They Don't)*. Wiley: Hoboken, NJ.

Shiller, Robert J. 2015. *Irrational Exuberance*. Princeton University Press: New York.

Thakor, Richard. 2016. "A Theory of Efficient Short-Termism." 17 September. *Harvard Law School Forum on Corporate Governance and Financial Regulation*. https://corpgov.law.harvard.edu/2016/09/17/a-theory-of-efficient-short-termism/.

Welch, Ivo. 2014. *Corporate Finance*. 3rd ed. Marina del Rey, CA.

CHAPTER 6

Short-Termism Transmission Mechanisms

The previous chapter concluded that there are legitimate questions around whether share prices accurately reflect the future value of listed companies given that asset owners and asset managers appear to excessively discount long-term returns. This excessive discounting of long-term returns by asset owners and asset managers may cause company managers to prioritize short-term financial returns and to take actions that improve share prices in the short-term. Before turning to an examination of whether this stock mater short-termism (SMST) is actually harmful, and if the SMST-driven reforms identified in Chapter 4 at least conceptually address SMST, it is first necessary to understand how such SMST is conveyed by the market into the board rooms of listed companies. More precisely, why do company managers care about share prices and keeping the stock market content?

As observed by Harvard Professor Mark Roe, for SMST to be a real problem, a transmission mechanism from the stock market to the board room is required.[1] Essentially, the argument goes that the short-term interests of asset owners and asset managers are transmitted into listed companies primarily through concerns about negative impacts on share prices—which may result in shareholder activism and impact executive compensation—thus causing company managers to forgo longer-term value maximization in favour of shorter-term financial returns, which

[1] Roe (2013, 987).

K. M. Willey, *Stock Market Short-Termism*,
https://doi.org/10.1007/978-3-030-22903-0_6

short-term returns are more favourably received by asset owners and asset managers.[2] In order to develop effective regulatory and financial industry reform, however, the transmission mechanisms of SMST and the connection to share prices require further unpacking. Analysis of SMST transmission is also required in the context of each element of the equity ownership chain: namely, asset owners, company managers, and intermediaries.

Consequently, this chapter identifies the types of asset owner and asset manager activity that appear to generate the greatest SMST concerns, and then examines how exactly such SMST is transmitted through the equity ownership chain to company managers. Central to this analysis is a review of the growth of the shareholder value maximization (SVM) concept, and the legal and corporate governance mechanisms that have developed alongside SVM, primarily in the United Kingdom (UK) and the United States (US), over the last five decades. These legal and corporate governance mechanisms include share-based executive compensation arrangements and shareholder capacity to make changes to the board of directors, and consequently, company management. These mechanisms appear to have enhanced shareholder rights, and further aligned company manager and shareholder interests, which in turn may have furthered the transmission of the SMST problem into listed companies.

A. Investor Short-Termism—Asset Owners

As discussed in Chapter 5, asset owners appear to exert pressure on intermediaries and company managers for short-term financial returns. But which asset owners apply this pressure? Claims have been made that not all asset owners are responsible for the pressure exerted on listed companies, rather it is hedge funds, i.e. activist investors,[3] or other asset owners who hold equity securities for very short-time periods who are

[2]For example, see Moore and Walker-Arnott (2014), Moore and Petrin (2017), and Dallas (2012), where the authors consider investor short-termism and how this results in managerial short-termism.

[3]For example, Trustee Leadership Forum (2016, 1), lists activist hedge funds as a primary driver for short-term behaviour noting that increasing payouts to shareholders is one of their most frequent demands.

accountable—i.e. there are short-termist and long-termist shareholders.[4] The short-termist asset owners—i.e. traders or speculative investors—have been seen as problematic, and calls have been made to rally against them to "fight the tyranny of the short-term."[5]

This *trading* argument—which, as demonstrated below, is questionable as a SMST cause as it lacks a transmission mechanism into the listed company—is premised on the idea that "because securities traders hold their stock for such a short duration, they look for strong corporate results during the period they hold the corporation's stock, so they can sell profitably."[6] The trading argument has been expanded on to separate *speculative* trading from *earnings-based investment*.[7] The SMST problem in the context of both of these types of trading is considered below. However, as set out below, I argue that it is excessive discounting of long-term returns by a wide-range of investors rather than the time-frames of specific investors that is more plausibly transmitting SMST into listed companies.

1. *Speculative Trading and HFT*

Speculative trading—including high frequency trading (HFT), which as discussed earlier involves using sophisticated technological tools and computer algorithms to rapidly trade securities—is argued to be based primarily on market opinion, rather than company-specific information, and it is viewed as the most extreme form of short-term investing.[8] This type of trading may not be a significant cause of SMST, however, as it lacks a clear transmission mechanism into the firm.[9] Quite logically, shareholders who hold their shares for a split second will have little impact on the behaviour of corporate managers. As observed by Roe, "even if the short-term traders furiously moved a company's stock every nanosecond, mangers would still be free to decide on corporate

[4] See Moore and Walker-Arnott (2014, 422) and Moore and Petrin (2017, 124) where the authors describe speculative trading.

[5] Barton (2011, 86) and Dallas (2012, 296).

[6] Roe (2013, 985).

[7] Moore and Walker-Arnott (2014, 423) and Moore and Petrin (2017, 124–128).

[8] Moore and Walker-Arnott (2014, 424) and Moore and Petrin (2017, 124).

[9] Moore and Walker-Arnott (2014, 425) and Moore and Petrin (2017, 125).

investments and time horizons, as the furious traders might simply pay no attention to the firm's horizons and would be incapable of intervening in corporate governance decision making."[10] Further, with respect to quantitative investors including HFT and other program traders, Charles Nathan of the US financial consulting firm, Finsbury, observes that "it is hard to see how such avowedly short-term traders have a meaningful effect on corporate behaviour and strategy."[11] Consequently, for the purposes of this book, speculative trading is largely disregarded as a separate category of SMST-driven concern. The focus instead is on earnings-based investors, on the basis that a large part of speculative trading rides on the back of the actions of earnings-based investment. The following Sect. A.2, accordingly, considers how such earning-based investors may transmit the SMST problem into listed companies.

2. *Earnings-Based Investors*

Another approach used to consider how SMST is transmitted into the firm, is to look at the pressures exerted primarily indirectly by earnings-based investors via the reactions of such investors to information relevant to the listed company's performance.[12] Earnings-based investors are not clearly defined but may include a range of asset owners and asset managers, including professional fund managers, institutional investors and activist hedge funds. In this approach, the timeframe of the investor is less of an issue than the significant weight placed by such investors on a listed company's actual or anticipated periodic corporate earnings when deciding to buy, sell or hold shares.

Expectations of earnings-based investors for steadily increasing earnings growth, often calculated on an earnings per share (EPS) basis, are enforceable on company managers via an investor's actual or threatened exit from the market if earnings—and thus share prices—decline.[13] Also, actual or anticipated low earnings numbers, which would be reflected in share prices, could bring with it the threat of an activist campaign, either by hedge funds or in the form of defensive activism by existing investors. Earnings guidance provided by listed companies projecting what the EPS

[10] Roe (2013, 985).

[11] Nathan (2015).

[12] Moore and Walker-Arnott (2014, 426) and Moore and Petrin (2017, 126).

[13] Moore and Walker-Arnott (2014, 427) and Moore and Petrin (2017, 127).

will be in the next reporting period may amplify this issue. However, earning guidance is mainly a US concept and is, for example, not as prevalent in the UK,[14] which has also identified a SMST issue in its capital markets. This analysis on earnings-based investment suggests it is not holding periods, but rather the emphasis on share price by a wide range of investors that transmits SMST into the firm.

3. *The Relevance of Investor Timeframes*

Simultaneously to the criticism of short-term investors, long-term asset owners—i.e. patient capital—have been elevated to the moral high ground.[15] The argument has been made that institutional asset owners that hold their shares briefly monitor the actions of listed companies less than asset owners that hold shares for longer periods.[16] However, "[t]he duration of any investor's holding period in a company's stock", it is argued, "is simply not relevant to issues involving corporate value creation."[17] Further, short-term traders are a 'big red herring' in the debate on how SMST is transmitted into listed companies.[18] There is definite merit to this argument, particularly with regard to speculative traders, whose actions, as discussed above, lack a clear transmission mechanism into the firm. Also, the assumption that long-term asset owners are more interested in long-term value than short-term shareholders might be problematic as evidence suggests long-term asset owners may knowingly pursue short-term returns at the expense of sustainable longer-term value.[19] Also, there are a myriad of reasons why long-term investors may be reluctant to intervene in long-term value generation.[20] The short

[14] Roach (2013).

[15] See the summary in Garratt and Hamilton (2016, 791), which sets out the many virtues of patient capital—i.e. long-term investors.

[16] See Dent (2010, 132) referring to Chen et al. (2007, 283) and Gaspar et al. (2005, 137).

[17] Nathan (2015).

[18] Martin (2015).

[19] See discussion in Fried (2015, 1554–1628) and generally in Dent (2010).

[20] See Pozen (2015), where the author lists reasons why institutional investors do not engage, including that they often prefer to hold index funds, participation in proxy contests has high costs which are often not justified on a cost-benefit analysis, and there are concerns about free-riding from other investors.

investment holding periods of offensive activist investors[21] such as hedge funds are also often cited as a source of SMST,[22] but this too has been questioned.[23] It follows, therefore, that investor timeframes alone do not provide a clear transmission mechanism of the SMST problem into the listed company.

How can we reconcile this conclusion that investor timeframes alone do not transmit SMST into listed companies with research showing that such investment timeframes investment does in fact matter? For example, a recent study by finance academics, Martijn Cremers, Ankur Pareek and Zacharias Sautner,[24] built on earlier research in this area.[25] This study used a wide-ranging data set of US common stocks from 1985 to 2011 with prices above US$1.00. Cremers et al. concluded that an inflow of short-term investors—which in the study were limited to US institutional investors with more than US$100 million under management and thus required to report to the US Securities and Exchange Commission (SEC) on Form 13F—appeared to exert pressure on management to cut research and development (R&D) investment in order to report higher earnings and generate positive earnings surprises, and also caused temporary boosts in firm valuations—i.e. higher stock prices.[26]

[21] 'Offensive' activism generally refers to the actions of investors that actively seek out opportunities to invest and pursue strategies aimed at unlocking the value of perceived underperforming listed companies. In contrast, 'defensive' activism refers to the activities taken by existing shareholders to pressure management to address the perceived under performance of a listed company.

[22] For example, see Strine (2015, 8–11), where Delaware Chief Justice Strine states that "[m]any activist investors hold their stock for a very short period of time … What is even more disturbing than hedge fund turnover is the gerbil-like trading activity of the mutual fund industry…."

[23] Squire (2014) and Sorkin (2015), in which the author refers to a study showing the average hedge fund holds shares for more than three years, which is about the same as average mutual fund holdings.

[24] Cremers et al. (2019).

[25] For example, a study by Matsumoto (2002), which concluded that firms with a large number of transient investors are more likely to manage earnings in order to meet analyst and investor expectations, and, a study by Francois Brochet, Maria Luomioti and George Serafeim (discussed in Brochet et al. 2012) that analyzed transcripts of earnings calls and found that firms that focus on the short term tend to have a more short-term oriented investor base and that these investors tended to reinforce a short-term focus within the firm.

[26] Cremers et al. (2019, 22–23).

Evidencing that short-term institutional investors caused such boost, the study indicated that the reductions in R&D were reversed when the inflow of short-term investors also reversed, thereby confirming that the cuts were only transitory.[27] However. Cremers et al.'s analysis may not generally be applicable as it was derived from firms on the Russell 2000 Index, which is an index of domestically-focused US listed 'small cap' companies.[28] Further, whether reducing R&D is problematic or a decent measure of SMST is considered further in Chapter 7. However, though there may be valid questions on the connection between SMST and R&D generally, Cremers et al.'s research on the impact of short-term investment suggests that shareholding duration is of some consequence.

It is certainly logical that earnings-based investors with shorter-term investment time frames may exert more pressure on companies for short-term results measured by EPS, than longer-term shareholders. However, I argue that the bigger concern is not the trading argument, but rather how company managers are taking problematic short-term actions to boost earnings in response to a general perceived or actual excessive discounting of long-term projects by a wide range of shareholders, perhaps amplified or initiated by short-term institutional investors, or the actions of activist hedge funds. The key point is that longer-term shareholding does not necessary remove the SMST issue. Logically, the focus of SMST-driven reform should, therefore, be less on investment durations, and more on addressing the underlying cause of such excessive discounting, or cutting off the transmission of SMST into the listed company.

As suggested above, the discussion around the perceived short-termism of activist investors, such as hedge funds, may be another 'red herring'. Activist hedge funds could just be the loudest voice in a much wider problem of excessive discounting by investors. Hedge funds arguably bear the brunt of the negative attention given the very public—and often adversarial—nature of their campaigns. It is argued that activist hedge funds may perhaps instead be the natural champions of dispersed shareholders, who are not economically capable of collective action in their own interest—i.e. they may bridge the separation of ownership and

[27] Ibid., 23.

[28] "What Is the Russell 2000 Index." Online: https://www.investopedia.com/terms/r/russell2000.asp.

control.[29] Evidence of the long-term impact of offensive hedge fund activism is mixed. Using a data set of 2000 activist interventions in the US from 1994 to 2007, Professors Bebchuk, Brav and Jiang claimed to have empirically shown that intervention by activist hedge funds does not have a detrimental effect on the long-term interests of companies and their shareholders.[30] To do so, Bebchuk et al. looked at the three years' prior and the three years' post-intervention, and they concluded that such interventions showed an increase rather than decrease in longer-term company performance.[31]

This study, and the earlier research upon which it is based, is the subject of considerable ongoing debate.[32] Most notably, Columbia Law Professor John Coffee, Jr. together with Professor Darius Palia from Rutgers Business School rejected the empirical evidence that Bebchuk et al. used to prove that activist attacks are beneficial on a number of grounds including that the time period is not reflective of the current wave of activism, and that more recent studies provide different results.[33] It may also be asked whether Bebchuk and et al.'s three-year time period is sufficient to test the long-term implications of activism. Regardless, activist hedge funds hold too few shares to act on their own to effect change[34]—even if as suggested by Coffee and Palia they may now act in 'wolf packs'.[35] Therefore, the bigger factor in the SMST discussion is not the measurable impact of activist interventions. Rather, the issue requiring further consideration is how the threat of hedge fund activism acts as a transmission mechanism contributing to the short-term actions taken by company managers, which is discussed the following Sect. B.

[29] As summarized in Coffee Palia (2015, 2, Note 2) where the authors refer to Gilson and Gordon (2013) and Bebchuk et al. (2015).

[30] Bebchuk et al. (2015).

[31] Ibid., 1154.

[32] See the summary in Lipton (2015).

[33] Coffee and Palia (2015, 8–10) for a discussion of the limitations of previous research discounting the negative effects of hedge fund activism, and 6 and Note 12 referring to the recent studies by Becht et al. (2015) and Allaire and Dauphin (2015).

[34] As noted in Pozen (2015), "an activist with 1% or 2% of a company's stock has no power to get its reform program adopted unless it can win the support of the institutional investors that own a majority of the company's stock."

[35] Coffee and Palia (2015, 7), which refers to this recent development of US hedge funds to work in a group in compliance with US securities law to gather small holdings before the 'wolf pack leader' files its Schedule 13D.

B. Managerial Myopia—Short-Termism of Company Managers

Myopic behaviour by company managers is seen as the flip side of the investor short-termism discussed above, as this managerial myopia "represents the internal response at the business enterprise level to the external financial-performance demands of the stock market."[36] Essentially, SMST at the listed company level involves company managers, "giving the market what it wants to hear."[37] The precise connection between investor short-termism and managerial behaviour is, however, difficult to establish.[38] Nonetheless, as discussed in more detail in Chapter 5, I conclude that this connection appears to be largely based on the share prices of listed companies, and the impact that excessive discounting of long-term returns has on such share prices. The main reasons why company managers care about share prices and how company managers respond to market preferences for high share prices are summarized in Fig. 1 and are discussed in more detail in the following sections.

1. *Why Do Company Managers Care About Share Prices?*

SVM as a concept is the widespread academic and business view that the primary objective of a listed company—at least in US, UK and Anglo-American influenced corporate models—is to maximize value for its asset

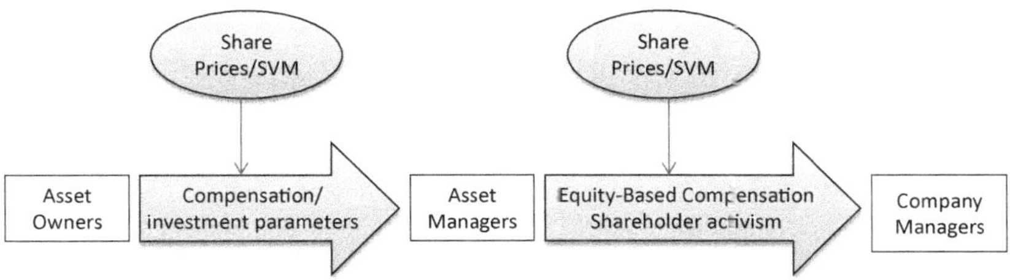

Fig. 1 Transmission of SMST into listed companies

[36] Moore and Walker-Arnott (2014, 427) and Moore and Petrin (2017, 123).

[37] Ibid.

[38] See Rieg (2015, 197), where the author reviews the literature in this area and concludes that "the interaction of investor myopia and managerial myopia is not straightforward."

owners.[39] As SVM and its interaction with SMST have been the subject of considerable discussion,[40] the starting point for the analysis in this section is a consideration of SVM and how the pursuit of value for investors by company managers, including in the form of high share prices, may contribute to SMST. Adherence to alternative corporate purpose theories, such as stakeholder theory or the 'enlightened' SVM, have been proposed as a way of addressing the SMST problem. The arguments discussed below that SVM is—or at least should be—about more than just short-term financial returns for investors are compelling. However, as demonstrated in Chapter 5, SMST is most probably getting inside listed companies through a focus on share prices which excessively discount future returns. Specifically, of interest is how SMST is transmitted into listed companies through corporate governance and legal mechanisms, i.e. executive compensation arrangements and the ability of asset owners to make change to the board. Better understanding these transmission mechanisms should assist policymakers and financial industry to develop conceptually effective SMST reform.

a. SVM and the Importance of Share Prices

In listed companies, SVM has been interpreted in practice to mean keeping share prices high and returning profits to asset owners through dividends and buybacks.[41] Although the purpose of corporate entities has been discussed for centuries,[42] the genesis of the modern SVM movement may be attributed to Milton Friedman, former leader of the Chicago school of economics, and the winner of Nobel Prize in Economics in 1976.[43] Mr. Friedman wrote an article for the *New York*

[39] SVM was first comprehensively articulated and popularized by Alfred Rappaport in Rappaport (1986) and refined by Rappaport in Rappaport (1998), where Rappaport observed that SVM has gained widespread acceptance in the US and increasing significance in the UK, Europe, Australia and Japan, and is on its way to becoming the global standard for business performance (at 1).

[40] See the summary of this discussion in Denning (2017) and the literature review on SVM and SMST provided by Rieg (2015, 195–198).

[41] Rappaport (2011), where Rappaport discussed how US companies in particular have attempted to maximize shareholder value by various means which keep share prices and payments to shareholders high.

[42] See Jensen (2010, 32) where Jensen asserts that the modern value maximization proposition has its roots in 200 years of research in economics and finance.

[43] Denning (2013).

Times in 1970 in which he said that the only social responsibility of a business is to increase its profits, and a manager's primary responsibility is to the owners of the firm.[44] SVM theory gained traction in the following decades primarily in US business and economics schools and with senior executives of US listed corporations, consequently becoming the highly influential doctrine that it is today.[45]

According to the SVM concept, a company builds value through aligning the interests of asset owners and company managers, primarily through equity-based compensation arrangements for company managers.[46] Asset owners may also encourage SVM by supporting governance structures that monitor the activities of management, such as independence requirements on the boards of listed companies.[47] These measures attempt to reduce managerial agency costs—the costs associated with the separation of management and control—which if not addressed may result in corporate managers enriching themselves or pursuing other motivations at the expense of building shareholder value.[48] This alignment of interests of asset owners and company managers in order to maximize asset owner value is also at the heart of the value based management (VBM) method, a popular method of corporate management compelling listed companies to focus on value maximization at all levels of corporate decision-making.[49]

There has been much discussion, particularly after the global financial crisis (GFC), on whether SVM should continue to be the primary objective in the Anglo-American corporate model, and, as a corollary consideration, if adherence to SVM by managers causes or amplifies the perceived SMST problem.[50] The provocative question asked is "should organizations operate as money-making machines solely for the benefit of managers and shareholders or as instruments that add value

[44] Friedman (1970).

[45] The Modern Corporation: Corporate Governance for the 21st Century, Statement on Management. Online: https://themoderncorporation.wordpress.com/management-and-msv/.

[46] See Rieg (2015, 195) and Rappaport (1986).

[47] Shapiro (2005).

[48] See Rieg (2015, 195).

[49] See the description provided in Koller (1994).

[50] Reland (2009) and Denning (2014).

to society?"[51] An argument has also been made that short-termism and a short-term orientation seem to be outcomes caused by SVM when placed in a real-world context—for example, where a firm has unrealistic expectations, there is uncertainty of future capabilities—with competitive rivalry and market disruptions.[52]

Noted US economist, Alfred Rappaport, who is also credited with popularizing the SVM concept,[53] defends the SVM theory by arguing that there is no inherent flaw with SVM as a corporate objective.[54] In the SVM model, Rappaport explains, "[m]anagement's responsibility is to pursue the maximization of long-term cash flows, regardless of the holding periods of shareholders."[55] This focus on long-term cash flows, he argues, builds company value and is the best framework for balancing the interests of all of the company's stakeholders. It is the market's current obsession with short-term earnings, rather than managing for long-term cash flows that Rappaport says is the real issue. "The shareholder value principle has not failed management," instead he argues that "management has betrayed the principle."[56] Far from being the "dumbest idea",[57] Rappaport's argument suggests that when correctly applied, the SVM model is a key driver of long-term corporate value rather than a basis for SMST concerns. This may be so, but it raises the important question of why company managers appear to focus on maximizing value of shareholders, and these links are explored further below.

SVM is not the only approach to corporate purpose. Stakeholder theory has emerged as the main contender to the SVM concept. Stakeholder theory is essentially a theory of management and ethics that holds that society is best served if companies are run for the benefit of all stakeholders—e.g. employees, customers, creditors, communities, etc.—rather than just asset owners.[58] Instead of focusing on returns to

[51] Denning (2014).

[52] Rieg (2015, 216–217).

[53] Ibid., 195.

[54] Rappaport (2011, 49–54).

[55] Ibid., 54.

[56] Ibid.

[57] A criticism levied against SVM by Jack Welch, former-Chairman and CEO of General Electric—see Guerrara (2009).

[58] Phillips (2003), where the authors outline what stakeholder theory encompasses, and elaborates on a number of common misconceptions of the theory.

shareholders, the argument goes that SMST could be addressed by listed companies if they instead prioritized the interests of a broader group of constituents. Stakeholder theory has been criticized, however, on the basis that it creates considerable uncertainty in the management of the firm, and, therefore, adherence to a stakeholder approach does provide a socially efficient outcome.[59]

In an attempt to address these criticisms and marry SVM with stakeholder theory, the theory of "enlightened shareholder value maximization"[60] has been put forward as a means of ameliorating the perceived SMST problem. For example, in his critique of the short-term focus of modern listed companies, Dominic Barton of McKinsey & Company (McKinsey) argued that it is essential for a listed company to serve the interests of all stakeholders to achieve value for shareholders. Barton asserts that companies should build corporate value by focusing on their main constituencies. Particularly, Barton stated that choosing between shareholders and stakeholders is a false choice,[61] and expanded on this point by saying that "executives must infuse their organizations with the perspective that serving the interests of all major stakeholders—employees, suppliers, customers, creditors, communities, the environment—is not at odds with the goal of maximizing corporate value; on the contrary, it's essential to achieving that goal."[62] There does appear to be significant convergence around the concept that company managers should consider more than just short-term returns to asset owners in the exercise of their duties.

As discussed above, the basis of the SMST concern is that listed companies are principally focused on maximizing shareholder value, which is purportedly manifested as short-term financial returns for asset owners. Although company managers should consider more than just short-term

[59] For example, see Jensen (2010), where Jensen argues that stakeholder theory is not a complete theory for the objective of a firm as it does not provide a clear purpose thereby requiring the firm to serve many masters, and when there are many masters all end up being short-changed (32–33).

[60] Jensen proposed enlightened shareholder value as the objective of a firm, which he says, "uses much of the structure of stakeholder theory but accepts maximization of the long-run value of the firm as the criterion for making the requisite tradeoffs among its stakeholders" (Jenson 2010, 33).

[61] Barton (2011, 88).

[62] Ibid., 86.

returns to asset owners in the exercise of their duties, this discussion is largely theoretical if corporate law and governance measures continue to facilitate the use of share prices—which as demonstrated in Chapter 5 are a questionable measure of long-term value—as the primary measure of the value of a listed company. However, as a realistic alternative to share prices is not readily apparent, the only feasible options currently remaining are to improve share pricing as a measure of long-term value or cut off the transmission of the short-termism of asset owners, via asset managers, into the listed company. The corporate governance and legal mechanisms by which such investor short-termism is transmitted into listed companies are, consequently, particularly important to understand in order to develop effective SMST reform.

The fiduciary duties of directors are briefly considered first as these could be seen as a legal means of transmitting SMST into the firm. However, fiduciary duties are rejected as a transmission mechanism given the broad deference given to boards of directors in applying such duties. A stronger transmission mechanism is arguably more evident in two main categories: (1) executive compensation, and (2) the asset owner/asset manager ability to change the board of directors, thereby facilitating a change of control of senior management of the listed company.

b. Fiduciary Duties—An Inefficient Transmission Mechanism

It may be argued that the undue focus on maximizing short-term shareholder value is transmitted into listed companies through the exercise of fiduciary duties by directors. These duties are codified in company law in the UK[63] and have been developed in case law in Delaware.[64] Such fiduciary duties require directors to consider the best interests of the company. These duties have been expanded in UK company law to state that directors should consider stakeholder interests, and, in particular, the

[63] UK Companies Act 2006, Chapter 46 (UK Companies Act), Section 172(1).

[64] In Delaware which is the domicile for over 50% of US listed companies (http://www.corp.delaware.gov/aboutagency.shtml), Section 141(a) of the Delaware General Corporation Law (Title 8, Chapter 1 of the Delaware Code) provides that the business and affairs of Delaware corporations shall be managed under the direction of a board of directors, and the duties of such board of directors have been developed in case law and require each of the directors to act in good faith to advance the best interests of the corporation (*Kaplan v. Centex Corp.*, 284 A.2d 119, 124 (Del. Ch. 1971)).

duty of directors in Section 172(1)(a) of the UK Companies Act to have regard to the likely consequences of any decision in the long term.[65]

There is significant deference by courts—particularly in the US and UK[66]—to the business judgment of directors. It is very possible, therefore, that directors could pursue a business strategy that does not prioritize short-term returns to shareholders without breaching their duties as directors. Fiduciary duties are, consequently, a tenuous basis for the transmission of SMST into listed companies. Instead further analysis is warranted on whether directors' duties could be further codified to require directors to take a longer-term approach when promoting the success of the company. More likely transmission mechanisms are the structure of executive compensation arrangements, and the corporate law and governance mechanisms that give shareholders the ability to make changes to boards of directors and thereby senior executives, which are discussed below.

c. *Equity-Based Executive Compensation*

A question that may be asked in the short-termism discussion, is why don't company mangers just accept share price fluctuations and manage to build long-term value for listed companies regardless of such fluctuations. The simple answer is that company managers may want to do so, but they are predominantly focused on maximizing share prices as low share prices cause a host of problems. These problems include personal financial implications as a significant portion of management compensation is often tied to share prices.[67]

As discussed in Chapter 3,[68] the use of equity-based compensation, which is meant to reduce managerial agency costs by aligning the interests of company managers and investors, grew exponentially in the

[65]The UK Companies Act introduced in 2006 clarified in Section 172(1) that a director has a duty to promote the success of the company for the benefit of its members as a whole, and then enumerated further considerations for directors in exercising this duty, including the likely consequences of any long-term decision in the long-term (Section 172(1)(a)), the interests of the company's employees (Section 172(1)(b)), the need to foster the company's business relationships (Section 172(1)(c)), and the impact of the company's operations on the community and the environment (Section 172(1)(d)).

[66]See the US decision in *Gimbel v. Signal Cos.*, 316 A.2d 599, 608 (Del. Ch. 1974) and the UK Companies Act 2006, Section 172 and *Re Smith & Fawcett Ltd* [1942] Ch. 304.

[67]Dallas and Barry (2016, 558).

[68]See Chapter 3, Sect. B.

1990s, predominantly in the US[69] and UK.[70] The rationale was that if company managers held shares in the listed company they managed, they would be incentivized to run the company to maximize share prices. The equity-based compensation of choice during this time period was stock options. For a variety of reasons—largely attributable to accounting and taxation rule changes—stock options have diminished in importance in the US[71] and also went out of favour earlier in the UK, due to the criticisms levied in number of influential reports.[72] However, as discussed below, other forms of equity-based compensation—such as performance and restricted shares—continue to make up a significant portion of executive pay packages in listed companies.

In the US, the long-term incentive (LTI) awards—stock awards and options—valued at the date of grant constituted 57.2% of the total chief executive officer (CEO) compensation reported in 2014 in the S&P 500, compared to 55.8% in 2010.[73] Research also shows that the usage of performance-vesting equity awards, meaning vesting based on achieving certain performance objectives, rather than time-based vesting to top executives in large US companies has grown from 20 to 70% from 1998 to 2012.[74] In the UK, while the salary component of FTSE 100 executive compensation has been relatively steady over the years, additional compensation in the form of share-based compensation has risen dramatically.[75] Of particular note are Long-Term Incentive Plans (LTIPs). These LTIPS are equity-based plans that are typically three years in length and usually constitute the largest element of UK executive pay in listed companies.[76] Approximately 90% of UK FTSE 100 companies used LTIPs in 2013, which is an increase of 30% from the mid-1990s.[77]

Payments to executives of listed companies in the EU also appear to be following a similar US/UK trend of greater reliance on equity-based plans.

[69] Bachelder (2014).

[70] Kay (2012, 77).

[71] Bachelder (2014).

[72] Kay (2012, 78).

[73] Tonello (2015) referring to the findings in The CEO and Executive Compensation Practices: 2015 Edition, by the Conference Board Inc. and Arthur J. Gallagher & Co.

[74] Bettis et al. (2018).

[75] Barty and Jones (2012, 16).

[76] Dawson (2017).

[77] Ibid.

As examined by the Hay Group in 2014, the trend of long-term compensation of European Union (EU) executives "is more akin to the US practice of making senior executives retain vested option and stock awards, thereby tying a significant part of their wealth to the company's fortunes."[78] The Hay Group's research with respect to equity-based pay observes that, "[f]or European CEOs such requirements now tend to be between 200 and 300 per cent of base salary and the shareholding is typically built up from vested deferred bonus and long-term incentive awards."[79]

The US executive compensation model—which includes a growing portion of equity-based compensation—is gaining momentum worldwide.[80] In Asia, the Kothuis and Chua (2014) observed that the fixed pay portions of executive salaries in listed companies have fallen significantly.[81] Kothuis and Chua (2014), also stated that the use of LTI plans in Asia has been increasing, however, they are still not provided in the same frequency or percentages of overall compensation as their Western counterparts.[82] Further, when LTIs are used to compensate executives, Asian listed companies are less likely to use share-based compensation than cash.[83] As noted in Kothuis and Chua (2014), "this is a trend that should wane as Asian companies become global."[84] Consequently, equity-based compensation may not be as large of a contributor to the SMST problem outside of the US and the UK. However, as the US model equity-based compensation model appears to be gaining ground in the EU and to a lesser degree in Asia, equity-based pay as a possible SMST transmission mechanism into listed companies should be considered seriously in all major markets.

Demonstrating the importance of the connection of share prices to executive compensation, it has been stated that "[t]oday, equity accounts for about 60% of the remuneration of executives at companies in the Standard & Poor's 500-stock index…[w]ith so much money tied up in stock options and the like, it is not surprising that executives

[78] Hay Group Report (2014).

[79] Ibid.

[80] See the Hay Group (2014) and Kothuis and Chua (2014).

[81] Kothuis and Chua (2014, 4).

[82] Ibid., 4–5.

[83] Ibid.

[84] Ibid., 5.

will do almost anything to give their share price a boost regardless of what costs this might incur after their options have vested."[85] This statement would only be accurate if the timeframes of the vesting provisions in the equity-based compensation plan were too short to properly align the interests of company managers with the long-term performance of a listed company. The average vesting period for CEO equity-based compensation long-S&P 1500 and UK FTSE 500 companies appears to be three-years.[86] The question then is whether three years is long enough. Arguably, this time period is not adequate for company management to be sufficiently invested in the long-term performance of the listed company.[87] However, even if the time frames of current equity-based compensation arrangements are sufficient, such compensation structures are not the only transmission mechanism of SMST into listed companies. Further analysis is also required on the implications of low share prices on company manager job security and the market for corporate control.

d. Job Security—Ability to Change the Board/Senior Management

Both boards of directors and senior management of listed companies may be concerned about job security as a result of negative impacts to share prices. Boards of directors—either via pressure from shareholders through proxy contests to change directors or on their own initiative through concerns about such proxy contests, or perhaps their incentive structures—may exercise their authority to remove senior management if the share price is not performing as desired. Shareholder delegation of the power to fire the CEO to the board of directors is central to corporate governance, particularly in US listed companies.[88] Research by Dirk Jenter, London School of Economics & Political Science—Department of Finance; Centre for Economic Policy Research and Katharina Lewellen, Dartmouth College—Tuck School of Business shows that CEO turnover is closely linked to performance—which includes a listed company's share price performance—, and performance-induced

[85] Denning (2014).

[86] "Equity Vesting Schedules for S&P 1500 CEOs." 26 April 2013 *Equilar*. Online: http://www.equilar.com/reports/3-equity-vesting-schedules.html and Dawson (2017).

[87] Kay recommended that "[l]ong-term performance incentives should be provided only in the form of company shares to be held at least until after the executive has retired from the business"—Kay (2012, 13).

[88] Fisman et al. (2005).

turnovers are significantly more frequent than forced turnovers.[89] Using data compiled on S&P 500, S&P MidCap, and S&P SmallCap companies from 1993 to 2011, Jenter and Lewellen estimate that between 38 and 55% of all CEO turnovers are performance induced, with an even higher percentage in the first years of tenure.[90] This research confirms the assumption that boards change senior management of listed companies if share prices are negatively impacted. In addition to the board's ability to fire CEOs for poor performance, shareholders may exert pressure on the board itself, and by extension company management.

The mechanisms by which shareholders are able to call a general shareholder meeting to make changes to the boards of directors of a listed company—thereby also facilitating a change to senior management—differ jurisdiction by jurisdiction. In the UK, for example, shareholders have considerable scope to instigate such changes. Only 5% of the voting rights of a listed company are needed to require the directors to call an extraordinary general meeting, at which meeting a resolution can be put forward make changes to the board of directors.[91] There is also a statutory process whereby shareholders may propose an ordinary resolution at the next annual general meeting of the listed company for the removal or addition of a director.[92] Further, the UK Companies Act also provides a process whereby shareholders holding at least 5% of the voting rights or 100 shareholders may put forward any resolution at scheduled annual general meetings of a listed company.[93]

In contrast, to the UK Delaware corporate law is more limited. The Delaware General Corporation Law does not mandate that shareholders have the ability to call a special general meeting. Rather, the Delaware General Corporation Law leaves it to the discretion of the corporation to decide whether its shareholders will have this ability. If the corporation decides to provide this process, the relevant thresholds to call special general meetings—at which changes may be made to the board—are

[89] Jenter and Lewellen (2017, 1).

[90] Ibid.

[91] UK Companies Act, Section 303, as amended by The UK Companies (Shareholders' Rights) Regulations 2009.

[92] UK Companies Act, Sections 168 and 312.

[93] Ibid., Section 338(3).

set in the constitutional documents.[94] Evidence shows that around half of S&P 500 Delaware incorporated companies include the ability for shareholders to call a special general meeting in their constitutional documents.[95] When this right is included, the ownership threshold required to call the meetings was much higher than in the UK, and in the range of 15% or greater, with many companies at 25%.

With a few exceptions, including where the director is part of a staggered or classified board, a majority of the shareholders of a Delaware corporation entitled to vote may decline to re-elect directors at an annual general meeting.[96] Attempts by corporations to entrench boards and increase this threshold above a majority vote have been found by the Delaware courts to contravene this provision of the Delaware General Corporation Law.[97] However, a majority vote, as in the UK, is still a high threshold for listed companies given that many listed companies are widely held and obtaining a majority vote at a meeting may be challenging. Consequently, given this high threshold and the inconsistency around shareholder's ability to requisition meetings, attempts to make changes to the board of directors and thus make changes to senior management, particularly in the US, have increasingly centered on proxy battles at annual general meetings.[98]

A proxy battle occurs when an activist shareholder—either offensively as part of a strategy to acquire shares and unlock value or defensively to protect the interests of existing shareholders—attempts to convince existing shareholders to use their proxy votes to install new directors or an entire new board, which may result in changes to management.[99] As an example, activist hedge fund Starboard Value LP (Starboard), entered into a proxy battle for full control of the board at Yahoo Inc. (Yahoo). Starboard's stated intent was to change control of the board, and push for

[94] See §221(d) of the Delaware General Corporation Law which provides that a special meeting "may be called by the board of directors or by such person or persons as may be authorized by the certificate of incorporation or by the bylaws."

[95] See the summary provided in Brown (2014).

[96] Delaware General Corporation Law, §141(k).

[97] See *Fretcher v. Zier*, No CV 12038-VCG, 2017 WL 345142 (Del. Ch. Jan. 24, 2017).

[98] See Frankl and Balet (2017), where the authors observe that there were 110 proxy fights in the US in 2016, up 43% from 2012.

[99] Investopedia. Online: http://www.investopedia.com/ask/answers/08/how-do-proxy-fights-work.asp.

an auction of Yahoo's core internet business in order to address flagging financial performance.[100] Starboard was partially successful, but a proxy battle was avoided and Starboard instead negotiated directly with management and obtained four of the nine board seats sought.[101] Activists such as Starboard generally hold a minority share position and, consequently, even if they act in wolf packs as discussed above,[102] cannot effect changes to the board without convincing other shareholders to vote with them. Consequently, proxy campaigns are certainly not always successful.

For example, Greenlight Capital, Inc. (Greenlight), a US activist hedge fund led by David Einhorn, proposed four nominees to be elected to the board of directors at the 2017 annual general meeting of General Motors (GM), which nominees were overwhelming rejected by GM shareholders in favor of GM's incumbent nominees.[103] Greenlight's stated intent for proposing the board changes was to address GM's lagging share prices by attempting to get GM to split its shares, one class of which would focus on steady dividends and the other on share buybacks.[104] Although proxy campaigns are undoubtedly not always successful, shareholder activism is on the rise, and not just in the US. A 2015 global survey by FTI Consulting revealed that US-style activism is no longer confined to US listed companies. Notable increases of activism are shown in the UK, Canada, continental Europe and the Asia-Pacific region—with board changes being a key focus by activists.[105] The research of FTI Consulting also shows that US activists, for example ValueAct Capital, Elliot Management Corporation and Starboard, are becoming increasingly global.[106]

It is clear that declining share prices of listed companies attract activists. In particular, if the shares of a listed company are perceived to be trading at less than the perceived fundamental value of the listed company, it makes the listed company a prime target for intervention by activist shareholders in the form of a proxy battle. Although proxy

[100] Flaherty (2016).

[101] Lee (2016).

[102] Coffee and Palia (2015, 7).

[103] Ferris (2017).

[104] Foley (2017).

[105] Global Activism (2016).

[106] Ibid.

campaigns to change the board are not always successful, they do pose a real threat to the job security of incumbent directors and therefore senior management. The threat alone of such an activist campaign may be enough to impact company manager behaviour.

As discussed in Chapter 3,[107] when hostile takeovers became prominent in the 1980s the argument was made that just the threat of such a takeover had a negative impact on the stock market as a whole. Company managers supposedly endeavored to pre-empt hostile takeovers by foregoing long-term planning and engaging in short-termism in order to boost share prices,[108] although others contested this assertion saying that such companies were just inefficiently run.[109] However, this market impact reasoning could still be relevant as the mere threat of an activist campaign, and the support such campaign may generate from existing shareholders and concerns by the board, may act as a mechanism to transmit short-termist into listed companies. Company managers may take short-term actions that keep share prices high, knowing that the market overvalues these actions and excessively discounts future profits, and fearing that low prices may make them susceptible to investor activism or dismissal by the board. Consequently, shareholder activism, and even the threat of activism, together with the negative personal compensation implications of low share prices[110]—and the benefits of higher share prices—to company managers, appear to be the main transmission mechanisms by which SMST enters listed companies. How exactly company managers respond to this SMST is considered below.

2. *Response of Company Managers to SMST of Asset Owners and Asset Managers*

As demonstrated above, share prices are an important communication tool among market participants, and share prices are particularly important as they impact company manager compensation and job security.

[107] See Chapter 3, Sect. A.

[108] Lipton (1979, 109–110), expanded on subsequently in Schnitzer (1997).

[109] Easterbrook and Fischel (1981, 1184).

[110] A summary of the reasons that company managers are concerned about share prices are set out at http://www.investopedia.com/articles/basics/03/020703.asp. See also Rieg (2015) referencing a study by Mergenthaler et al. (2011), which study provides evidence of the career penalties to company managers for not meeting analyst forecasts (197).

The mechanisms by which company managers give the market what it wants to hear and thereby keep share prices high are arguably through "a consistently positive rate of periodic EPS growth, preferably coupled with a corresponding rise in declared rate of dividend."[111] Consistently positive EPS which meet earnings expectations are a key part of this equation, as are stable dividends. This steady rate is important as, "profits are observable and boost the investor's impression of managerial ability."[112] The response of company managers to the short-termism of asset owners and asset managers in respect of dividends and earnings management is considered below.

a. SMST and Dividends

Based on 2016 numbers, dividends were paid by 82.6% of S&P 500 companies, 69.3% of the companies on the S&P 400 Mid Cap Index MID, and 51.6% of companies included on S&P Small Cap 600 Index SML.[113] It is widely documented that company managers strive to maintain smooth dividends, and in particular institutional investors place considerable value on dividend-smoothing.[114] The concern raised is that share prices will be negatively impacted if dividend rates are not maintained. Demonstrating this concern, a survey of US executives focused on dividend policy, showed that concerns about strong market reactions drove executives to avoid cutting dividends at all costs, even if it meant by-passing net present value (NPV) projects.[115]

This concern was echoed by BlackRock Inc. (BlackRock) CEO Larry Fink in a letter addressed to CEOs of S&P 500 and large EU companies. Fink declared, that "[i]n the wake of the financial crisis, many companies have shied away from investing in the future growth of their companies…[t]o many have cut capital expenditure and even increased debt to boost dividends and increase share buybacks."[116] Fink concluded that, "[w]hen done for the wrong reasons and at the expense of capital investment, [returning cash to shareholders] can jeopardize a company's ability

[111] Moore and Walker-Arnott (2014, 428).

[112] Davies et al. (2014, 17).

[113] Vlastelica (2017).

[114] See the discussion in Larkin et al. (2017, 4114).

[115] Brav et al. (2005).

[116] BlackRock's Fink (2014).

to generate sustainable long-term returns."[117] The harms caused by declaring dividends and making share buy-backs at the expense of capital investment are considered further in Chapter 7.[118]

The point made in this section is that short-termism of asset owners and asset managers transmitted to company managers via negative impacts on share prices may cause company managers to prioritize consistent dividend payments to shareholders. However, not all listed companies pay dividends—perhaps for the reason that short-termism may cause them to have to prioritize dividend payments over capital expenditure. In addition to this pressure for consistent dividend payments, such short-termism may also lead to earnings management.

b. SMST and Earnings Management

Earnings per share (EPS) may be increased via 'earnings management', a practice involving creative manipulation of the numbers presented in a company's accounts by company managers.[119] Earnings management may be divided into two basic forms:

1. *accounting earnings management*—which essentially involves a fraud on the market (fraudulent earnings management), and
2. *real earnings management*—which uses legitimate means to present income stability (non-fraudulent earnings management).[120]

Fraudulent earnings management involves the direct manipulation of financial information or the use of off-balance sheet transactions to obscure a listed company's fundamental value.[121] This kind of activity is outright fraud or certainly verges on fraudulent behaviour, and it was associated with the high-profile corporate scandals of the early 2000s—such as Enron Corporation and WorldCom,[122] which were discussed further in Chapter 3.[123] As noted by Professor Lynne Dallas, this type of clearly objectionable earnings management appears to have decreased in

[117] Ibid.

[118] See Chapter 7, Sect. D.3.b.

[119] Davies et al. (2014, 428) and see Dallas (2012, 278–281).

[120] Dallas (2012, 278).

[121] Ibid.

[122] Ibid.

[123] See Chapter 3, Sect. C.

the US since the passage of legislation meant to specifically prohibit such activity.[124] Such fraudulent earnings management is undoubtedly objectionable as it blatantly obscures the real value of a listed company from the market, and should be legislated against regardless of any SMST reform motivations. The line between such fraudulent earnings management and non-fraudulent earnings management is admittedly blurred.[125]

Non-fraudulent earnings management, however, is more nuanced, and involves legitimate company manager actions that "present to the market an effective façade of corporate income-stability."[126] Non-fraudulent earnings management has caught the attention of those concerned about the SMST issue. As stated by Rappaport, "[s]hort-termism continues to be the disease, and earnings obsession the carrier."[127] Such non-fraudulent earnings management involves a range of activities by company managers of listed companies all of which are designed to 'smooth' periodic earnings—and thus EPS numbers—results on a continuing basis, and meet market earnings expectations.[128] These activities include offering price discounts to temporarily increase sales, engaging in overproduction to lower costs of goods sold, reducing discretionary expenses aggressively to improve margins, deferring incurred costs or losses to future accounting periods, managing the timing of major business announcements, effecting stock buy-backs, and even in certain circumstances creating illusory growth through corporate acquisitions.[129] The intent with all of these actions by company managers is to create an increasing EPS growth curve so as to avoid punishment from the stock market in the form of an end-of-period share price fall—which fall is inevitable if the listed company entirely relies on such non-fraudulent earnings management to build value.[130] This is particularly significant where earnings expectations are communicated to the market by company management and analysts.

These earnings expectations generally consist of guidance by company managers or analysts setting out an estimate of future revenue as well as

[124] Ibid., where Dallas refers to the US Sarbanes-Oxley Act of 2002.

[125] Millstein (2005).

[126] Moore and Walker-Arnott (2014, 428).

[127] Rappaport (2011, 55).

[128] Moore and Walker-Arnott (2014, 428).

[129] See Dallas (2012, 279) and Moore and Walker-Arnott (2014, 429–431).

[130] Moore and Walker-Arnott (2014, 428).

capital spending estimates and an estimated EPS for a specific period, e.g. a quarter.[131] Listed companies are not required to disclose earnings expectations, but there is considerable market pressure from asset owners to do so for US listed corporations, and, regardless of whether the company managers provide such guidance, financial industry analysts may do so independently of the listed company.[132] The concern raised is that a failure to meet these earnings expectations results in increased selling of the listed companies shares, causing a downward pressure in share prices.[133] There are questions on the actual impact of earnings guidance, with some analysis suggesting that it does not impact share price volatility, but just trading volumes.[134] Regardless of the actual impact of a failure to meet earnings guidance on share prices, there is considerable survey evidence suggesting that the threat of a negative market reaction of a failure to meet earnings guidance or demonstrate steadily increasing EPS and smooth dividends is sufficient to cause company managers to undertake non-fraudulent earnings management.

There is a considerable body of research evidencing that non-fraudulent earnings management is occurring.[135] Most notably, a detailed survey of 401 senior executives of US companies built on earlier survey evidence and found that: (1) managers would reject a positive-NPV project if it lowered earnings below quarterly consensus expectations, and (2) over 75% of the sample would give up economic value in order to smooth earnings.[136] When asked why earnings manipulation occurs, a large majority of chief financial officers (CFOs) have indicated that it is most often an attempt to influence stock price, because of outside and inside pressure to hit earnings benchmarks, and to avoid adverse compensation and career consequences for senior executives.[137] A more recent survey of 375 CFOs of US companies in 2015 confirmed that at least 20% of companies surveyed intentionally distorted earnings, even while adhering to generally accepted accounting

[131] Investopedia. Online: https://www.investopedia.com/terms/g/guidance.asp.

[132] Hsieh et al. (2016).

[133] Moore and Walker-Arnott (2014, 427).

[134] Hsieh et al. (2016).

[135] See the evidence presented in Dallas (2012, 279 at Note 80).

[136] Graham et al. (2005), updated in Graham et al. (2006).

[137] Graham et al. (2005), updated in Graham et al. (2006) and Dichev et al. (2016, 29).

principle (GAAP) standards—which admittedly may indicate an issue with GAAP disclosure requirements rather than specific SMST-driven concerns.[138]

As considered in Chapter 5,[139] survey evidence also undoubtedly has its limitations including that company managers may not be truthful in their responses. Further, survey evidence outside of the US is also limited. However, there is some empirical evidence from the UK demonstrating a quantitative connection between share-based compensation and non-fraudulent earnings management. Research on UK companies on the FTSE All Share Index showed that non-fraudulent earnings management increased when company managers owned between 5 and 10% of the equity of a listed company.[140] Though the evidence on non-fraudulent earnings management is largely US/UK centric and lacking in quantitative rigor, the depth of US survey evidence that has been conducted on this issue is compelling. The growing global influence of US investors and US-style management also means that non-fraudulent earnings management should be treated as a valid concern outside of just the US and UK capital markets.

Such non-fraudulent earnings management would not be a problem if it actually increased the fundamental value of the listed company, which was in turn reflected in share prices. However, the concern raised is that these actions do not generate real value, and once known eventually negatively impact share prices—or cause listed companies to miss out on projects that may produce greater financial returns in the long run. The evidence on the impact of SMST and non-fraudulent earnings management is considered further in Chapter 7.[141] It is sufficient for the purposes of this Section, however, to state that SMST appears to be transmitted to company managers by the importance of share prices in executive compensation and job security, which in turn appears to result in company managers taking actions to smooth earnings and meet market earnings expectations and, consequently, avoid any negative pricing impacts on share prices.

[138] Dichev et al. (2016).

[139] See Chapter 5, Sect. A.1.

[140] Bos et al. (2013).

[141] See Chapter 7, Sect. D.

C. Intermediaries

As discussed in Chapter 2,[142] intermediaries—meaning all of the entities in the equity ownership chain between the asset owner and the listed company, and also auxiliary intermediaries such as proxy advisers—play an important role in how the interests of asset owners are transmitted to listed companies. The most significant of these intermediaries are asset managers, given their scope and the level of control they have over investments—including as relevant to this book, the equity securities of listed companies.[143] It has been suggested that SMST is transmitted into listed companies from asset owners via asset managers. Asset managers, as agents for asset owners, act on their client's expressed preference for short-term returns interests, and in doing so pressure listed companies to deliver results by selling shares if the listed company does not meet expectations.[144] This is similar to the transmission mechanisms discussed above in the context of asset owners. If this is the case, then SMST-driven reform efforts should focus primarily on addressing the short-termism of asset owners, of which institutional investors are the most significant group. However, the contribution of asset managers to the SMST problem requires further analysis.

1. *Asset Managers*

Rather than just being a flow-through for asset owner interests, it has been suggested that asset managers themselves could be causing, or at least adding to, the SMST problem.[145] Key to this analysis is the assertion that "the agency relationship between institutional investors—asset owners—and their managers contributes to capital markets' increasing short-termism and to mispricing."[146] Particularly, as investors have imperfect knowledge of an asset manager's ability, they may conclude

[142] See Chapter 2, Sect. C.2.

[143] Kay (2012, 11), where Kay asserts that at least in the UK asset managers are the dominant players in the investment chain and in the US, US-registered investment companies managed $13 trillion in assets for more than 92 million US investors at year-end 2012 (Investment Company Institute, 2012 Investment Company Fact Book).

[144] Dallas and Barry (2016, 562).

[145] Ibid., and see also Dallas (2012, 295), Pozen (2015), and Aspen Institute (2009, 2).

[146] European Union Green Paper (2011, 12) referencing Woolley (2010).

that any reduction in asset value is due to an asset manager's incompetence and may react by switching their asset manager—provided that such asset management function is not in house.[147] The short reporting time periods for the assessment of asset managers are seen to be part of this problem.

Obviously, investors should not be locked into funds if such funds do not provide financial returns or if the investment is in consistent decline. However, the concern is that the timeframe for assessing whether an investment is viable is too short to meaningfully assess long-term value. The argument is that "[a]n active investment manager to be successful in the current environment must pay heed to its performance on a quarterly basis."[148] Asset managers "may be biased in favor of short-term initiatives than longer-term ones, even if the latter are likely to produce higher net value in the long-run" because "the search for 'alpha' by active asset managers is not just constant, but because of the pressure of being measured quarterly, immediate."[149] This need to constantly produce positive reports could be why asset managers disregard long-term interests and instead pressure companies for short-term returns. Asset managers also often facilitate quick redemption by asset owners of their investments on request.[150]

Dallas and Barry suggest that "[a] loyal asset manager who expects her clients to cash out soon, or who anticipates that short-term losses will cause clients to redeem their interests (at a loss), should focus on short-term stock prices."[151] This pressure for liquidity from asset owners may be an amplifying factor in how SMST is transmitted into listed companies, as it could also motivate asset managers to pressure listed companies to provide short-term returns by selling shares of listed companies that do not have steadily increasing share prices. Given these concerns, it has been said that the way forward is to "stop treating the finance sector as a pass-through that has no impact on asset pricing and risk."[152] While accepting the assertion that the asset manager/asset owner relationship may amplify the SMST concerns, the flaw in attributing the

[147] Woolley (2010, 126).

[148] Nathan (2015).

[149] Ibid.

[150] Dallas and Barry (2016, 562).

[151] Ibid.

[152] Woolley (2010, 127).

SMST problem primarily to asset managers is that they do not operate in a vacuum.

As noted by Dallas and Barry, asset managers may apply pressure for short-term results while acting as "loyal asset managers."[153] Accordingly, much of the impetus for such short-termist behaviour may be traced back to asset owners as they set the compensation and investment parameters in their contractual relationships with asset managers. Undeniably, the compensation structure of the asset management industry is varied. As observed by Professor John Kay, "[e]ach intermediary has its own remuneration structure and business model."[154] However, many asset managers are by and large compensated on a percentage of the assets under management (AUM), which consists of a performance and/or a fixed fee component.[155]

The fixed fee portion of asset manager compensation generally ranges from 0.01 to 2.0% of the value of the AUM, with fees on the higher end being paid for more actively managed funds.[156] Asset manager compensation may also include performance fees calculated as a percentage of the investment profits of the AUM. This method of compensation is typical of the hedge fund industry, which often has a '2 and 20' model, meaning that the hedge fund receives a 2% fixed fee, and performance fee of 20% of the profits generated on AUM.[157] These compensation structures reward returns to the asset owners, and may cause asset managers to forgo longer term investments in favour of identifying listed companies with short-term profitability. This may manifest as short-term trading and asset re-allocation by asset managers meant to maximize short-term performance numbers, which has the added benefit of generating fees.[158]

[153] Dallas and Barry (2016, 562).

[154] Kay (2012, 34).

[155] Standard asset management fees are generally a small percentage (e.g. 2%) on the asset value, and a larger percentage (e.g. 20%) on the annual performance of the assets (Garratt and Hamilton 2016, 799).

[156] Investopedia. Online: http://www.investopedia.com/terms/m/managementfee.asp and Maton (2016).

[157] Investopedia. Online: http://www.investopedia.com/terms/p/performance-fee.asp.

[158] Garratt and Hamilton (2016, 794), where the authors discuss the self-interest of asset managers and their payment structures which incentivize short-term trading and asset re-allocation activity.

Such short-termist behaviour by asset managers may not be well aligned with the long-term interests of asset owners, and the ultimate investors that asset managers are supposed to serve. Therefore, the possible amplifying impact of asset managers and the agency implications should be considered in SMST reform efforts, particularly around ensuring that asset manager compensation and investment parameters matches the investment objectives of their asset owner clients. However, such SMST-driven reforms directed at asset managers will need to be implemented in conjunction with reform efforts meant to nudge asset owners away from their current preference for short-term returns.

2. *Other Intermediaries*

It is also worth briefly considering possible transmission mechanisms of SMST concerns into listed companies by other intermediaries in the equity ownership chain, namely depositaries and proxy advisors. As mentioned in Chapter 2,[159] the argument has been raised that the complexity of this intermediary heavy ownership structure, where shares are not held directly by investors, raises SMST concerns. Further concerns have also been raised about proxy advisors not fully considering the long-term interests of investors. However, as argued in further details below, although regulatory and financial industry reforms may be justified to the depository and proxy advisory process generally, the links to a SMST issue are tenuous and such reform is not justified on this basis alone.

As discussed in Chapter 2,[160] listed companies shares are usually registered in the name of a central depositary—CREST in the UK, Euroclear in the EU, and Cede & Co in the US—and held in nominee accounts rather than directly in the name of an asset manager or asset owner. Theoretically, this type of intermediary should be neutral in the relationship between asset owners, asset managers and listed companies and they should just act as a flow-through mechanism. Further, in the digital age, company disclosure and voting information may be provided directly or made accessible to asset owners, although there will still need to be a reconciliation of beneficial shareholdings with the depositary.

[159] See Chapter 2, Sect. C.

[160] See Chapter 2, Sect. C.2.

The precise SMST concern related to central depositaries is unclear but centers on how the complexity of share ownership impedes engagement with listed companies by asset owners interested in long-term value. In particular, asset owners may have difficulty accessing or receiving information about the long-term projects of listed companies given that such information needs to flow through complex equity ownership chains.[161] These difficulties in communication could also be related to the causes of SMST originating from asset owners and asset managers discussed in Chapter 5, as the disconnection between asset owners and listed companies may increase the excessive discounting of future returns of such listed companies by asset owners. As they are unable to determine the value of long-term projects and effectively monitor such projects, in part due to this complexity of share ownership, asset owners may apply large discounts to future returns and instead prioritize shorter-term financial returns.

These links to SMST and central depositaries are theoretical and tenuous at best. Further, the argument could be made that such complexity may have the opposite effect and could mute short-term pressures placed on company managers by asset owners. Consequently, the focus of financial industry and regulatory reform to the depository process should arguably be guided by improving and simplifying information flows generally in order to increase market efficiency rather than any specific SMST concerns. Given this conclusion, depositaries, although certainly an important part of the equity ownership chain, are not considered further in this book in the context of SMST-related reforms.

As discussed in Chapter 2,[162] proxy advisors are also argued to be part of the SMST problem. The main concern raised is that investment decisions are often essentially outsourced to third party proxy advisory firms, such as Institutional Shareholder Services (ISS) and Glass Lewis & Co in the US. Asset owners and asset managers, particularly with investments outside of their home markets, tend to rely heavily on the recommendations of these proxy advisors.[163] There are without a doubt concerns about the proxy advisory process, including around transparency on how recommendations are made and how conflicts of interest are disclosed given that proxy advisors may also act for listed companies and advise on

[161] Kay (2012, 84).

[162] See Chapter 2, Sect. C.2.

[163] European Union Green Paper (2011, 14) and Nathan (2015).

specific proposed shareholder resolutions.[164] Chief Justice Leo Strine has also argued that the proxy advisory process needs to be more transparent so that investors can determine if the recommendation made takes into account an investor's longer-term interests, and there should be significantly less reliance by investors generally on proxy advisor recommendations.[165] These concerns surely should be addressed given the importance of the role of proxy advisors, as there is considerable reliance on proxy advice by asset owners/managers.[166] However, it is not at all clear to see how the voting recommendations of proxy advisors contribute to the SMST concerns discussed in Chapter 5. Without such a link, SMST should not be used as a driver for reforms to the proxy advisory process.

As set out in this chapter, the SMST issue appears to be transmitted into listed companies primarily via share pricing, and more particularly through company manager concerns around the implications of reductions to share prices. Although activist investors have been a lightning rod for SMST concerns, it seems most probable that the preferences for the certainty of short-term financial returns exhibited by a wide range of asset owners are the driving cause of the SMST problem. The short-term interests of such asset owners, arguably intensified by asset managers who act in their clients' interests, are then transmitted inside the listed company by the equity-based compensation packages of company managers, and certain corporate governance and legal mechanisms which give the board the ability to change senior management and asset owners the ability to change the board, which in turn may facilitate change in senior management of listed companies. The response of company managers to this short-term preference is to prioritize short-term financial returns and/or engage in non-fraudulent earnings management in an effort to keep share prices consistent or on an upward trend temporarily. Consequently, any remedy to the SMST issue requires either addressing the issues around share pricing or cutting off transmission mechanisms. However, before considering the conceptual effectiveness of SMST reforms on this basis, Chapter 7 first assesses if the preference for short-term financial returns and/or non-fraudulent earnings management has had a harmful effect.

[164] European Union Green Paper (2011, 14).

[165] Strine (2015, 24).

[166] Tonello (2012).

References

Allaire, Yvon and Dauphin, Francois. 2015. "Hedge Fund Activism: Preliminary Results and Some New Empirical Evidence." 1 April. Institute for Governance of Public and Private Corporations.

Aspen Institute. 2009. "Overcoming Short-Termism: A Call for a More Responsible Approach to Investment and Business Management." 9 September.

Bachelder, Joseph E. 2014. "What Has Happened to Stock Options?" 2 October. *Harvard Law School Forum on Corporate Governance and Financial Regulation*. https://corpgov.law.harvard.edu/2014/10/02/what-has-happened-to-stock-options/.

Barton, Dominic. 2011. "Capitalism for the Long Term." March. *Harvard Business Review*. 84–90.

Barty, James and Jones, Ben. 2012. *Executive Compensation: Rewards for Success Not Failure*. July. Policy Exchange.

Bebchuk, Lucien, Brav, Alan, and Wei, Jiang. 2015. "The Long-Term Effects of Hedge Fund Activism." 115:5 *Columbia Law Review*. 1085–1156.

Becht, Marco, Franks, Julian, Grant, Jeremy, and Wagner, Hammes F. 2015. "The Returns to Hedge Fund Activism: An International Study." 15 March. Center for Economic Policy Research Discussion Paper No. 10507. http://ssrn.com/abstract=2376271.

Bettis, J. Carr, Bizjak, John M., Coles, Jeffrey L., and Kalpathy, Swaminathan L. 2018. "Performance-Vesting Provisions in Executive Compensation." 25 April. http://dx.doi.org/10.2139/ssrn.2289566.

"BlackRock's Fink Urges CEOs to Focus Capital on Long-Term Growth." 26 March 2014. Investment News. https://www.investmentnews.com/article/20140326/free/140329929/blackrocks-fink-urges-ceos-to-focus-capital-on-long-term-growth.

Bos, Sebastian, Pendleton, Andrew, and Toms, Steve. 2013. "Earnings Management in the UK: Managerial Share Ownership, Minority Shareholder Protection and Discretionary Accruals." 14 January. https://ssrn.com/abstract=1747919.

Brav, Alon, Harvey, Campbell R., Graham, John R., and Michaely, Roni. 2005. "Payout Policy in the 21st Century." November. Tuck Contemporary Corporate Finance Issues III Conference Paper. https://ssrn.com/abstract=571046.

Brochet, Francois, Serafeim, George, and Loumioti, Maria. 2012. "Short-Termism: Don't Blame Investors." June. *Harvard Business Review*. 28.

Brown, J. Robert. 2014. "Delaware Law and the Right of Shareholders to Call Special Meetings." 13 August. *TheRacetotheBottom.org*. http://www.theracetothebottom.org/home/delaware-law-and-the-right-of-shareholders-to-call-special-m.html.

Chen, Xia, Harford, Jarrad, and Li, Kai. 2007. "Monitoring: Which Institutions Matter." November. 86:2 *Journal of Financial Economics*. 279–305.

Coffee, John C., Jr. and Palia, Darius. 2015. "The Wolf at the Door: The Impact of Hedge Fund Activism: Evidence and Implications." 4 September. Working Paper No. 521. http://wlrk.com/docs/The_Wolf_at_the_Door_The_Impact_of_Hedge_Fund_Activism_on_Corporate_Governance.pdf.

Cremers, K. J. Martijn, Pareek, Ankur, and Sautner, Zacharias. 2019. "Short-Term Investors, Long-Term Investments, and Firm Value: Evidence from Russell 2000 Index Inclusions." 26 March. https://ssrn.com/abstract=2720248.

Dallas, Lynne L. 2012. "Short-Termism, the Financial Crisis, and Corporate Governance." 2011–2012. 37:2 *The Journal of Corporation Law.* 265–364.

Dallas, Lynne L. and Barry, Jordan. 2016. "Long-Term Shareholders and Time-Phased Voting." 40:2 *Delaware Journal of Corporate Law* 541–646.

Davies, Richard, Haldane, Andrew G., Nielsen, Mette, and Pezzini, Silvia. 2014. "Measuring the Costs of Short-Termism." 12 *Journal of Financial Stability.* 16–25.

Dawson, Nick. 2017. "LTIP-ing Point: Is This the End of Long-Term Incentive Plans?" 12 May. *Harvard Law School Forum on Corporate Governance and Financial Regulation.* https://corpgov.law.harvard.edu/2017/05/12/ltip-ing-point-is-this-the-end-of-long-term-incentive-plans/.

Denning, Steven. 2013. "The Origin of the 'World's Dumbest Idea': Milton Friedman." 26 June. *Forbes.* https://www.forbes.com/sites/stevedenning/2013/06/26/the-origin-of-the-worlds-dumbest-idea-milton-friedman/#6d58c973870e.

Denning, Steve. 2014. "Why Can't We End Short-Termism." 22 July. *Forbes.* https://www.forbes.com/sites/stevedenning/2014/07/22/why-cant-we-solve-the-problem-of-short-termism/#45c7ba7b3376.

Denning. Steve. 2017. "Resisting the Lure of Short-Termism: Kill 'The World's Dumbest Idea'." 8 January. *Forbes.* https://www.forbes.com/sites/stevedenning/2017/01/08/resisting-the-lure-of-short-termism-how-to-achieve-long-term-growth/#1d2287451ca0.

Dent, George. 2010. "Essential Unity of Shareholders and the Myth of Investor Short-Termism." 35:1 *Delaware Journal of Corporate Law.* 97–150.

Dichev, Ilia, Graham, John, Harvey, Campbell R, and Shiva, Rajgopal. 2016. "The Misrepresentation of Earnings." 2016. 72:1 *Financial Analysts Journal.* 22–35.

Easterbrook, Frank H. and Fischel, Daniel R. 1981. "The Proper Role of a Target's Management in Responding to a Tender Offer." April. 94:6 *Harvard Law Review.* 1161–1204.

European Union Green Paper. 2011. "The EU Corporate Governance Framework." COM (2011)164. 5 April.

Ferris, Robert. 2017. "GM Shareholders Overwhelmingly Defeat Greenlight' Proposal." 6 June 2017. *CNBC.* http://www.cnbc.com/2017/06/06/general-motors-defeats-greenlight-capitals-board-nominations-and-stock-plan-proposal.html.

Fisman, Raymond J., Khurana, Rakesh, and Rhodes-Kropf, Matthew. 2005. "Governance and CEO Turnover: Do Something or Do the Right Thing?" January. EFA 2005 Moscow Meetings Paper. https://ssrn.com/abstract=656085 or http://dx.doi.org/10.2139/ssrn.656085.

Flaherty, Michael. 2016. "Starboard Launches Proxy Fight to Remove Entire Yahoo Board." 29 March. *Reuters*. http://www.reuters.com/article/us-yahoo-starboard-proxy-idUSKCN0WQ0D7.

Foley, Stephen. 2017. "Einhorn Drives Proxy Battle for 4 Seats on GM Board." 28 March. *Financial Times*. https://www.ft.com/content/c74171d5-698d-37a7-a6b4-2019ae30054a?mhq5j=e1.

Frankl, J. and Balet, S. 2017. "The Rise of Settled Proxy Fights." 22 March. *Harvard Law School Forum on Corporate Governance and Financial Regulation*. https://corpgov.law.harvard.edu/2017/03/22/the-rise-of-settled-proxy-fights/.

Fried, Jesse M. 2015. "The Uneasy Case for Favoring Long-Term Shareholders." 124 *The Yale Law Journal*. 1554–1628.

Friedman, Milton. 1970. "The Social Responsibility of Business Is to Increase Its Profits." 13 September. *New York Times*. https://www.colorado.edu/studentgroups/libertarians/issues/friedman-soc-resp-business.html.

Garratt, T. and Hamilton, K. 2016. "The Loneliness of The Long-Term Investor: A Comment on Patience in Practice." 14:4 *Socio-Economic Review*. 789–806.

Gaspar, Jose Miguel, Massa, Massimo, and Matos, Pedro. 2005. "Shareholder Investment Horizons and the Market for Corporate Control." April. 76:1 *Journal of Financial Economics*. 135–165.

Gilson, Ronald J. and Gordon, Jeffrey N. 2013. "The Agency Costs of Agency Capitalism: Activist Investors and the Revaluation of Governance Rights." January. 113 *Columbia Law Review*. 863–928.

"Global Activism on the Rise." 4 October 2016. FTI Consulting. http://fticommunications.com/2016/10/global-activism-rise/.

Graham, John R., Cam, Harvey, and Shiva, Rajgopal. 2005. "The Economic Implications of Corporate Financial Reporting." December. 40 *Journal of Accounting and Economics*. 3–73.

Graham, John R., Cam, Harvey, and Shiva, Rajgopal. 2006. "Value Destruction and Financial Reporting Decisions." 62 *Financial Analysts Journal*. 27–39.

Guerrara, Francesco. 2009. "Welch Condemns Share Price Focus." 12 March. *Financial Times*.

Hay Group Inc., Summary Report. 2014. "Top Executive Compensation in Europe 2014."

Hsieh, Peggy, Koller, Timothy, and Rajan, S. R. 2016. "The Misguided Practice of Earnings Guidance." March. *McKinsey & Company, Strategy and Corporate Finance*. https://www.mckinsey.com/business-functions/strategy-and-corporate-finance/our-insights/the-misguided-practice-of-earnings-guidance.

Jensen, Michael C. 2010. "Value Maximization, Stakeholder Theory, and the Corporate Objective Function." 22:1 *Journal of Applied Corporate Finance*. 32–42.

Jenter, Dirk and Lewellen, Katharina. 2017. "Performance-Induced CEO Turnover." 27 July. http://dx.doi.org/10.2139/ssrn.1570635.

Kay, John. 2012. 'The Kay Review of UK Equity Markets and Long-Term Decision Making." Final Report. July.

Koller, Timothy. 1994. "What Is Value-Based Management?" August. *McKinsey Quarterly*. http://www.mckinsey.com/business-functions/strategy-and-corporate-finance/our-insights/what-is-value-based-management.

Kothuis, Hans and Chua, Jiawen. 2014. "Executive Compensation in Asia—Best Practices in a Dynamic Environment' Mercer LLC." https://www.mercer.com/content/dam/mercer/attachments/asia-pacific/asia/Mercer_Executive_Compensation_in_Asia_Best_Practices_10525A-HC.pdf.

Larkin, Yelena, Leary, Mark T., and Michealy. Roni. 2017. "Do Investors Value Dividend-Smoothing Differently." December. 63:12 *Management Science*. 3999–4446.

Lee, Wendy. 2016. "Yahoo Settles with Starboard, Avoiding Messy Proxy Fight." 27 April. *San Francisco Gate*. http://www.sfgate.com/business/article/Yahoo-settles-with-Starboard-7378599.php.

Lipton, Martin. 1979. "Takeover Bids in the Target Boardroom." November. 35 *The Business Lawyer*. 101–134.

Lipton, Martin. 2015. "The Threat to the Economy and Society from Activism and Short-Termism Updated." 27 January. *Harvard Law School Forum on Corporate Governance and Financial Regulation*. https://corpgov.law.harvard.edu/2015/01/27/the-threat-to-the-economy-and-society-from-activism-and-short-termism-updated/.

Martin, Roger. 2015. "Yes, Short-Termism Really Is a Problem." 9 October. *Harvard Business Review*. 2–7.

Maton, Brendan. 2016. "Asset Management Fees: What Is the Going Rate?" March. *IPE*. https://www.ipe.com/investment/asset-management-fees-whats-the-going-rate/10012128.fullarticle.

Matsumoto, Dawn A. 2002. "Management's Incentives to Avoid Negative Earnings Surprises." July. 77:3 *The Accounting Review*. 483–514.

Mergenthaler, R. D., Rajgopal, S., and Srinivasan, S. 2011. "CEO and CFO Career Penalities to Missing Quarterly Analysts Forecasts." Working paper, University of Iowa.

Millstein, Ira. 2005. "When Earnings Management Becomes Cooking the Books." 26 May. *Financial Times*.

Moore, Marc T. and Petrin, Martin. 2017. *Corporate Governance: Law, Regulation and Theory*. Palgrave Corporate and Financial Law: London, UK.

Moore, Marc T. and Walker-Arnott, Edward. 2014. "A Fresh Look at Stock Market Short-Termism." 41:3 *Journal of Law and Society*. 416–445.

Nathan, Charles. 2015. "Observations on Short-Termism and Long-Termism." 12 October. *Harvard Law School Forum on Corporate Governance and Financial Regulation*. https://corpgov.law.harvard.edu/2015/10/12/observations-on-short-termism-and-long-termism/.

Phillips, Robert A., Freeman, R. Edward, and Wicks, Andrew. 2003. "What Stakeholder Theory Is Not." 13:4 *Business Ethics Quarterly*. 479–502.

Pozen, Robert C. 2015. "Institutional Investors and Corporate Short-Termism." 24 August. *Harvard Law School Forum on Corporate Governance and Financial Regulation*. https://corpgov.law.harvard.edu/2015/08/24/institutional-investors-and-corporate-short-termism/.

Rappaport, Alfred. 1986. *Creating Shareholder Value: The New Standard for Business Performance*. Free Press: New York.

Rappaport, Alfred. 1998. *Creating Shareholder Value: A Guide for Managers and Investors*. Free Press: New York.

Rappaport, Alfred. 2011. *Saving Capitalism from Short-Termism: How to Build Long-Term Value and Take Back our Financial Future*. McGraw-Hill: New York.

Reland, Jacques. 2009. "The Dangers of the Cult of Shareholder Value in Reforming the City: Responses to the Global Financial Crisis." *London Forum Press*. http://www.academia.edu/923008/The_Dangers_of_the_Cult_of_Shareholder_Value.

Rieg, Robert. 2015. "Dynamics of Value-Based Management: Does Shareholder Value Cause Short-Termism?" August. 26:2/3 *Journal of Management Control*. 193–224.

Roach, Garnet. 2013. "Less Than 10 Percent of FTSE 100 Forms Provide Quantitative EPS Guidance." 21 February. *IR Magazine*. https://www.irmagazine.com/articles/earnings-calls-financial-reporting/19328/ftse-100-shuns-us-style-earnings-guidance/.

Roe, Mark J. 2013. "Corporate Short-Termism—In the Boardroom and in the Courtroom." August. 68 *Business Lawyer*. 977–1006.

Schnitzer, Maria. 1997. "Short-Termism and the Market for Corporate Control." 36–58. In Picot, A. and Schlicht, E. (eds.). *Firms, Markets, and Contracts: Contributions to Economics*. Physica-Verlag: Heidelberg, Germany.

Shapiro, Susan P. 2005. "Agency Theory." 31 *Annual Review of Sociology*. 275–284.

Sorkin, Andrew Ross. 2015. "Activists May Be Less Myopic That Their Reputation Suggests." 4 November. *New York Times*.

Squire, Ken. 2014. "Are Activists Short-Term Investors: No More Than Mutual Funds." 28 May. *FA Magazine*. http://www.fa-mag.com/news/are-activists-short-term-investors—no-more-so-than-mutual-funds-18123.htmland.

Strine, Leo E., Jr. 2015. "Securing Our Nation's Economic Future: A Sensible, Nonpartisan Agenda to Increase Long-Term Investment and Job Creation in The United States." University of Pennsylvania Institute for Law & Economics Research Paper No. 15-41.

Tonello, Matteo. 2012. "The Influence of Proxy Advisory Firm Voting Recommendations." 8 April. *Harvard Law School Forum on Corporate Governance and Financial Regulation*. https://corpgov.law.harvard.edu/2012/04/08/the-influence-of-proxy-advisory-firm-voting-recommendations/.

Tonello, Matteo. 2015. "CEO and Executive Compensation Practices: 2015 Edition." 15 September. *Harvard Law School Forum on Corporate Governance and Financial Regulation*. https://corpgov.law.harvard.edu/2015/09/15/ceo-and-executive-compensation-practices-2015-edition/

Trustee Leadership Forum for Retirement Security. 2016. "A Note on Short-Termism." The Initiative for Responsible Investment. http://iri.hks.harvard.edu/files/iri/files/tlf-note-on-long-term-investing.pdf.

Vlastelica, Ryan. 2017. "S&P 500 Dividend Payouts Hit a Record in the Third Quarter." 3 October. *MarketWatch*. https://www.marketwatch.com/story/sp-500-dividend-payouts-hit-a-record-in-the-third-quarter-2017–10-03.

Woolley, Paul. 2010. "Chapter 3: Why Are Financial Markets so Inefficient and Exploitative—And a Suggested Remedy." In The Future of Finance: The LSE Report.

CHAPTER 7

What Are the Harms of Short-Termism?

But where is the harm from short-termism?—so what if a listed company's shares are unduly high, or if there is pressure on management of listed companies to keep share prices up or pay-back cash rather than re-investing in the business? Similarly, why does it matter if company managers are consistently saying that they prioritize short-term returns? As observed by Harvard Law School professor Jesse Fried, "[t]he question … is not whether short-termism can exist, but rather: how bad is it?"[1] 'Bad' is obviously a relative term. Academics Gregory Jackson and Anastasia Petraki—after concluding, rather optimistically, that researchers agree generally that short-termism is a preference for strategies that add less value but have an earlier payoff—add specificity to this question by observing that "[i]t is hard to establish whether short-term decisions are actually detrimental to long-term value creation."[2] Given the nature of short-termism as a social process whereby short-termist behaviour is reinforced by the actions of others through a complex system of incentives, they say, it is very hard to measure the effects of short-termism.[3] Consequently, Jackson and Petraki suggest that short-termism will be difficult to address through simple policy instruments aimed at one group of stakeholders.[4]

[1] Fried (2015, 1569).

[2] Jackson and Petraki (2011, 5).

[3] Ibid.

[4] Ibid.

K. M. Willey, *Stock Market Short-Termism*,
https://doi.org/10.1007/978-3-030-22903-0_7

The stock market is also a complex adaptive system, and we may fall afoul of the 'micro-macro' problem by attempting to understand the issue by only looking at one part.[5] Michael Mauboussin and Dan Callahan, financial strategists with Credit Suisse, noted that this concept is best encapsulated by Phil Anderson, a physicist who won the Nobel Prize and claimed quite simply that "more is different."[6] More precisely, the micro-macro problem holds that "[co]mplex adaptive systems generally have properties and features that are difficult to predict by examining the individual agents."[7] The argument can be made, therefore, that stock market short-termism (SMST) may produce negative consequences for individual firms or company managers, but this is not indicative of a broader market failure. Conversely, SMST may "not necessarily be negative for a single investor or manager, since an individual can gain from it in the short run while transferring the burden to others in the short or long run."[8] Mauboussin and Callahan went on to argue that "if you want to assess and evaluate the impact of short-termism, the right level of analysis is not what individuals say but rather what the stock market does."[9] Thus, it may be difficult to measure the harms of SMST, but there should at least be some broad demonstrable harm connected to the SMST problem in order to justify reform.

As illustrated in Fig. 1, numerous harms caused by the SMST issue have been articulated. This chapter summarizes the research that has been conducted to demonstrate the harms of SMST into four salient—albeit potentially overlapping—categories. These four core categories are:

1. reduced firm productivity,
2. reduced trust in the stock market,
3. societal costs,[10] and
4. wealth transfer from future to current asset owners.

[5] Mauboussin and Callahan (2015, 72).

[6] Ibid., 71, referencing Anderson (1972).

[7] Ibid., 71.

[8] Rieg (2015, 212).

[9] Ibid.

[10] Admittedly, any of the four categories could validly be defined as 'societal costs.' However, the term 'societal costs' is used here to mean the implications of certain negative behaviours of company managers allegedly connected to SMST and the impacts of SMST on sustainability generally. These negative behaviours of corporate managers include excessive risk-taking, corporate greed, fraud and disregard for, or harm to, the interests of other stakeholders of the listed company, including environmental interests.

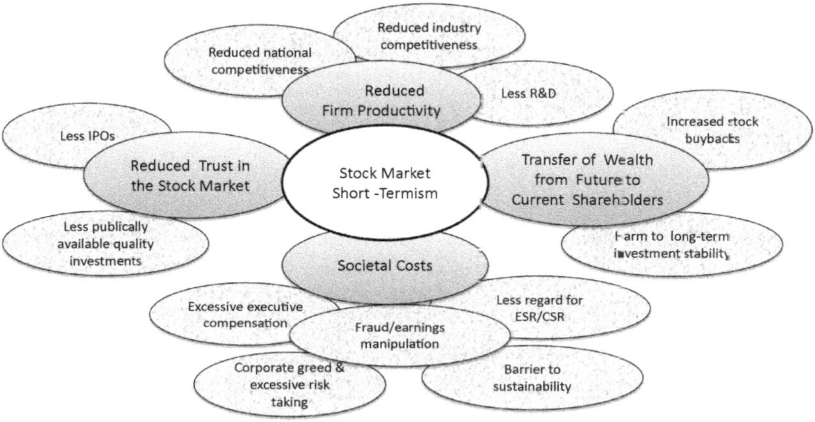

Fig. 1 Alleged harms of SMST

In considering this research on the harms of SMST, this chapter assesses the strength of the arguments made and the evidence provided in support of each of these four categories. Based on an assessment of the research in each category, each of the arguments of (1) reduced firm productivity, and (2) societal costs, are rejected as a sufficiently viable basis justifying SMST-driven reform. Though significant questions remain around the evidence presented in support of the arguments (3) reduced trust in the stock market, and (4) wealth transfer from future to current asset owners, these categories are the most probable areas of harm from SMST.

A. Reduced Firm Productivity

A frequent allegation made by those arguing that short-termism is problematic, is that SMST reduces listed company productivity, and by extension, industry and national productivity.[11] If the allegation that SMST is contributing to under-investment in research and development (R&D), and thereby reducing corporate productivity, is substantiated it would be

[11] See the Mason (2015) and Lazonick (2014), discussing the impact of short-termism on economy activity in the United States (US), and Hughes (2014) (Hughes Report) for similar analysis in the United Kingdom (UK).

a compelling basis for regulatory reform. Accordingly, the allegation that SMST impacts productivity is considered first in this chapter. The impact of SMST on productivity is primarily considered through an analysis of spending on R&D. However, as demonstrated by the analysis below, using R&D statistics alone as an evidentiary basis for SMST-driven reform does not seem justified, as R&D appears irrelevant to the SMST discussion. Even if R&D is relevant, the results of the impact of SMST, as considered below, are ambiguous. Consequently, overall productivity measures may be a more useful indicator of a SMST problem. However, it will be difficult, if not impossible, to even roughly isolate how SMST impacts overall firm, industry or national productivity.[12]

R&D spending is a particular focus for SMST analysis as R&D projects commonly have upfront costs, and returns are more heavily concentrated at the end of their life cycle.[13] The problem, it was asserted by the Aspen Institute, for example, is that "[t]o show short-term profits, public companies increasingly defer investments in market research, product design, or prototype development."[14] To back up this assertion, the Aspen Institute referred to a survey of chief executive officers (CEOs), the results of which survey indicated that "80 percent will cut discretionary spending – for R&D, maintenance, advertising, etcetera – to avoid missing a quarterly forecast."[15] The Aspen Institute went on to argue that "potential systemic underinvestment in R&D will lead to long-term challenges to U.S. competitiveness."[16]

But is this short-termist perspective of company managers actually impacting long-term investment by listed companies? Some evidence has been presented that it is. For example, in the United Kingdom (UK), the UK Government commissioned a report from Professor Alan Hughes, which report built on the conclusions of the Kay Review[17] and was

[12] Graham et al. (2005, 4).

[13] Hughes (2014, 11).

[14] Aspen Institute (2010, 1).

[15] Ibid., 2, referring to a survey conducted by Graham et al. (2005), which was updated and enhanced in Graham et al (2006), of 401 senior financial executives and in-depth interviews with an additional 22 executives which concluded that the destruction of shareholder value through legal means is a persuasive, if not routine way of doing business.

[16] Ibid.

[17] Kay (2012) (Kay Review).

designed to assess the extent to which business decision making in the UK was affected by "short-termism."[18] The Hughes Report concluded that for the period from 1999 to 2010 there was a fall in the ratio of business expenditures on R&D relative to gross domestic product (GDP), and that the UK was at the lower end of the international spectrum in the ratio of overall gross expenditure R&D to GDP.[19]

The Hughes Report also observed that the UK had a relatively high dependence on overseas funding, and, therefore, the UK was characterized by a very high reliance on the performance of R&D in the UK by foreign owned businesses.[20] Accordingly, the Hughes Report concluded that "[i]f US businesses and investors are subject to similar short-term pressures as UK investors and boards, this will reinforce any such tendencies which exist in the UK and vice versa if stock market strength enhances radical long-term innovation."[21] Thus, the R&D numbers in the UK may be concerning.[22] However, the situation is much murkier in the United States (US).

In the US, general statements have been made on the negative state of the economy, in particular as it relates to national productivity growth. Recently, Jamie Dimon, JPMorgan Chase Chairman and CEO, noted in his 2017 annual report to shareholders that "it is clear something is wrong – and it is holding us back."[23] In support of this claim, Mr. Dixon observed that the US "economy has been growing much more slowly in the last decade or two than in the 50 years before then…[f]rom 1948 to 2000, real per capita GDP grew 2.3%; from 2000 to 2016, it grew 1%."[24] However, the main proxy used to measure the SMST problem, R&D expenditures, does not appear to match this assertion re GDP growth.

[18] Hughes (2014).

[19] Ibid., 8.

[20] Ibid., 8–9.

[21] Ibid., 9.

[22] See Tovey (2015) which notes that R&D in 2014 was up 5% from the prior year, but remained constant at 1.1% of GDP, considerably lower than other nations.

[23] CEO Letter to Shareholders, J. P. Morgan Chase (4 April 2017), 32. Online: https://www.jpmorganchase.com/corporate/investor-relations/document/ar2016-ceolettershareholders.pdf.

[24] Ibid.

As adeptly pointed out by James Surowiecki in *The New Yorker*, it has been shown that as a whole in the US, "corporate spending on R&D has risen steadily over the years and has stayed relatively constant as a share of GDP and as a share of sales."[25] A pertinent question has been raised; if SMST is a real problem, "what explains the fact that businesses are investing so much in research and development?"[26] It could be that R&D has just not been measured correctly in the US. Other measures show that the real growth of business investment in the US has actually slowed since 2000, which is perplexing as corporate profits having been rising during this period and borrowing costs are at historic lows.[27]

However, even if R&D expenditures are falling in the UK, and productivity measures in the US raise concerns, the link to the SMST issue as a cause or contributing factor has not been convincingly demonstrated. It is possible that today's economy just does not have the capacity for growth as was seen in earlier times. Professor John Kay raised this point in the Kay Review with regards to the UK's perceived declining competitiveness. Kay commented that "[p]erhaps there were few good opportunities for British companies to invest – fewer opportunities than those available to their industry competitors based in other countries."[28] Counter to this argument, it has been argued that "[w]hile R&D is a useful proxy of long-term orientation, this measure is incomplete."[29]

The argument has been made that in many businesses R&D is the focal point of their ongoing operation, and therefore "it is unlikely that managers would choose to reduce it in favour of other investments with faster and more certain payoff."[30] Businesses may instead make other negative short-term decisions. Such "[o]ther long-term drivers of value may not be picked up (e.g. employee skills, corporate reputation, etc.), and these investments may be at least equally relevant."[31] Further, it is argued that, "...the salience of R&D as a key measure may differ across

[25] Surowiecki (2015).

[26] Zandi (2015).

[27] Jarsulic et al. (2015).

[28] Kay (2012, 15).

[29] Jackson and Petraki (2011, 19).

[30] Ibid.

[31] Ibid.

different types of firms and industries."[32] Therefore, using R&D statistics alone as an evidentiary basis for SMST-driven reform does not seem justified. Overall productivity measures may be a more useful indicator of a SMST problem. However, it will be difficult, if not impossible, to directly isolate how SMST impacts overall firm, industry or national productivity. Consequently, neither R&D nor productivity numbers alone convincingly evidence a macro problem necessitating SMST-driven reform.

B. Reduced Trust in the Stock Market

A central theme in the Kay Review was on restoring trust and confidence in UK financial markets.[33] Although certainly not the only cause, Kay suggested that SMST was contributing to the erosion of trust and confidence in the UK stock markets.[34] Kay alleged that this was because "companies' expectations of the quantum of future earnings they will have to allocate to meet the needs of prospective new shareholders – their view of the cost of capital – differed substantially from the perceptions of these prospective shareholders of the likely value of these earnings to them – their view of the return on capital."[35] Kay went on to attribute this divergence to the "increased distance between companies and savers which results from the lengthening of the chain of intermediation, and the growth in complexity of the modern corporation."[36]

The basic argument is that this wide divergence on capital costs caused in part by SMST—i.e. excessive discounting by investors of longer-term investments by listed companies contributes to stock markets being an unattractive option for many businesses. This section considers the evidence presented showing that SMST is contributing to reduced trust in the stock market primarily evidenced by a reduction in initial public offerings (IPOs) and an increase in companies opting out of public market structures. Counter-arguments to this interpretation are also considered. The conclusion reached is that although the evidence is

[32] Ibid.

[33] Kay (2012, 5).

[34] Ibid.

[35] Ibid., 26.

[36] Ibid.

not definitive, there is sufficient substance to conclude that SMST is—or has the potential to—undermine confidence in the stock market, and this problematic perception is worth addressing.

1. *Reduced IPOs*

Kay referred to evidence that primary equity issuances in the UK have declined.[37] Similar figures have been offered in the US. US IPOs have declined generally followed a downward trend from 486 IPOs per year in 1999 to 160 IPOs per year in 2017.[38] Concerns about SMST—along with costs, market volatility and litigation risks—have been expressly cited as a reason that European, Asian and North American companies have reservations about undertaking an IPO.[39] Anecdotal evidence indicates that that public market listings are not particularly desirable. A technology analyst stated that "every other software CEO I speak with has little or no interest in the capital markets…the way markets operate are of little value to a company that has a strong customer base, cash flow and even in some cases, profitability."[40]

The problem with the allegation that SMST is contributing to fewer IPOs is that global market launches appear to be flourishing.[41] However, this abundance does not necessarily equate to quality, and also is questionable given that the overall the number of US public companies has declined—from a peak of about 8000 in 1999 to approximately 4000 in 2017.[42] Foreign companies listed on the US stock exchanges have increased slightly during this period—from approximately 800 in 2000 to 873 in 2017, although this increase is not significant enough to offset the reduction in domestic listings. It does not appear that this gap

[37] Kay (2012, 24).

[38] "Number of IPOs in the United States from 1999 to 2017." *Statista*. Online: https://www.statista.com/statistics/270290/number-of-ipos-in-the-us-since-1999/.

[39] See Reid Smith and Merger Market Report, "Taking Stock: Going Public in Uncertain Times" (2016), where a survey of market participants indicated that short-termism of investors was a major reservation in going public.

[40] McNevin (2016).

[41] Wasik (2017) in which it is observed that although UK IPOs are down—likely largely due to Brexit uncertainty—'[t]here have been more fresh stock market listings globally than any other similar period since 2000, while the value of global IPOs for the same period has more than doubled compared to last year'.

[42] Ritholtz (2015) and Brorsen (2017).

is taken up elsewhere in the world, as total figures for listed companies globally have also declined during this period, albeit calculated on the basis of the number of listed companies per million people.[43]

This global decline in number of companies is broadly supported by declines in numbers of domestically listed companies in the 35 countries that have signed the Convention on the Organization for Economic Co-operation and Development (OECD)—which went from approximately 26,000 in 2005 to approximately 22,000 in 2016.[44] Although the number of companies and IPOs may be declining, the quantity of listed companies may not be the only relevant measure of a declining interest in capital markets. The increasing market value of listed companies in the US and globally is also significant.

The remaining public companies have grown in size. In the US, market value of listed companies relative to US GDP grew from 40% in the 1990s to almost 160% in 2016.[45] These numbers are reflected in OECD domestic listed companies with market value relative to GDP moving from approximately 60% in 1990 to 110% in 2015.[46] In total dollar terms, in the US for example, this means that the market value of 4000 domestic listed companies is now in excess of US$30 trillion.[47] This increased value does not mean that there are more investment options or demonstrate investor confidence in the market. Rather, wealth appears to have consolidated in fewer listed companies. The largest 1% of US public companies now represent 29% of the total market capitalization.[48] Further, about 140 companies now each exceed US$50 billion in market value, representing more than half of the total US market capitalization.[49] There may be issues around industry

[43] Number of Listed Companies for the World (1975–2015) FRED Economic Data Economic Research, Federal Reserve Bank of St Louis. Online: https://fred.stlouisfed.org/series/DDOM01USA644NWDB.

[44] Listed domestic companies, total (OECD countries), The World Bank. Online: https://data.worldbank.org/indicator/CM.MKT.LDOM.NO?locations=OE.

[45] Brorsen (2017).

[46] Market capitalization of listed domestic companies (% of GDP) (OECD countries), The World Bank. Online: https://data.worldbank.org/indicator/CM.MKT.LCAP.GD.ZS.

[47] Market capitalization of listed domestic companies (current US$) (United States), The World Bank. Online: https://data.worldbank.org/indicator/CM.MKT.LCAP.CD?locations=US.

[48] Brorsen (2017).

[49] Ibid.

consolidation as a result of this trend, although these concerns could be offset by robust competition laws. Other reasons for concern due to this consolidation could include issues around stock dispersion and the quality of the remaining stocks, which are considered in greater detail in Sect. B.3 below.

2. *Increased Going-Private Transactions and Use of Private Equity*

It could be argued that public-to-private buyouts, also known as 'leveraged buy-outs' or 'going-private transactions'—an acquisition strategy where private equity is used to acquire and de-list a company[50]—should be occurring at an increased rate if SMST is driving public companies from public markets. There is some evidence that going-private transactions have—with various notable dips including in 2009 as a result of the GFC—significantly increased in number and dollar value since the 1990s. In the US, for example, going-private transactions have gone from six deals valued at less than US$1 billion in 1995 to 328 deals valued at over US$300 billion in 2016.[51] Also, in the European Union (EU) generally, Bain Capital observed that the value of going-private merger and acquisition (M&A) transactions part way through 2017 was nearly €12bn, its highest level since 2007 and more than double each of the previous three years.[52] There is some anecdotal evidence that SMST is to blame for this increase.

Notable going-private transactions include Del and Tibco Software. Speaking on the decision to take Del private in 2013, Michael Dell stated, "I'd say we got it right…[p]rivatization has unleashed the passion of our team members who have the freedom to focus first on innovating for customers in a way that was not always possible when striving to meet the quarterly demands of Wall Street."[53] Echoing these sentiments, Tibco Software CEO Vivek Ranadive, when speaking about the decision to go private said that, "[t]he whole philosophy is not to think about the short term and focus on having a highly profitable long-term

[50] Renneboog and Vansteenkiste (2017, 3).

[51] Global Private Equity (2017, 2).

[52] Bower (2017).

[53] Dell (2014).

business."[54] Ranadive speculated that "I think there will be a large number of companies who will think answering to the Street is too much of a hassle and will decide to go private… I see this as an increasing trend."[55]

This could just be rhetoric, but when viewed together with the survey evidence discussed in Chapter 5 whereby CEOs express concerns about SMST,[56] it is suggestive that SMST is a contributing factor to less use of public market structures. It also appears that many companies are electing not to enter public markets at all due to SMST concerns, but rather pursuing financing through private equity routes.[57] Although the upward trend of private equity has not been consistent, 2017 looked to be a record high year since the global financial crisis (GFC) for private equity buy-outs generally in both the US[58] and the UK.[59] Evidence of going private activity and the increasing use of private equity ownership structures coupled with survey and anecdotal evidence may be indicative that SMST is contributing to a preference for non-public structures. If we accept that SMST is a contributing factor, the question remains as to if this trend is problematic.

3. *Are Less IPOs and More Going-Private Transactions/Private Equity a Problem?*

Even if IPOs are declining and there is an increase in non-public structures, the argument has been made that the slack caused in the public markets is taken up elsewhere in the financial markets. Harvard Professor Mark Roe posited that "[i]f the public markets are inducing a publicly held firm to be excessively short-term oriented…then private equity holders…could buy the company, take it off the public market, and reorient its business model toward the longer term."[60] Showing that this rebalancing occurs, Kay observed that "[t]he diminished importance of public equity markets as a source of new funds for business investment has been paralleled by a rise in private equity and in the use of corporate

[54] Qualtrough (2014).

[55] Ibid.

[56] See Chapter 5, Sect. A.1.

[57] See the discussion by Colvin (2017).

[58] Espinoza (2017).

[59] Wastell (2017).

[60] Roe (2013, 987–988).

debt."[61] This may be so, and stock markets may no longer be the important source of capital for business investments that they once were.[62] Further, it could be argued that stock markets are only a by-product of a healthy economy and may no longer be relevant if sufficient capital can be raised privately. However, robust public markets continue to be important for many reasons.

As considered in Chapter 2,[63] well-functioning stock markets may reduce investing risk by providing liquidity for asset owners and asset managers,[64] be viable exit options for founders, and also serve as important bench marks for valuations of businesses in the private sector.[65] More research is required to explore the impact of the stock market on non-public companies, but the interconnectedness of public and non-public entities is considerable. Liquid and robust stock markets are an important part of a healthy financial system. Consequently, SMST should not be discounted just because some of its effects may be ameliorated in the capital markets as a whole. But what exactly are the problems created by fewer IPOs, an increase in going-private transactions and the use of private equity, caused perhaps in part by SMST? Rather than being harmful, is this consolidation indicative of market efficiency and maturity? The main harms hypothesized are concerns about access and quality in the remaining listings, including a 'lemons problem.'

a. Access Issues

The argument made is that the reliance on private capital has made it harder for investors to get exposure to younger companies that would have otherwise listed on a stock exchange more quickly.[66] For example, in 1997, Amazon went public as a small-cap stock and has since

[61] Kay (2012, 25).

[62] Ibid., 22, where Kay observes that "[e]quity markets have not been an important source of capital for new investment in British business for many years…[l]arge UK companies are self-financing – the cash flow they obtain from operations through profits and depreciation is more than sufficient for their investment needs."

[63] See Chapter 2, Sect. A.1.

[64] Arestis et al. (2001, 18).

[65] "Valuing Private Companies." Investopedia (16 November 2016). Online: http://www.investopedia.com/articles/fundamental-analysis/11/valuing-private-companies.asp, and see the discussion in Chapter 2, Sect A.1.

[66] Wursthorn and Zuckerman (2018).

ballooned into a US$566 billion company, providing early investors with a significant fortune.[67] In contrast, in the current market, companies like Facebook Inc. wait until they are multibillion-dollar businesses before publicly listing, and other major players such as Uber Technologies Inc. and Airbnb Inc. have so far resisted going public.[68] In order for investors to gain exposure to faster-growing industry segments and companies, they must rely on "various forms of private equity"[69]—which are not available to all investors.

Supporting the position that if companies list at all, they are listing larger and later, US academics Paul Rose and Steven Davidoff Solomon argued that "[t]he small company IPO is dead."[70] Rose and Davidoff attribute the cause of such 'death' not to regulatory increases in the US—i.e. Sarbanes-Oxley—but rather primarily to a lack of investor appetite for riskier small-cap companies.[71] It may just be that these types of companies are not suited to the public space. However, it is equally possible that SMST concerns are driving these entities out of public markets. "If a fix is to come," Rose and Davidoff argued, "it will require creating a patient market environment that fosters growth in small companies both before and after a small company's IPO."[72] These arguments are certainly not conclusive that there is a harmful SMST problem limiting access to investment at least in the US stock market, but if we accept that diversity of investment options in stock markets is beneficial, claims of a SMST problem reducing the attractiveness of public markets should be addressed, otherwise further consolidation of the stock market into a few large-cap companies appears probable.

b. Quality Issues

Another concern raised about the consequences of the impact of SMST on the quality of public equity markets is the 'lemons problem.' US Professor Lynne Dallas summarizes this 'lemons problem' as occurring "when a firm is unable to differentiate itself from other firms with poorer

[67] Ibid.

[68] Ibid.

[69] LaCroix (2018).

[70] Rose and Solomon (2016).

[71] Ibid., 87.

[72] Ibid.

prospects."[73] Also, in a report for the Centre for American Progress, Jarsulic et al. link SMST to this 'lemons problem.'[74] Specifically, they say that "[s]ince higher short-term earnings signal higher long-run value, some managers may attempt to fool investors by engaging in short-termism to raise current earnings."[75] As discussed in Chapter 6,[76] there is some plausible evidence suggesting that this results in real earnings management by company managers—which is subtler than fraud, and involves management acting to smooth short-term earnings thereby not causing any undue decline to stock prices. This behaviour, Jarsulic et al. go on to say, "poses the danger that investors will believe the stock market is a lemons market, forcing even long-termist managers into short-termism in order to appear as profitable as short-termist firms."[77] The end result, Jarsulic et al. argue is that "this dynamic could cause growing firms to forgo or even exit public markets entirely."[78] Coupled with the anecdotal examples provided above, and the actual reduction in IPOs and the number of listed companies generally, the SMST issue—either real or perceived—appears to be leading to the degradation of the quality of public markets. The result may be that there will continue to be fewer and fewer IPOs, and that stock market listings will be consolidated into fewer and fewer—albeit potentially higher dollar value—listed companies.

C. Societal Costs of SMST

The point has also been raised that "[i]f one is worried about the sustainability of corporations from an environmental, social, or political perspective, the problem of 'short-termism' has to be a central worry."[79] The well-known collapses of corporate giants, Enron, Worldcom and Nortel, have all been cited to show how unrealistically high expectations from the market can lead to short-term thinking, and behavior by a listed company's management in order to fulfill these expectations encourages

[73] Dallas (2012, 313).

[74] Jarsulic et al. (2015).

[75] Ibid.

[76] See Chapter 6, Sect. B.2.b.

[77] Ibid.

[78] Ibid.

[79] Greenfield (2011, 628).

a culture of greed and promotes excessive risk taking.[80] It has been argued that this encouragement of excessive short-term behaviour leads to a 'culture of greed', providing a fertile breeding ground for excessive executive pay and corruption, which can then have impacts that go far beyond the scandalized corporate managers.[81] It has also been argued that the SMST issue could actually cause harmful environmental impacts as company managers would take environmentally harmful actions in order to see short-term financial benefits.[82] Although these arguments may be intuitively compelling, it is difficult to viably demonstrate the connection between the actual or perceived excessive discounting by asset owners and the societal costs of SMST, and convincing arguments or evidence establishing this connection have not been presented.

Furthermore, it has been suggested that "markets that are focused primarily on the short term will almost certainly excessively discount even price-relevant ESG information limiting further the role that markets are able to play in driving sustainable behaviour…[t]hus, markets that focus only on the short run cannot be said to be sustainable in any form."[83] The United Nations Environmental Program (UNEP) referred to an expert poll of business, non-governmental (NGO), academia and government respondents conducted by GlobeScan and SustainAbility in 2011. This survey indicated that a large majority (88%) of the 642 experts polled saw pressure for short-term financial results as a barrier to businesses becoming more sustainable.[84] Details of exactly how SMST prevented sustainability were not provided by respondents, but presumably this would be because company managers feel pressure from investors to provide short-term financial returns at the expense of funding longer-term sustainable business initiatives.

Sustainable initiatives, the UNEP has suggested, often have long investment horizons, and therefore may be particularly impacted by

[80] See the discussion in Dallas (2012, 268) at Note 7, and Aspen Institute (2010, 2).

[81] Salter (2012), where the author explains using the example of Citigroup and its settlement with the US Securities and Exchange Commission (SEC) on fraud charges, how the firms focus on short-term profit invited corruption.

[82] See the Aspen Institute (2010, 4), which cites a survey of corporate directors of Fortune 200 boards, 31 of 34 of which state that they would "cut down a mature forest or release a dangerous, unregulated toxin into the environment in order to increase profits."

[83] Cleary (2015, 23).

[84] Financial Short-Termism (2012).

SMST.[85] Although longer-term thinking is certainly a component of sustainability initiatives, the UNEP in its report on Stock Exchanges and Sustainability, has acknowledged that there may be a disconnection between longer-term company management and sustainable business. Particularly, a longer-term approach does not necessarily mean a focus on environmental, social and governance (ESG) factors. Consequently, the UNEP argued, "lengthening time horizons is a necessary but insufficient condition for ensuring a transition to a more sustainable economy."[86] There may be numerous factors, and not just SMST, which jeopardize corporation's becoming more sustainable, including for example climate change and geo-political instability. Consequently, regulatory and financial industry solutions should tailor solutions addressing all factors impeding sustainability. Addressing sustainability issues collaterally though SMST reform alone does not appear to be a viable approach.

D. Transfer of Wealth from Future to Current Asset Owners

It has been argued that on a market-wide basis, SMST issue elicits "a direct and uncompensated transfer of wealth from future to current shareholders."[87] This uncompensated wealth transfer effect is more than merely an issue of asset distribution between sophisticated financial professionals that are able to protect themselves. Rather, according to this theory, current asset owners and asset managers—those holding shares in the present—apply pressure to unduly extract short-term lesser value returns from a listed company in the form of cash distributions, buybacks and/or high share prices, which causes a resulting net loss to the investing public. As discussed below, this wealth transfer appears to manifest in two main ways: (1) when future shareholders suffer a loss in share price; or (2) if short-term expenditures result in company managers 'missing long-term investment opportunities' that would be more profitable.

[85] Cleary (2015, 11).

[86] Ibid.

[87] Moore and Walker-Arnott (2014, 423) and Moore and Petrin (2017, 124), which discussed and referenced Greenfield (2011, 636).

1. *Loss in Share Price*

It has been argued that if the shares of listed companies are over-priced in the market and are not reflective of the long-term value of the firm, "the future investors holding the relevant shares at the point in time when the overpricing is widely detected will suffer a resulting loss in value."[88] The wealth transfer from high share prices occurs as a listed company's existing asset owners may exit their investment prior to the over-valuation being detected, thereby leaving future shareholders to suffer a loss in value as the share price declines.[89] The question may be asked as to why regulators and the financial industry should intervene in the absence of fraud: why should the financial returns of future investors be protected? Accepting that there is at least some evidence of a SMST problem as discussed in Chapter 5, the difficulty lies in the ability of asset owners and asset managers to adequately assess these losses and their ability—or individual interest—to act to recoup such losses. Individual losses to asset owners may not be significant enough—or the causation of such loss sufficiently clear—to compel the negatively impacted parties to seek a remedy at the time they suffer the loss, but collectively the lost value could be considerable. This scenario raises questions on how investor pressure and company manager responses to such investor pressure impacts whether share prices accurately represent long-term value.

2. *Missed Opportunities*

It has also been argued that SMST involves management "taking steps that boost the short-term stock but reduce the size of the pie."[90] The theory is that the excessive discounting discussed in Chapter 5 may cause company managers to favour short-term cash returns to shareholders rather than pursuing longer-term and more beneficial projects. Davies et al. have articulated this concept as opportunity costs, which include investment projects and hence future output.[91] These 'missed opportunities' mean current shareholders may receive lesser value at the expense of revenues which could have greater benefit to future shareholders.

[88] Ibid.

[89] Ibid.

[90] Fried (2015, 1568).

[91] Davies et al. (2014, 16).

It may be that if listed company shareholders are not properly valuing these types of long-term projects, then the company should be taken private, where such investments could be more accurately valued. This may be occurring in some circumstances, and the increasing role of public-to-private buyouts suggests that companies believe longer-term returns may be more accurately valued in the private sector.

However, as noted above and in Chapter 2,[92] there is value in these opportunities being available in a robust widely held public market. The harms caused by such short-term approach and the resulting 'missed opportunities' may not be readily apparent to the market. As observed by Davies et al. "[unlike] crises, these opportunity costs are neither violent nor visible...[r]ather they are silent and invisible."[93] This suggests that these missed opportunities for longer-term investment are not just relevant for a limited number of listed companies but could apply across the market. The survey evidence discussed in Chapter 5[94] supports this position, as a significant portion of company managers consistently indicate that due to shareholder pressure for short-term financial returns they forgo longer-term projects.[95] As discussed Chapter 5,[96] survey evidence, although compelling, has inherent weaknesses, and, therefore, the specific analysis on the evidence of wealth transfer and potential losses to future shareholders caused by SMST is considered below.

3. *Evidence of This Wealth Transfer/Loss*

As discussed in Chapter 5,[97] it is practically very difficult—if not impossible—to quantitatively measure the wealth transfer or loss caused by the supposed SMST issue because there is no readily available control group against which to measure a market without SMST. However, attempts have been made to measure this wealth transfer or loss through an analysis of the impacts of stock buybacks—which are cash purchases by the

[92] See Chapter 6, Sect. B.2.b.

[93] Davies et al. (2014, 16).

[94] See Chapter 5, Sect. A.1.

[95] See the surveys summarized in Graham et al. (2005), updated in Graham et al. (2006).

[96] See Chapter 5, Sect. A.1.

[97] See Chapter 5, Sect. A.

company of its own outstanding shares on the open market,[98] and by various other measures including using the private/public company comparison and attempting to measure the benefits of a longer-term investing approach by asset owners and asset managers. Each of these evidentiary measures is considered below.

a. Stock Buybacks

The substantial surge in US stock buybacks over the last decade—allegedly caused in part by SMST via an interest by company managers to boost earnings per share (EPS) and satisfy shareholder desires for short-term financial returns—has been offered as evidence of a loss of wealth and a problematic wealth transfer from future to current shareholders.[99] Though US stock buybacks may have declined in the last few years, they are still well above where they were a decade ago.[100] Recent figures also put such stock buybacks at record highs for 2018.[101]

It appears possible that such stock buybacks are not occurring for valid business reasons, but instead are driven by SMST and are harmful to long-term value. Three main arguments raised by company managers to justify open market purchases of their shares are:

1. buybacks are necessary to offset the dilution of employee stock options;
2. the company is mature and has run out of investment opportunities; and
3. buybacks are investments in undervalued shares meant to signal confidence in the company's future.[102]

[98] Definition of 'buyback', Investopedia. Online: https://www.investopedia.com/terms/b/buyback.asp.

[99] See Lazonick (2014) summarizing the research that Professor Lazonick has done in this area. This research shows that 54% of the earnings of the 449 companies in the S&P 500 index which were publicly listed from 2003 to 2012 were used to buy back stock, and dividends absorbed an additional 37% of earnings (Lazonick 2014, 48). This rate has also doubled from the previous 10-year period—See Ro (2014).

[100] Samson et al. (2017).

[101] Cowen (2018).

[102] Lazonick (2014, 51–52) and Yallapragada (2014), which sets out a range of reasons why stock buybacks are carried out by listed companies.

The first point used to justify buybacks—i.e. that such buybacks are necessary to offset the dilution caused by employee stock option plans—is arguably not a viable justification for the high level of buybacks, as research shows that buybacks are often in excess of a multiple of exercised employee options.[103] The second point used to justify buybacks—i.e. that the company is mature and has run out of investment opportunities—is more difficult to assess.

It is possible that mature companies do not have viable investment options and that the capital is best deployed elsewhere. The increasing percentage of S&P 500 listed company earnings dedicated to buybacks rather than reinvestment is considerable. However, it is possible that these buybacks free up capital and allow investors to reinvest in more profitable opportunities. With respect to buybacks, economist Tyler Cowen noted that funds transferred to shareholders and real resources are not destroyed. Rather, Cowen observed that the money from buybacks could still go to a venture capital fund, or into private equity or a real estate investment trust, in addition to numerous other undertakings, all of which might boost investment and real wages.[104] Cowen's observation may be true, but it is also likely that these funds may not be valuably invested. They could be squandered by the recipients or reinvested in capital raises by similar listed companies and thus used as fodder for further buybacks—thereby contributing to an ongoing cycle of cash transfers without building any underlying value. A study on this point indicated that US corporate investment has fallen below levels indicated by Tobin's Q, a measure of the prospective profitability of investment projects, and concluded that this underperformance in part owes to "changes in governance that encourage shares buyback instead of investment."[105]

Further, it has been argued that existing listed companies have significant organizational and financial advantages when they expand and enter new markets.[106] They may be giving this up in exchange for a short-term positive bump to their share prices caused by the buyback. In addition to pressure from shareholders to provide short-term financial returns,

[103] Lazonick (2014, 51).

[104] Cowen (2018).

[105] Gutierrez and Philippon (2016).

[106] Lazonick (2014, 52).

a reason that company managers may pursue buybacks is because such buybacks increase EPS numbers by reducing the total number of issued shares.[107] Buybacks, therefore, facilitate company managers meeting EPS targets and keeping shareholders happy.[108] In support that this is use of buybacks occurring, a study of US listed companies from 1988 to 2010 evidenced that a considerable amount of buybacks occur when a company would otherwise miss its EPS target if not for the resulting lift provided by a stock buyback.[109] It is important to note that such EPS-driven buyback actions do not increase the total earnings for the period. Consequently, in the long-term, these share buy-backs would only have a temporary positive impact on share price. A correction would result in a decline in share price for the shareholders who did not have their shares bought back. The argument is also made that stock buybacks may undermine income equality, job stability and growth—i.e. the interests of future shareholders—, because the capital used to implement the stock buyback is not invested in longer-term more profitable investments of the listed company.[110]

As discussed in Sect. A above, productivity levels, particularly with regard to UK and US listed companies, are arguably not optimal as compared to what they could be. The point raised by Lazonick and others[111] is that a listed company's productivity, and by extension national productivity, will not improve unless firms retain earnings and fund investment, rather than returning cash to shareholders, in part through stock buybacks. Yallapragada observes "[m]any analysts attribute this phenomenon [buybacks] to weakening economy, falling prices of financial stocks and the sovereign debt crisis in Europe."[112] However, as discussed in Sect. A above in the context of corporate competitiveness, the leap to national productivity is problematic as it is difficult to precisely extrapolate the causes of national productivity decline. More significant, however, are concerns about the impact of buybacks on the listed company that buys

[107] Lazonick (2014, 48) and Yallapragada (2014, 193).

[108] Ibid.

[109] Almeida et al. (2016).

[110] Ibid., 48.

[111] Ibid., 53, which also references Gary P. Pisano and Willy C. Shih of Harvard Business School, in their 2009 *Harvard Business Review* article "Restoring American Competitiveness" and their book *Producing Prosperity*.

[112] Yallapragada (2014, 193).

its own shares. As noted above, stock buy-backs would only have a temporarily positive impact on share price, and a correction would result in a decline in share price for the shareholders who did not have their shares bought back.

On the third point—i.e. that buybacks are investments in undervalued shares meant to signal confidence in the company's future—buybacks may be beneficial to listed companies if the shares purchased are in fact undervalued. However, evidence suggests that rather than picking up undervalued shares, listed companies tend to buy back shares when the market is high, which penalizes continuing shareholders when the share price drops.[113] General Electric has been cited as an example of a listed company with a poor buyback policy. It has spent more than US$50 billion on buybacks since 2015, and yet the share price has collapsed over that period.[114] Consequently, there is evidence suggesting that buybacks are occurring when shares are overvalued therefore negatively impacting remaining shareholders. There is no evidence to suggest that the funds from share buybacks are being more valuably invested by recipients of the buyback funds. Consequently, the current level of buybacks provides some indication of SMST harm.

b. Research on Long-Term Focused Companies

As a rough proxy for a control group to evidence the harms of SMST, private companies have been used. As discussed in Chapter 5,[115] matched samples of private and public companies provide some evidence that private companies invest more in a firm's long-term operations than public companies.[116] Although intuitively compelling, the evidence does not on its own convincingly demonstrate that short-termism is a significant contributor to this public/private investment gap. It could just be that businesses with longer-term interests are self-selecting into the private sector—so the method is, therefore, arguably comparing apples to oranges. To address this lacuna in the research, attempts have also been made to divide listed companies into companies that have a long-term focus and those that do not have such a focus, as a means of

[113] Lazonick (2014, 51).

[114] Lazonick (2014, 51) and Trainer (2017).

[115] See Chapter 5, Sect A.4.

[116] See the summary in Roe (2013, 986) at Note 33 and Davies et al. (2014, 22–24).

determining if the longer-term focused companies exhibit superior financial performance.

McKinsey & Company (McKinsey) has set out to measure this purported wealth transfer by isolating short-term and long-term focused sample groups of listed companies. If a company with a long-term focus does better than a short-term focused company, this should indicate that long-termism creates more value and firms that fail to have this orientation are transferring wealth to their current shareholders at the expense of greater value for future investors. To do so, McKinsey developed a corporate horizons index (CHI) based on a set of variables that McKinsey claimed indicate how long-term oriented companies behave differently from short-term focused firms.[117] These variables include investment, earnings quality, margin growth, quarterly management and earnings-per-share growth.[118]

Using a data set of 615 large- and mid-cap US publicly listed companies from 2001 to 2015, the McKinsey Report 2017 provided evidence that, based on the CHI, the listed companies classed by McKinsey as 'long-term' significantly outperformed their 'short-term' classed peers in terms of revenue, R&D spending, market capitalization and job creation.[119] The out-performance by the long-term companies suggests that a longer-term focus creates more value for investors than that of short-term oriented companies. Admittedly, the McKinsey Report 2017 does not attempt to directly demonstrate that SMST is harmful. Instead, it presents research that a longer-term approach may be more beneficial than a shorter-term approach, based on a select set of variables. Further, this study raises the question of how the longer-term oriented companies in the sample group were able to pursue their long-term approach given the significant pressures for short-term returns identified in the stock market.

The argument could be made that the longer-term companies are just better managed, and the discussion should be around superior verses mediocre performing managers—with the stock market keeping mediocre managers on a tighter leash through calls for short-term financial returns. This accords with the discussion in Chapter 5[120] that owners of

[117] Barton et al. (2017, 3) (McKinsey Report 2017).

[118] Ibid.

[119] Ibid., 2.

[120] See Chapter 5, Sect. B.2.b.

listed companies pursue short-termism in project choice in order to limit managerial rent-seeking behaviour. Although the longer-term companies may do a better job of communicating long-term value to the market, this does not confirm that the remaining companies are poorly managed. It is equally possible that these short-term focused companies could particularly benefit from regulatory and financial industry reforms meant to reduce the excessive discounting causing SMST.

The analysis in this chapter suggests that if SMST is harmful, such harm most plausibly relates to reduced trust in the stock market and a wealth transfer from future to current shareholders. The evidence presented in this chapter does not, however, definitively demonstrate any market-wide failings caused at least in part by SMST. Given the evidentiary issues inherent in viably measuring the deleterious effects of SMST, definitive proof of such harms may never be convincingly provided. Regardless of the evidentiary issues in definitively proving that there is a harmful SMST problem, the analysis provided in Chapter 4 demonstrates that there has been—albeit limited—SMST reform. Consequently, policymakers and the financial industry appear to be, at least to some degree, accepting the evidence provided that SMST is a problem. As there is some compelling evidentiary basis affirming the validity of such a response by regulators and the financial industry, SMST concerns cannot entirely be written off as delusional or only a rhetorical cover for other reform efforts. Possibly in response to the lack of evidentiary substantiation of the harms of SMST, reform efforts to date have mainly been 'light' touch and a 'gentle nudge' rather than a 'push.' The next chapter assesses these reforms and whether such reforms at least conceptually address the SMST problem based on the conclusions reached in Chapters 5 and 6.

References

Almeida, Heitor, Fos, Vyacheslav, and Kronlund, Mathias. 2016. "The Real Effects of Share Repurchases." 119:1 *Journal of Financial Economics*. 168–185.

Anderson, P. W. 1972. "More Is Different." August 4. 177:4047 *Science*. 393–396.

Arestis, Philip, Demetriades, Panicos O., and Luintel, Kul B. 2001. "Financial Development and Economic Growth: The Role of Stock Markets." 33:1 *Journal of Money, Credit and Banking*. 16–41.

Aspen Institute. 2010. "Short-Termism and U.S. Capital Markets: A Compelling Case for Change." https://assets.aspeninstitute.org/content/uploads/files/content/images/Compelling%20Case%20for%20Change_August2010.pdf.

Barton, Dominic, Manyika, James, Koller, Timothy, Palter, Robert, Godsall, Jonathan, and Zoffer, Joshua. 2017. "Measuring the Economic Impact of Short-Termism." February. *McKinsey Global Institute*. Discussion Paper. https://www.mckinsey.com/~/media/mckinsey/featured%20insights/Long%20term%20Capitalism/Where%20companies%20with%20a%20long%20term%20view%20outperform%20their%20peers/MGI-Measuring-the-economic-impact-of-short-termism.ashx.

Bower, Max. 2017. "LBOs to Fly as Activists Poised to Bring More M&A Activity to Europe." 22 June. *GlobalCapital*

Brorsen, Les. 2017. "Looking Behind the Declining Number of Public Companies." 18 May. *Harvard Law School Forum on Corporate Governance and Financial Regulation*. https://corpgov.law.harvard.edu/2017/05/18/looking-behind-the-declining-number-of-public-companies/.

Cleary, Siobhan. 2015. "Stock Exchanges and Sustainability." December. UNEP. Inquiry Working Paper. http://unepinquiry.org/wp-content/uploads/2015/12/Stock_Exchanges_and_Sustainability.pdf.

Colvin, Geoff. 2017. "Take This Market and Shove It." 16 May *Fortune*. http://fortune.com/going-private/.

Cowen, Tyler. 2018. "Massive Share Buybacks' Are Nothing to Fear." 6 March. *Bloomberg*. https://www.bloomberg.com/view/articles/2018-03-06/stock-buybacks-triggered-by-trump-s-tax-cuts-aren-t-scary.

Dallas, Lynne L. 2012. "Short-Termism, the Financial Crisis, and Corporate Governance" 2011–2012. 37:2 *The Journal of Corporation Law*. 265–364.

Davies, Richard, Haldane, Andrew G., Nielsen, Mette, Pezzini, Silvia. 2014. "Measuring the Costs of Short-Termism." 12 *Journal of Financial Stability*. 16–25.

Dell, Michael. 2014. "Going Private Is Paying Off for Dell." 24 November. *The Wall Street Journal*.

Espinoza, Javier. 2017. "Private Equity Buyouts Hit Highest Level in Decade." 29 June. *Financial Times*. https://www.ft.com/content/7e99c000-5c1e-11e7-b553-e2df1b0c3220.

"Financial Short-Termism a Major Obstacle to Sustainable Change in Business: Expert Poll." 26 January 2012. *Press Release of the United Nations Environmental Program (UNEP)*.

Fried, Jesse M. 2015. "The Uneasy Case for Favoring Long-Term Shareholders." 124 *The Yale Law Journal*. 1554–1628.

Gaspar, Jose Miguel, Massa, Massimo, and Matos, Pedro. 2005. "Shareholder Investment Horizons and the Market for Corporate Control." April. 76:1 *Journal of Financial Economics*. 135–165.

"Global Private Equity Report." 2017. *Bain & Company, Inc*. https://psik.org.pl/images/publikacje-i-raporty—publikacje/BAIN_REPORT_Global_Private_Equity_Report_2017.pdf?.

Graham, John R., Cam, Harvey, and Shiva, Rajgopal. 2005. "The Economic Implications of Corporate Financial Reporting." December. 40 *Journal of Accounting and Economics*. 3–73.

Graham, John R., Cam, Harvey, and Shiva, Rajgopal. 2006. "Value Destruction and Financial Reporting Decisions." 62 *Financial Analysts Journal*. 27–39.

Greenfield, Kent. 2011. "The Puzzle of Short-Termism.". 46 *Wake Forest Law Review*. 627–640.

Gutierrez, German and Philippon, Thomas. 2016. "Investment-Less Growth: An Empirical Investigation." December. *National Bureau of Economic Research*. Working Paper 22897. https://www.nber.org/papers/w22897.

Hughes, Alan. 2014. "Short-Termism, Impatient Capital and Finance for Manufacturing Innovation in the UK." UK Government Office for Science.

Jackson, Gregory and Petraki, Anastasia. 2011. "Understanding Short-Termism: The Role of Corporate Governance." *Report to the Glass House Forum*. http://www.sofi-goettingen.de/fileadmin/Textarchiv/WIP2/Praesentationen/jackson-petraki_short-termism.pdf.

Jarsulic, Marc, Duke, Brendan, and Madowitz, Michael. 2015. "Long-Termism or Lemons: The Role of Public Policy in Promoting Long-Term Investments." 21 October. *Centre for American Progress*. https://www.americanprogress.org/issues/economy/reports/2015/10/21/123717/long-termism-or-lemons.

Kay, John. 2012. "The Kay Review of UK Equity Markets and Long-Term Decision Making." Final Report. July.

LaCroix, Kevin. 2018. "Fewer U.S. Listed Companies—Is That a Problem?" 9 April. *The D&O Diary*. https://www.dandodiary.com/2018/04/articles/ipos/fewer-u-s-listed-companies-problem/.

Lazonick, William. 2014. "Profits Without Prosperity." September. *Harvard Business Review*. 47–55.

Mason, J. W. 2015. "Understanding Short-Termism: Questions and Consequences." 6 November. *The Roosevelt Institute*.

Mauboussin, Michael and Callahan, Dan. 2015. "A Long Look at Short-Termism: Questioning the Premise." September. 27:3 *Journal of Applied Corporate Finance*. 70–82.

McNevin, Ambrose. 2016. "Keeping It Private or Making It Public – the CEO's of Tibco, Informatica and Zscaler Answer If and Why Software Companies Need Capital Markets?" 15 February. *Computer Business Review*. https://www.cbronline.com/enterprise-it/keeping-it-private-or-making-it-public-the-ceos-of-tibco-informatica-and-zscaler-answer-if-and-why-software-companies-need-capital-markets-4811289.

Moore, Marc T. and Petrin, Martin. 2017. *Corporate Governance: Law, Regulation and Theory*. Palgrave Corporate & Financial Law: London, UK.

Moore, Marc T. and Walker-Arnott, Edward. 2014. "A Fresh Look at Stock Market Short-Termism." 41:3 *Journal of Law and Society*. 416–445.

Qualtrough, Edward. 2014. "Tibco CEO Says More Companies Will Follow Dell and Go Private." 5 November. *CIO*. https://www.cio.co.uk/it-strategy/tibco-ceo-says-more-companies-will-go-private-3584225/.

Renneboog, Luc and Vansteenkiste, Cara. 2017. "Leveraged Buyouts: A Survey of the Literature." January. ECGI Finance Working Paper No. 492/2017.

Rieg, Robert. 2015. "Dynamics of Value-Based Management. Does Shareholder Value Cause Short-Termism?" August. 26:2/3 *Journal of Management Control*. 193–224.

Ritholtz, Barry. 2015. "Where Have All the Public Companies Gone?" 24 June. *Bloomberg View*. https://www.bloomberg.com/view/articles/2018-04-09/where-have-all-the-u-s-public-companies-gone.

Ro, Sam. 2014. "The Rate of Share Buybacks Has Doubled in the Last Decade." 5 April. *Business Insider*. http://www.businessinsider.com/sp-500-stock-buyback-history-2014-4?IR=T.

Roe, Mark J. 2013. "Corporate Short-Termism—In the Boardroom and in the Courtroom." August. 68 *Business Lawyer*. 977–1006.

Rose, Paul and Solomon, Steven Davidoff. 2016. "Where Have All the IPOs Gone: The Hard Life of the Small IPO". 6 *Harvard Business Law Review*. 83–128.

Salter, Malcolm S. 2012. "How Short-Termism Invites Corruption…and What to Do About It." 12 April. *Harvard Business School*. Working Paper 12-094.

Samson, Adam, Platt, Eric, and Wigglesworth, Robin. 2017. "US Share Buyback Plan Approvals Plunge." 1 May. *Financial Times*. https://www.ft.com/content/694fa0b0-2e84-11e7-9555-23ef563ecf9a.

Surowiecki, James. 2017. "The Short-Termism Myth." 24 August. *The New Yorker*. http://www.newyorker.com/magazine/2015/08/24/the-short-termism-myth.

Tovey, Allan. 2015. "British R&D Spending Rises to £19.9bn But Worries Persist Over Government Cuts." 20 November. *Telegraph*.

Trainer, Davis. 2017. "Bad Buybacks Can Destroy Shareholder Value." 26 December. *Forbes*. https://www.forbes.com/sites/greatspeculations/2017/12/26/bad-buybacks-can-destroy-shareholder-value/#71a740ef294a.

Wasik, Zosia. 2017. "Number of UK IPOs at 4-Year Low." 28 March. *Financial Times*. https://www.ft.com/content/4bdd4888-a20a-3cc4-b683-6d0c2d0d606f.

Wastell, Kenny. 2017. "UK Buyout Activity Reaches Post-Crisis Peak in 2017." 21 December. *Unquote*. http://www.unquote.com/uk/analysis/3007966/uk-buyout-activity-reaches-post-crisis-peak-in-2017.

Wursthorn, Michael and Zuckerman, Gregory. 2018. "Fewer Listed Companies: Is That Good or Bad for Stock Markets?" 5 January. *Dow Jones Newswires*.

Yallapragada, RamMohan R. 2014. "Stock Buybacks: Good or Bad for Investors." 12:2 *Journal of Business and Economics Research*. 193–198.

Zandi, Mark. 2015. "What Hillary Clinton Gets Wrong About 'Quarterly Capitalism': Businesses Are Actually More Than Ever in R&D." 24 July. *New York Daily News*. http://www.nydailynews.com/opinion/mark-zandi-hillary-wrong-quarterly-capitalism-article-1.2303721.

CHAPTER 8

Dual Pathway for Short-Termism Reform

The previous chapters demonstrate that a harmful stock market (SMST) problem appears to be occurring, and a significant contributing factor is the excessive discounting of future financial returns by asset owners and asset managers. This undue discounting causes company managers to prioritize short-term financial returns and actions that improve, or at least do not negatively impact, share prices. As discussed in Chapter 6, such excessive discounting by asset owners and asset managers requires a transmission mechanism into listed companies. The likely conduits for such SMST are the actions of a wide range of investors primarily via the approval of short-term equity-based compensation of company managers, and corporate governance and legal mechanisms which give asset owners the ability to make changes to the board of directors, and, as a result, the management of a listed company. This SMST may be intensified by asset managers who are incentivized to act in their clients' short-term interests, and by asset manager compensation structures focused on short-term financial returns. As discussed in Chapter 7, there is plausible evidence suggesting that SMST results in a reduced trust in the stock market as a capital raising venue, which is problematic as a robust stock market is intrinsically important to modern capital markets, and that SMST may also result in an uncompensated wealth transfer from future to current asset owners, which is also problematic as it causes a net loss to the investing public.

Based on this analysis, notionally effective reforms to address the SMST problem require either:

K. M. Willey, *Stock Market Short-Termism*,
https://doi.org/10.1007/978-3-030-22903-0_8

1. minimizing the excessive discounting of future returns; or
2. cutting off the transmission mechanisms of SMST into the listed company

This dual pathway to SMST reform is explored further in Sect. A of this chapter. Section B then provides an examination of whether the implemented SMST reforms identified in Chapter 4 address the SMST problem by employing either of Option (1) or Option (2) identified in Sect. A as necessary corrective measures. Based on this examination, the conclusion reached in Sect. B is that few of the implemented SMST reforms considered in Chapter 4 adequately hit the mark and conceptually address the SMST issue. Given these issues, and the resulting difficulty in effectively regulating to correct the SMST issue, it is not surprising that the implemented SMST reforms to date have been minimal and are relatively 'light' touch. Section C then goes on to explore whether this 'light' touch approach may not be particularly problematic providing that it is focused on reducing excessive discounting. The chapter concludes that with the appropriate regulatory and financial industry messaging, this 'light' touch approach may be, if not the ideal, rather the most feasible and realistic method of providing a gentle 'nudge' to correct the SMST problem.

A. Dual Pathway for SMST Reform

If SMST is a harmful material problem, any potential regulatory or financial industry solution requires either:

1. minimizing the excessive discounting issues around future returns—i.e. assisting capital markets to more accurately assess long-term financial performance and encouraging asset owners to take a longer-term approach; or
2. cutting off the transmission mechanisms of SMST into the listed company—i.e. preventing the asset owner/asset manager preference for short-term financial returns getting into listed companies at all.

This dual pathway is illustrated in Fig. 1. Before analyzing whether the SMST reforms identified in Chapter 4 conceptually address the SMST issue through either of these options, it is, however, first necessary to delve deeper into the theory behind how such options would work to counter SMST.

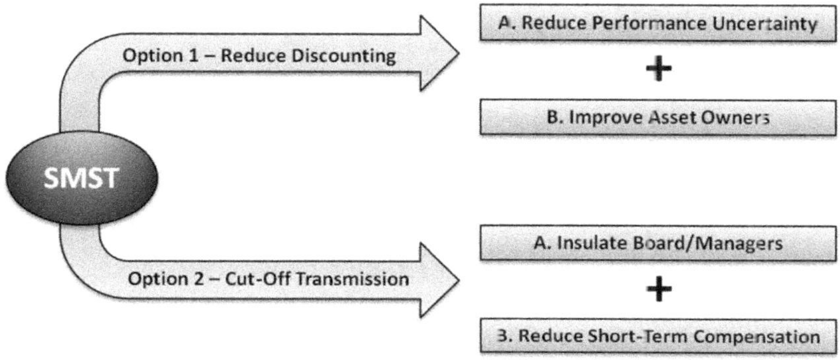

Fig. 1 Dual pathway for SMST reform

1. *Option 1: Reduce Excessive Discounting*

It is certainly reasonable that asset owners and asset managers may apply deep discounts to future profits of listed companies given the myriad of uncertainties inherent in actually delivering on long-term performance objectives. Also, as discussed earlier in Chapter 5,[1] it has been argued that rather than being a problem, this significant discounting might instead merely be a crude way of adjusting for—and even constraining—company manager optimism and market uncertainties.[2] However, as further considered in Chapter 5, the evidence is suggestive that this discounting appears to be in excess of what is reasonably necessary to account for company manager optimism and market uncertainties.[3] As company managers are aware of this excessive discounting and the resulting negative share price impact, they may pursue actions to provide short-term financial gains which are more favorably received by the market, but do not build fundamental value. This may result in a later share price correction and, consequently, a net loss to the investing public—despite there potentially being individual winners and losers.

As a result, the SMST problem should either be addressed by reducing this excessive discounting, or, as discussed in Sect. A.2 below, by cutting off the transmission of such excessive discounting entirely. There are

[1] See Chapter 5, Sect. B.2.b.

[2] See the summary of research in Dobbs (2009, 118).

[3] See Chapter 5, Sect. A.

several logical ways of reducing excessive discounting in share pricing. One approach—as considered in further detail in Sect. A.1.a below—involves the challenging proposition of increasing asset owner and asset manager confidence that company managers will actually deliver on stated long-term performance objectives. For this approach to be at least conceptually effective, asset owners—and correspondingly asset managers—will also need to appreciate the benefits of a longer-term approach.

Accordingly, Sect. A.1.b below considers the option of 'improving' asset owners—and by extension asset managers—mainly by facilitating engagement and collective action and by 'enlightening' asset owners on the existence of a harmful short-term bias, and the corresponding benefits of a longer-term approach. Another approach that may work to reduce excessive discounting is using structures with a controlling asset owner—such as dual class structures.[4] These structures involve tackling the agency problem underlying the excessive discounting by facilitating listed companies towards a controlling asset ownership structure. Structures with controlling asset owners are considered in Sect. A.1.c below, but ultimately rejected for the time being as a viable basis for SMST reform in the absence of further research.

a. Reduce Performance Uncertainty

As indicated above, reducing the excessive discounting that appears to be causing SMST is a two-part process that involves both reducing performance uncertainty and 'improving' asset owners (discussed in Sect. A.1.b below). Key to this process is that listed company long term performance objectives, and results of such performance, should be clearly communicated to the market. Providing such clear communication may reduce the actual or perceived excessive discounting of future returns by asset owners, and, thereby, assist asset owners and asset managers to rely to a lesser degree on short-term financial returns.

The extent to which the SMST-driven reforms identified in Chapter 4 attempt to tackle the SMST issue by reducing performance uncertainty of listed companies are considered in Sect. B of this chapter and are summarized in tabular form in Appendix 'C'. As will be demonstrated in the analysis in Sect. B of this chapter, these SMST reforms primarily include introducing long-term strategic reporting requirements linked to listed

[4] See discussion of dual class structures in Chapter 4, Sect. A.1.c.

company remuneration reports. For these reforms to effectively reduce excessive discounting, it is not enough for company managers to more clearly communicate long-term performance strategy. Asset owners—and by extension asset managers—will also need to recognize the existence of a harmful short-term bias, and the corresponding benefits of a longer-term approach.

b. 'Improve' Asset Owners

For the reform approach of reducing performance uncertainty to be at least conceptually effective, asset owners—and correspondingly asset managers—also need to appreciate the benefits of a longer-term approach—i.e. the current behaviour of asset owners and asset managers needs to be 'improved'. Unlike Sect. A.1.a above, this 'improvement' approach does not center on the communication of long-term performance objectives and corresponding results on such objectives by company managers. Instead, the 'improvement' approach focuses on:

1. collective action and engagement by asset owners and asset managers in order to reduce concerns contributing to excessive discounting by increasing confidence that company manager actions are being monitored; and
2. educating—and thus 'enlightening'—asset owners and asset managers on the existence of a harmful short-term bias, and the corresponding benefits of a longer-term approach.

As discussed further in Sect. B below, there are numerous reservations around increased engagement and collective action by asset owners, including that such actions could amplify existing SMST concerns if asset owners continue to pursue short-termist objectives. It has also been suggested that engagement and collective action reform efforts may be most effective if lead by institutional investors, provided that they are 'enlightened' towards the harms of SMST and the benefits of a longer-term investing approach.[5] Consequently, institutional investor

[5]See Ambachtsheer (2014, 9), where the author suggests that "institutional investors around the globe, led by the pension fund sector, are well placed to play a 'lead wagon' fiduciary role" in efforts to end SMST and Barton and Wiseman (2014, 44), where the authors argue that big investors have an obligation to "end the plague of short-termism."

'enlightenment' is a key part of the SMST reform process. The concept of 'enlightenment' involves SMST reforms that inform investors of the benefits of a longer-term approach and the potential negative impacts of an undue short-term focus in investing. The extent to which the SMST-driven reforms identified in Chapter 4 attempt to tackle the SMST issue by 'enlightening' asset owners—and by extension asset managers—are considered in Sect. B and summarized in tabular form in Appendix 'C'.

c. Controlling Asset Owners

Another option that has the potential to reduce the excessive discounting by asset owners is for a listed company to have a controlling shareholder. However, this option as a standalone solution is ultimately rejected as a viable basis for reform given the current uncertainty around whether such approach positively impacts firm value. The argument that the presence of a controlling asset owner may reduce SMST is best understood in the context of agency theory.

Excessive discounting may occur as a result of a perceived information asymmetry and the resulting costly monitoring.[6] This monitoring needs to be incurred by asset owners—often via asset managers, as principals—, to scrutinize and ensure the long-term financial value generation of listed companies by their agents—namely boards of directors and by extension, company managers. Holding a 'significant ownership stake' could provide motivation for a principal to incur such monitoring costs.[7] These principals may be incentivized to incur monitoring costs to protect their investment as they may in practice have a reduced ability to 'vote with their feet,' the so-called 'Wall Street Walk'—i.e. sell their share position at a favourable price—, because selling a control block tends to depress the share price.[8]

There is no bright line test for what constitutes a 'significant ownership stake' in the context of listed companies. As a starting point, the term 'control' in corporate law generally means holding a majority of the

[6] As discussed in the seminal work of Jensen and Meckling, William (1976) on agency theory, where at 308 the authors state that "monitoring includes more than just observing the behaviour of the agent…[i]t includes efforts on the part of the principal to 'control' the behaviour of the agent through budget restrictions, compensation policies, operating rules, etc."

[7] Cheffins (2002, 360).

[8] Dasgupta and Piacentino (2015, 2853).

voting shares of a company, or having the right—via shareholdings or contract—to appoint a majority of the board of directors.[9] With respect to business combinations, the Delaware General Corporation Law[10] reduces the presumption of control to 20% of the voting rights of a company, which threshold applies in the absence of any evidence to the contrary.[11] As listed companies have dispersed shareholdings, particularly in Anglo-American corporate markets, by and large the percentage of shares actually voted on significant matters is considerably less than 100%. In the United Kingdom (UK) in the 2017 annual general meeting (AGM) season, for example, only 70% of FTSE 250 company shares were voted, and less than 50% the capital was voted in other UK listed companies.[12] As not all shares are voted given dispersed shareholdings in listed companies, as a general observation, an ownership position of 20% may be considered to be a 'significant ownership stake' in a listed company.

The effect of ownership and control on listed firm value is a long standing question in finance.[13] Such control may be considered in the context of 'inside' control—i.e. control by a founder as discussed in Chapter 5,[14] and 'outside' control—i.e. the presence of a significant shareholder unconnected to the business of the listed company.[15] Either of these may be evident in a dual class structure. The presence of either type of significant shareholder could conceivably provide confidence to the market on the listed company's ability to produce long-term results, which in turn could reduce the excessive discounting. To advocate for facilitating significant shareholders as a SMST-reform, there needs to be some evidentiary basis to suggest that a significant shareholder has a positive impact on firm value.

[9]For example, see the—UK Companies Act, 2006, Chapter 46 (UK Companies Act), Section 1159, which defines control in the context of subsidiaries, and the discussion of the Delaware court position in Wolf (2014).

[10]Delaware General Corporation Law (Title 8, Chapter 1 of the Delaware Code) (Delaware General Corporation Law).

[11]Delaware General Corporation Law, §203(c)(4).

[12]AGM Trends (2017, 15).

[13]For example, see Demsetz and Lehn (1985), Bolton and Thadden (1998), Cho (1998), and Demsetz and Villalonga (2001).

[14]See Chapter 5, Sect. C.1.a.

[15]See the discussion in Nguyen and Nielsen (2013).

The impact of significant shareholders on firm value remains, however, ambiguous.[16] Studies indicate that significant shareholders may play a beneficial role in mitigating the potential conflict of interest—i.e. agency costs—between managers and shareholders and, thereby, improve firm performance, benefiting all shareholders.[17] For example, US Professor George Dent summarizes the evidence of the potential benefits that a company may receive from the presence of a large block holder. These benefits may include more effective chief executive officer (CEO) performance pay, increased share prices and increased investment by the listed company in research and development.[18]

Conversely, evidence suggests that listed companies with significant shareholders may in practice have lower firm values than their non-controlled counterparts.[19] This lower valuation of firm value does not, however, appear to be due entirely to inefficient monitoring. Rather, the discounting may come from the market perception that private benefits are extracted from listed companies for the benefit of the significant shareholder.[20] In support of this position, there is some research to suggest that significant shareholders may influence firm policies to the detriment of minority shareholders' interests[21] or reduce the liquidity of a firm's shares.[22]

It stands to reason that these negative effects may be mitigated through strong legal protections for minority shareholders. However, monitoring by a controlling shareholder even with strong legal minority protections may not add long term value, as a shareholder with a significant stake may, as a result of such stake, be poorly diversified.[23] Though the controlling shareholder may be incentivized to monitor its investment, as its capital is tied up in one firm, such shareholder may also be risk adverse and therefore incentivized to "preserve wealth rather than create it."[24] This risk aversion would reduce the monitoring benefits of

[16] Ibid, 5.

[17] Grossman and Hart (1980), Shleifer and Vishny (1986), and Cheffins (2002, 366).

[18] Dent (2010, 116–117)

[19] Lin (2017, 458) and see the discussion in Cheffins (2002, 366).

[20] Ibid.

[21] Demsetz (1983).

[22] Glosten and Milgrom (1985) and Maug (1998).

[23] Cheffins (2002, 357).

[24] Ibid., referencing "In the Family's Way" *The Economist* (London) 15 December 2001, 75.

having a significant shareholder.[25] Given the ambiguity of the evidence available and that any monitoring benefits gained by having a significant shareholder may be negated by the perceived extraction of value by significant shareholders or risk aversion, increasing control is not advocated at this time in this chapter as a viable standalone option for effecting SMST reform. However, this position could be reconsidered as further research is undertaken in this area.

2. *Option 2: Cut-off Transmission Mechanisms*

As an alternative to reducing excessive discounting, another notionally effective option for SMST reform is to cut-off the transmission of SMST. As discussed in Chapter 6,[26] the most probable cause of SMST transmission is through the impact of an actual or perceived decline in share prices. The primary reason why company managers care about declining share prices is the impact on their compensation and job security. If executive compensation is structured to reward short-term financial objectives and if asset owners and asset managers remove directors—and senior managers—who fail to provide positive short-term financial results, then SMST will continue to be an issue in equity markets. Consequently, one option for SMST reform is to insulate boards and thereby company managers from the short-termism of asset owners and asset managers, and to impose legal or corporate governance restrictions on executive compensation that rewards short-term financial performance. The theory behind how each of these methods may act to reduce SMST is considered further below, and whether any of the reforms identified in Chapter 4 employ these methods are then considered in Sect. B below.

a. Board Insulation

The concept of cutting off potential SMST by insulating boards from asset owners and asset managers was put forward in the 1990s by well-known corporate lawyers, Martin Lipton and Steven Rosenblum of the New York firm, Wachtell, Lipton, Rosen & Katz. Their precise proposal was to replace the annual election of directors with a 'quinquennial' election—i.e. five-year terms—and to bar non-board approved changes in control

[25] Ibid.

[26] See Chapter 6, Sect. B.1.

between board elections.[27] Lipton and Rosenblum's stated intent was to provide "a framework that permits the corporation to carry out long-term plans and permits stockholders to assess their results before deciding whether to they are satisfied with their director's performance."[28]

Arguments for board insulation have been broadly advanced not only by legal practitioners such as Lipton and Rosenblum, but also by a wide variety of other parties. Advocates include prominent legal academics,[29] economics and business professors,[30] management thought leaders,[31] business columnists,[32] organizations such as the Aspen Institute,[33] and in the Kay Review,[34] the recommendations of which were endorsed by the UK government.[35] The unifying principle held by those persons advocating a board insulation approach, as observed by Professor Lucien Bebchuk, is that "the long-term costs of short termism, produced by both shareholder interventions and fears of such interventions, make it desirable to shield boards from shareholders."[36] Insulating boards from short-term shareholder pressure, it is argued by Bebchuk, "enables them to focus on enhancing long-term value and thereby better serve the long-term interests of companies and their shareholders."[37]

After acknowledging the considerable influence of the arguments to insulate boards on policymakers and public officials,[38] Bebchuk disputed the benefits of doing so. While acknowledging that board insulation may produce some long-term benefits, he argued "insulation advocates overlook the fact that these benefits might be outweighed by significant countervailing costs."[39] These costs are the benefits of shareholder

[27] Lipton and Rosenblum (1991, 225).

[28] Ibid., 228.

[29] Stout (2012), Bainbridge (2006), and Bratton and Wachter (2010).

[30] Fox and Lorsch (2012) and Porter (1992).

[31] For example, see Drucker (1986) at A32 arguing outside pressures push top managements toward short-term decisions.

[32] For example, see Nocera (2011) and Sorkin (2013).

[33] Aspen Institute (2009, 2010).

[34] Kay (2012) (Kay Review).

[35] Implementation (2014).

[36] Bebchuk (2013, 1639).

[37] Ibid.

[38] Ibid., 1640.

[39] Ibid., 1643.

engagement, Bebchuk asserted, and the accountability and discipline such engagement produces. This accountability and disciple "provide incentives to avoid shirking, empire building and other departures from shareholder interests that are costly both in the short and long term."[40]

The potential collateral damage inherent in insulating boards requires further analysis in the context of any specific reform proposal. However, if asset owners and asset managers are transmitting harmful short-termism into listed companies, cutting off such transmission is one possible option for reform. The extent to which the reforms reviewed in Chapter 4 act to counter the harms of SMST by insulating the board are considered in Sect. B.

b. Reduce Short Term Compensation

Another transmission method by which SMST may enter listed companies is through short-term focused executive or asset manager compensation structures. As discussed in Chapter 6,[41] declining share prices may have personal financial implications for company managers as a significant portion of management compensation—particularly in the United States (US) though this US model is gaining momentum worldwide—is often tied to share prices. The argument has been made that eliminating stock-based compensation, and other forms of short-term rewards, will help reduce the incentive for executive leadership to focus on the short term.[42] To be effective, however, cutting off SMST transmission via changes to executive compensation structures will need to be 'hard' law restrictions or such compensation structures will be susceptible to the short-termism of shareholders, or will need to occur in tandem with board insulation measures.

If deviations away from short-term performance objectives in executive compensation are encouraged on a voluntary basis, but asset owners and asset managers continue to have considerable latitude to change the board of directors, SMST will, theoretically at least, continue to be transmitted into listed companies. Consequently, insulating boards and altering execution compensation structures may not be an 'either/or' scenario. This was recognized by Lipton and Rosenblum.[43]

[40] Ibid.

[41] Chapter 6, Sect. B.1.

[42] Martin (2011) and Kay (2012, 13) (Recommendation 15).

[43] Lipton and Rosenblum (1991).

Their proposal for the 'quinquennial concept' involved not only five-year board terms, but also linked this board insulation to a five-year strategic report, which would be independently evaluated. This five-year report would serve as the basis for executive compensation and, in doing so, would "link a significant portion of the financial risks and rewards for managers to corporate performance against the corporation's five-year goals."[44] Consequently, Sect. B of this chapter considers whether any of the SMST-driven reforms at least conceptually attempt to cut off SMST either on a non-voluntary 'hard-law' basis, or by both insulating the board and limiting short-term executive compensation.

In addition to executive compensation structures, concerns have also been raised that the compensation structures of asset managers may contribute to SMST.[45] The argument made is that asset managers are not incentivized towards long-term investing as their compensation may be based on quarterly assessments of performance of assets under management. Although SMST may be transmitted from asset owners to asset managers through short-term oriented compensation structures, the method of addressing this transmission is through Option 1(b) discussed above. If asset owners are 'improved', asset manager compensation structures will theoretically at least be less short-term focused, and the SMST issue will be minimized. Consequently, the only method to cut-off SMST transmission between asset owners and asset managers considered in respect of this Option 2(b) in Sect. B are 'hard' law changes, which specifically restrict the short-term compensation of asset managers.

B. Analysis of Implemented SMST Reforms

This section analyzes each of the implemented SMST reforms summarized in Appendix 'A', to determine whether any of these implemented SMST reforms conceptually address the SMST problem by employing one or more of the options identified in Sect. A above. The results of this analysis are presented in tabular form in Appendix 'C'. As demonstrated

[44] Bebchuk (2013, 239).

[45] See the discussion in Chapter 6, Sect. C.1.

below, this analysis indicates that of the implemented SMST reform in this area, very few of the reforms at least theoretically meaningfully address the SMST concerns.

1. *Conceptual Effectiveness of Implemented Asset Owner Oriented SMST Reforms*

The following Sect. A.1 analyzes each of the implemented Asset Owner Oriented SMST reforms summarized in Appendix 'A', Table 1. These implemented SMST reforms are assessed on the basis of whether they, at least theoretically, act to address the SMST problem by employing one or more of the options identified in Sect. A above. The results of this analysis are then presented in tabular form in Appendix 'C', Table 5. As demonstrated below, this analysis indicates that of the implemented SMST reform in this area, few of the reforms at least theoretically meaningfully address the SMST concerns.

a. Measures Favouring Long-Term Share Ownership

The first grouping of SMST-driven reforms considered is reforms providing additional voting rights and rewards for long-term shareholders, as this area has received considerable attention. Despite much discussion, however, implemented reforms are modest, and consist only of the Florange Law[46] in France,[47] the use of L-Shares in certain European Union (EU) countries,[48] and the limited introduction of dual class shares structures on the Singapore Stock Exchange (SGX)[49] meant to give additional voting rights to certain asset owners. As discussed further in Chapter 4,[50] these reforms are meant to encourage longer-term shareholding and shareholding by insiders of listed companies, the rationale being that such shareholders are more likely to consider the long-term interests of listed companies and are less likely to use their voting authority solely to further their own short-term financial gain.

[46] LOI n° 2014-384 du 29 mars 2014 visant à reconquérir l'économie réelle (1) NOR: EFIX1322399L enacted in April 2014 (Florange Law).

[47] See Chapter 4, Sect. A.1.a.

[48] Ibid.

[49] See Chapter 4, Sect. A.1.c.

[50] Ibid., Sect. A.1.

The Florange Law enacted 'hard' law SMST-driven legislative change in 2014 meant to counter SMST by re-setting the corporate law default position in France to provide that double voting rights must be given to all shareholders who hold their shares for at least two years. Companies may opt out of this new default position, provided that the requisite 2/3rd shareholder approval is obtained. Increasing voting rights of all shareholders holding shares for over two years does not reduce SMST via Option 2—Cutting Off Transmission Mechanisms. Boards are not insulated from short-term interests, and short-term compensation structures are not restricted by measures in the Florange Law. Similarly, there are no provisions in the Florange Law designed to reduce performance uncertainty as per Option 1(a), which would include improved reporting of long-term objectives by company managers. There is also no indication that the Florange Law would 'improve' asset owners as per Option 1(b) either through increased communication and engagement with company managers, or 'enlightenment' towards a longer-term approach.

It is arguable that the Florange Law may create significant asset owners through the granting of double voting rights. However, there are no assurances that this will occur in practice, and even if it does, as discussed in Sect. A.1.c there are questions around whether this would positively impact firm value. In fact, there is suggestion of the opposite, as existing shareholders who get such rights may use the opportunity to realize on their investments by selling some shares while retaining their previous voting positions. Consequently, as shown in Appendix 'C', Table 5, the Florange Law is not considered a conceptually effective SMST reform.

Based on the same reasoning applied to the Florange Law, voluntary uses of loyalty shares or L-Shares granting bonus shares by French listed companies and other L-Share structures used by listed companies in certain EU jurisdictions that provide either bonus shares or increased voting rights to long-term shareholders are not considered a conceptually effective SMST reform. Such L-Shares do not cut off the transmission of SMST into the listed company or reduce excessive discounting central to the SMST concern either by furthering communication between asset owners, improving reporting of long-term objectives by company managers, or 'enlightening' asset owners as to the benefits of a longer-term approach.

As discussed in Chapter 4,[51] dual-class share structures, long permitted in certain jurisdictions including the US and Canada, have also been touted as a means of ameliorating the negative effects of SMST. The general argument raised is that such dual class structures allow founders or other insiders to retain a controlling voting position, thus allowing management to ignore the short-termism often seen in financial markets. Despite much discussion of the potential benefits of dual class structures, the only instance of dual class structures being introduced based on SMST concerns is the permission granted for dual-class listings of secondary listings on the SGX. However, dual class listings do not cut off the transmission of SMST as per Options 2(a) and 2(b) as boards of directors are not fully insulated from shareholders nor is management compensation tied to long-term performance in these structures. Further, dual class listings do not reduce performance uncertainty as set out in Option 1(a) by better disclosing long-term performance objectives or 'improving' asset owners as per Option 1(b) by facilitating communication or 'enlightenment' towards a longer-term approach.

There may be benefits to having a controlling shareholder as facilitated by dual class structures. Nevertheless, as discussed in Sect. A.1.c below there are questions around whether this would positively impact firm value, and further, there are no assurances that the controlling shareholder created in the dual class structure would pursue a longer-term approach. Thus, of the SMST-driven reforms that introduce measures favouring long-term share ownership, none conceptually address the SMST issue. This, however, is not the end of the story for dual class structures as a measure to ameliorate SMST. Further analysis is warranted, and evidence should be obtained investigating whether less pressure for short-term performance is observed by company managers in dual class structures. Similarly, analysis on short-termism in the share pricing of dual class structures relative to their industry piers with a non-dual class structure would be informative, although the difficulty in such analysis would be accounting for any potential negative effects of controller self-interest.

[51] Ibid.

b. Disclosure Reforms

Reforms to the timing and quality of information disclosed to the market by listed companies have also been a focus for SMST reformers. As considered further in Chapter 4,[52] the specific concerns raised are that the content of public disclosure is too focused on short-term financial objectives, and also the pace of such dissemination may exacerbate SMST concerns, as company managers feel pressured to constantly generate short-term results to produce fresh news. These concerns have generated some SMST reform, specifically 'hard' law changes to mandatory quarterly reporting the EU and UK, and 'hard' and 'soft' law changes to corporate governance reporting in the EU and UK.

Based on a recommendation in the Kay Review, the UK Government adopted regulations removing mandatory quarterly reporting requirements.[53] The UK changes took effect in November 2014, a year ahead of when amendments to the EU Transparency Directive[54] removed mandatory quarterly reporting for all EU Members. These reforms do not reduce performance uncertainty as per Option 1(a), as the reforms take away information from the market rather than provide greater disclosure around longer-term performance. However, it may be argued that removing mandatory quarterly reporting 'improves' asset owners, and by extension asset managers, as per Option 1(b). Arguably, asset owners, often via their asset manager, are too focused on short-term performance metrics. A significant contributor to such short-term approach is quarterly reporting by listed companies. The removal of mandatory quarterly reporting, therefore, provides space for companies to report results to the market over a longer time period, and could thus act to 'improve' asset managers and asset owners by facilitating longer-term reporting. As discussed in Chapter 4,[55] however, the impact of such reforms may be minimal as these changes are optional and US investors may still prefer quarterly reporting.

[52] See Chapter 4, Sect. A.3.

[53] UK Financial Services and Markets Act (Transparency) Regulations 2014 giving authority to the UK Financial Conduct Authority (FCA) to remove the requirement from the Disclosure and Transparency Rules in the FCA Handbook. https://www.handbook.fca.org.uk/.

[54] Directive 2013/50/EU (EU Transparency Directive).

[55] See Chapter 4, Sect. A.3.a.

Removing mandatory quarterly reporting could cut off the transmission of SMST into the listed company as per Option 2(a), as this action may insulate boards from having to provide short-term financial reporting. This is not an effective severing of the transmission of SMST concerns because, as noted above, the change is optional, and shareholders may still push for such reporting. Further, these reforms do not limit short-term executive compensation as per Option 2(b), which as noted in Sect. A, is also necessary for such reform to effectively cut off SMST. However, as the removal of EU and UK mandatory quarterly reporting requirements may 'improve' asset owners, and by extension asset managers, these are included as conceptually effective SMST reforms in Appendix 'C', Table 5.

The changes in the EU and the UK providing for longer-term strategic reporting could also be considered a means of reducing excessive discounting pursuant to Options 1(a) and (b). As discussed in Chapter 4,[56] these reforms include the strategic reporting requirement for all UK listed companies adopted in October 2013 in the UK[57] and the Financial Reporting Council (FRC) guidance on such reporting issued in June 2014,[58] together with EU changes including the EU recommendation in 2014 on the quality of corporate governance reporting[59] and the EU directive on non-financial reporting in place in EU Member States by December 2016.[60] As analyzed in Chapter 4,[61] these reforms essentially intend to (1) connect corporate actions with long-term strategy and focus less on short-term—e.g. quarterly—earnings results; and (2) emphasize corporate social responsibility (CSR) and environmental, social, governance (ESG) factors in addition to financial measures of performance of a listed company, which factors, notionally at least, represent inherently longer-term interests than short-term earnings.

These reforms certainly do not cut-off transmission of SMST into listed companies pursuant to Option 2. However, as noted above, they may, theoretically at least, act to reduce excessive discounting

[56] See Chapter 4, Sect. A.3.b.

[57] The Companies Act 2006 (Strategic Report and Directors' Report) Regulations 2013.

[58] Financial Reporting Council, Guidance on the Strategic Report (June 2014).

[59] EU Recommendation 2014/208/EU.

[60] Directive 2014/95/EU, which was in place in EU Member States by December 2016.

[61] See Chapter 4, Sect. A.3.b.

by asset owners or asset managers on a listed company's long-term performance as per Options 1(a) and (b). This would occur by such disclosure reducing performance uncertainty and 'improving' asset owners, and by extension asset managers, through emphasizing the benefits of a longer-term approach. Particularly, the changes to corporate governance reporting could better assist asset owners and asset managers to more accurately assess and measure long-term performance objectives.

As an example, the UK strategic report[62] may provide asset owners and asset managers with a yard stick by which to measure a company's long-term performance, and the details of how such objectives will be achieved and measured may give the market confidence that it will occur thereby reducing excessive discounting. Whether these measures will act to reduce excessive discounting thereby correcting SMST in practice remains to be seen. However, these reporting reforms are noted in Appendix 'C', Table 5, as at least conceptually effective SMST reforms.

c. Direct Communication/Engagement

As dissed in Chapter 4,[63] the argument has been presented by SMST reformers that channels between asset owners and company managers should be strengthened, and asset owners and company managers should communicate and engage directly. Such actions are meant to counter SMST by facilitating engagement between companies and long-term asset owners, which asset owners supposedly have a greater interest in long-term growth of listed companies than short-term shareholders. 'Hard' law reforms in this area are limited to Articles 3a and 3b of the EU Amended Shareholder Rights Directive,[64] which require that EU Members must ensure that: (1) intermediaries provide listed companies with information on asset owner identity; and (2) information on listed companies must be directly communicated to asset owners either via

[62]The Companies Act 2006 (Strategic Report and Directors' Report) Regulations 2013.

[63]See Chapter 4, Sect. A.4.

[64]Directive (EU) 2017/828 of the European Parliament and of the Council, of 17 May 2017, amending Directive 2007/36/EC as regards the encouragement of long-term shareholder engagement (effective as of 9 June 2017) (EU Amended Shareholder Rights Directive).

the company's website or transmitted without undue delay.[65] Another SMST-driven initiative is the UK Investor Forum,[66] meant to facilitate collective discussion and engagement with UK listed companies, arising from recommendations in the Kay Review.

Neither the reforms in Articles 3a and 3b of the EU Amended Shareholder Rights Directive nor the UK Investor Forum cut off SMST via Option 2. In fact, both reforms may have the opposite effect. These reforms could act to increase the transmission of SMST interests of asset owners into the listed company, as not only long-term focused asset owners may take advantage of such communication channels. The question then is whether either of these reforms may act to counter SMST by reducing the excessive discounting inherent in share pricing. It is difficult to see how the reforms in the EU Amended Shareholder Rights Directive could act to reduce excessive discounting as per Option 1(a) or 1(b), as they facilitate the flow of all information and do not require any specific reporting on long-term objectives by listed companies or encourage asset owners to take a longer-term approach.

The UK Investor Forum, however, has the potential to reduce excessive discounting by 'improving' asset owners pursuant to Option 1(b). The intent of the UK Investor Forum is to facilitate dialogue by asset owners and asset managers, and company managers and its stated purpose is to "[p]osition stewardship at the heart of investment decision-making by facilitating dialogue, creating long-term solutions and enhancing value."[67] Such 'enlightened' collective action and discussion may act to reduce monitoring costs of long-term performance by any one individual asset owner or manager, and thereby encourage listed companies to take a longer-term approach. There is no indication that this initiative will overcome the numerous hurdles related to collective action including concerns over free-riding and regulatory issues around insider dealings. Therefore, although the UK Investor Forum is shown in Appendix 'C', Table 5 as a conceptually effective SMST reform, there are serious questions around whether this initiative will be an effective counter to SMST in practice.

[65] EU Amended Shareholder Rights Directive, Article 3a and 3b.

[66] The UK Investor Forum. https://www.investorforum.org.uk/ (UK Investors Forum).

[67] https://www.investorforum.org.uk/about/purpose/.

d. Restrictions on Stock Lending

As discussed in Chapter 4,[68] stock-lending has occasionally been raised in connection with SMST concerns. Although not clearly articulated, the concern appears to be that stocks may be 'lent', often by an asset manager, to a third-party borrower, which third party borrower is not interested in the long-term viability of an organization. In the Kay Review, Kay proposed that asset owners should have more information on when their shares are being lent to third parties, and, therefore, be able to exercise greater judgment on when such lending is appropriate. This theme of disclosure as a means of correcting SMST was picked up by the EU and adopted as a 'hard' law reform in the EU UCITS Directive.[69] The EU reform requires that investors in EU UCITS, EU collective investment schemes, receive all income from stock-lending net of operational costs. These EU changes do not have any impact on the SMST issue via Option 2—Cutting Off Transmission Mechanisms as they do not cut-off the short-termism of asset owners and managers from listed companies. Further, these changes do not reduce excessive discounting either by reducing performance uncertainty or 'improving' asset owners as per Options 1(a) and (b). Consequently, this reform is not included in Appendix 'C', Table 5 as a conceptually effective SMST reform.

e. Long Term Funds

Based on concerns that it is difficult for asset owners, often via asset managers, to adequately assess if a listed company is generating sustainable longer-term corporate value, the LTVC Index was developed in 2016. As considered further in Chapter 4,[70] the LTVC Index is an index of about 250 companies identified through a Dow Jones proprietary system to take a long-term view, which companies are also meant to have a sustained history of financial quality. This financial industry initiative does not directly cut off transmission of SMST into listed companies pursuant to Option 2. Rather, the purpose of the LTVC Index is to reduce excessive discounting by identifying listed companies with

[68] See Chapter 4, Sect. A.5.

[69] ESMA Guidelines for competent authorities and UCITS management companies on ETFs and other UCITS issues, ESMA/2012/832EN (UCITS Directive).

[70] See Chapter 4, Sect. A.6.

proven track-records of long-term value generation to asset owners and asset managers who are 'enlightened' to the benefits of a longer-term approach.

If the LTVC Index is successful, companies on this LTVC Index may feel more confident that their long-term prospects are not being excessively discounted and, therefore, company managers may be more confident when proceeding with long-term objectives and less likely to focus on short-term financial objectives. This LTVC Index could also 'improve' asset owners if the indexed listed companies generate returns over the long-term that are superior to other stock market indexes, and these results are communicated to the market. Theoretically, therefore, this initiative may reduce SMST via Options 1(a) and (b), and this reform is thus included in Appendix 'C', Table 5 as a conceptually effective SMST reform. However, this is a big ask for a relatively untested financial industry voluntary initiative, particularly one which has struggled to gain support from leading global investors. Consequently, it remains to be seen whether this LTVC Index will have a material impact on excessive discounting.

Of the asset owner-oriented reforms analyzed in Sect. B.1, as illustrated in Appendix 'C', Table 5, only half address the SMST issue using one of the options identified in Sect. A as necessary for SMST reform. None of the reforms cut-off SMST transmission as per Option 2. The implemented asset owner SMST reforms that address SMST using one of the options identified in Sect. A appear to do so through Options 1(a) and/or (b)—reducing excessive discounting by asset owners either by reducing performance uncertainty or 'improving' asset owners. These SMST reforms include the EU and UK removal of mandatory quarterly reporting, 'soft' law UK and EU strategic and governance reporting requirements, and the UK Investor Forum and the US LTVC Index, each of which is a voluntary financial industry initiative. As discussed above, there are questions around how effective such SMST reforms may be in practice. However, in theory at least, these implemented asset owner reforms could conceptually reduce SMST concerns.

2. *Analysis of Intermediary Oriented Reforms*

The following section analyzes the implemented intermediary oriented SMST reforms summarized in Appendix 'A', Table 2. As with the asset owner oriented SMST reforms analyzed in Sect. B.1 above, these intermediary reforms are assessed on the basis of whether they, at least theoretically, address the SMST of intermediaries by employing one or more of the options identified in Sect. A above. The results of this analysis are presented in tabular form in Appendix 'C', Table 6. As demonstrated below, as with the asset owner oriented SMST reforms, of the implemented reforms meant to address intermediary SMST, few of these implemented reforms actually meaningfully address the SMST concerns.

a. Stewardship and Disclosure

An area that has witnessed significant discussion and generated some implemented reform, is the concept of guiding principles establishing desired behaviour for market participants and the disclosure of adherence to such principles. These guiding principles are meant to encourage accountability, mainly from intermediaries who manage other people's money, by focusing on sustainable long-term returns. As set out in Chapter 4,[71] specific SMST-driven reforms in this space include the Stewardship Code in the UK,[72] which the UK Government indicated was amended in 2012 in line with the recommendations in the Kay Review to require asset managers to engage with listed company on long-term strategy in order to deliver long-term sustainable returns[73] and the adoption of a Japanese Stewardship Code[74] based on the UK Stewardship Code, promoting engagement by asset managers with listed companies in order to deliver long-term sustainable returns, Additionally, the UK National Association of Pension Funds (NAPF) Stewardship Disclosure Framework[75] encouraged asset managers to clearly articulate stewardship approaches on long-term investment objectives to their clients.

Similar to requirements contained in many stewardship codes, and Articles 3h and 3i of the EU Amended Shareholder Rights Directive require institutional investors to publicly disclose an investment strategy

[71] See Chapter 4, Sect. B.1.

[72] https://www.frc.org.uk/investors/uk-stewardship-code (UK Stewardship Code).

[73] Implementation (2014, 11).

[74] Japanese Financial Services Authority, "Stewardship Code; 227 institutional investors have signed up to the Principles for Responsible Institutional Investors as of April 5, 2018". Online: https://www.fsa.go.jp/en/refer/councils/stewardship/20160315.html.

[75] Stewardship Disclosure Framework. Online: http://www.plsa.co.uk/PolicyandResearch/Corporate-Governance/Stewardship/Stewardship-disclosure-framework.aspx (NAPF Stewardship Disclosure Framework).

and report on such strategy to institutional investors. The UK Investor Forum has also been cited as a SMST-driven reform meant to facilitate collective engagement and encourage best practice by asset managers. Financial industry initiatives in this space include Dominic Barton of McKinsey & Company (McKinsey) and Canada Pension Plan Investment Board (CPPIB)'s online platform developed in 2013, Focusing Capital on the Long Term (FCLT),[76] which intended to develop practical structures, metrics, and approaches for longer-term behaviour in the investment and business worlds, and the calls to action by Larry Fink, CEO of BlackRock Inc. (BlackRock), in 2016,[77] 2017,[78] and 2018[79] for asset managers to be more involved in holding listed companies to account for delivering long-term sustainable value (BlackRock Letters).

Although this is an area of SMST reform that has seen some action, questions remain as to how these reforms actually act to counter SMST. They do not cut-off the transmission of SMST into listed companies via Options 2. These reforms instead encourage or require asset managers—and asset owners—to support listed companies in their efforts to deliver long-term sustainable value. This approach attempts to 'improve' asset owners as per Option 1(b). Although admirable, the difficulty with this approach, based on the analysis provided in this book, is that such 'improvement' will only work if efforts are made in tandem to reduce performance uncertainty as per Option 1(a). The excessive discounting appears to be occurring precisely because asset managers and asset owners have a short-term preference in large part because they are not able to adequately rely on the ability of company managers to deliver long-term results.

Consequently, merely asking asset managers to commit to greater long-term value generation, theoretically at least, will not act to reduce excessive discounting. Such 'improvement' needs to coincide with better quality long-term reporting by company managers. As discussed in Chapter 4,[80] there are also real questions around whether there has been meaningful buy-into stewardship principles by market participants. Therefore,

[76] http://www.fclt.org.

[77] Turner (2016).

[78] Oyedele (2017).

[79] Fink (2018).

[80] See Chapter 4, Sect. B.1.

although these reforms are included in Appendix 'C', Table 6 as a conceptually effective SMST reform on the basis of Option 1(b), questions remain around whether such reforms will actually be effective in practice.

b. Asset Manager Remuneration

As discussed in Chapter 4,[81] concerns have been raised that asset managers are not sufficiently incentivized towards long-term investing as their compensation may be based on quarterly assessments of performance of assets under management. The UK Government pointed to the UK NAPF Stewardship Disclosure Framework and other financial industry initiatives such as the Investment Management Association (IMA's) guidance on disclosure of charges by funds,[82] as examples of how the financial industry in the UK was addressing such SMST concerns. Rather than prescribing how asset managers should charge for their services, these measures instead simply provide for disclosure of asset manager fee structures to asset owners. This compensation disclosure is meant to assist asset owners ensure that the actions of asset managers are appropriately aligned with the asset owner's interests.

These reforms do not act to reduce excessive discounting as per Option 1(a) by reducing performance uncertainty. Nor do these reforms insulate boards from the short-termist pressures of asset owners or asset managers as per Option 2(a). It could be argued that these changes 'improve' asset managers as per Option 1(b) as they focus on transparency of asset manager pay structures. Further, it is arguable that such reforms may act to reduce the short-term focus of asset managers compensation as per Option 2(b). However, as discussed further in Chapter 6,[83] the flaw in this reasoning is that asset managers may loyalty be pursuing their client's interests by engaging in short-termist behaviour. Such short-termism may be traced back to asset owners as they set the compensation and investment parameters in their contractual relationships with asset managers.

Though better-quality disclosure of remuneration structures is useful to ensure the interests of asset owners and asset managers are aligned, there is nothing to suggest that such additional disclosure will reduce short-term focused compensation structures of asset managers.

[81] Ibid., Sect. B.3.

[82] Implementation (2014, 37–39).

[83] See Chapter 6, Sect. C.1.

Therefore, these reforms are not included in Appendix 'C', Table 6 as an effective SMST reform. To be conceptually effective, such measures would need to specifically limit short-term compensation, which is what is done in reforms to the EU UCITS Directive.

As set out Chapter 4,[84] the EU UCITS Directive—which only applies to the management of certain EU collective investment schemes—, does include restrictions on the short-term compensation of asset managers. These reforms include that:

1. guaranteed variable remuneration—e.g., guaranteed bonus of x% of returns—is only to be paid in exceptional circumstances;
2. remuneration policies must be reviewed yearly and should be consistent with effective risk management;
3. a substantial portion of remuneration must be paid in EU UCITS units and deferred for a reasonable period of time; and
4. staff cannot use personal hedging strategies or insurance in remuneration.

These restrictions with respect to EU UCITS may act to reduce SMST by imposing 'hard' law restrictions on executive compensation that rewards short-term financial performance which cuts off SMST as per Option 2(b). These 'hard' law restrictions may, theoretically at least, act to reduce SMST by linking asset manager remuneration to longer-term fund performance, thereby reducing the incentive of asset managers to push for short-term financial returns from listed companies. These changes are also mandated regardless of the interests of investors, and, therefore, would apply even if the investors in such programs would prefer shorter-term returns. These changes are limited as they only apply to EU UCITS. However, these reforms are included in Appendix 'C', Table 6 as a conceptually effective SMST reform.

c. Voting Restrictions

As discussed in Chapter 4,[85] SMST concerns have been raised in the context of voting by intermediaries. The concern is that such intermediaries have discretion to vote on behalf of asset owners, but such intermediaries

[84] See Chapter 4, Sect. B.3.

[85] See Chapter 4, Sect. B.4.

may be pursuing their own short-term interests rather than the long-term interests of asset owners. Reforms in the UK and at the EU level have focused on disclosure of the voting process as a means of ameliorating such SMST concerns. In the UK, changes to the UK Stewardship Code placed a duty on intermediaries to disclose voting policies and to make use of such voting power.[86] At the EU level, the EU Amended Shareholder Rights Directive includes provisions meant to ensure that intermediaries facilitate the exercise of asset owner rights, including voting rights, or explain why they do not.[87] Reforms in Switzerland, based on the Minder Initiative,[88] went further, and restricted voting by intermediaries. Specifically, the Swiss Constitution now prohibits all proxy voting by an intermediary or by a depositary in respect of any Swiss public companies listed on stock exchanges in Switzerland or abroad, and Swiss pension funds must vote in the interests of the beneficiaries and disclose how they voted.

None of the changes to the UK Stewardship Code, the EU Amended Shareholder Rights Directive, or the Minder Initiative act to reduce SMST via Option 1(b) by 'improving' asset owners, or via Option 2, by cutting off SMST transmission mechanisms. Instead, these measures are meant to encourage voting by existing asset owners, rather than intermediaries. Arguably, such reforms could reduce performance uncertainty as per Option 1(a) by better connecting asset owners with listed companies and reducing intermediary self-interest. Further, such reforms may be commendable as they help ensure that the interests of asset owners are better communicated into the listed company. However, from a SMST perspective, rather than alleviate SMST concerns, such measures may actually make the perceived SMST issue worse.

For the reasons discussed in this book, if there is a SMST problem it appears to originate from asset owners excessively discounting long-term returns thereby causing company managers to prioritize short-term financial returns. Consequently, if asset managers are acting on the parameters set by their clients and asset owners are short-termist, increasing asset owner voting channels into listed companies could just exacerbate the SMST issue. Such concerns in respect of the EU Amended

[86] UK Stewardship Code, 9, principle 6.

[87] EU Amended Shareholder Rights Directive, Article 3c.

[88] Thomas Minder initiative in English, 'Maurice's Musings' (1 March 2013) (Minder Initiative).

Shareholder Rights Directive were also raised by Johnston and Morrow, who expressed concern that the changes "will further empower shareholders with a short-term perspective."[89] As a result, these reforms are not included in Appendix 'C', Table 6 as a conceptually effective SMST reform.

d. Proxy Advisors

As discussed in Chapter 4,[90] the connection between SMST and the proxy advisory process is tenuous at best. However, the claim made is that proxy advisors—entities which provide voting advice to asset owners and asset managers—may contribute to SMST as asset owners and asset managers rely heavily on voting recommendations that could contain conflicts or do not reflect the investment horizons of asset owners. The only implemented reform in response to such concerns has been in the EU Amended Shareholder Rights Directive.[91]

The EU Amended Shareholder Rights Directive includes 'hard' law provisions requiring proxy advisors to adopt and adhere to a code of conduct or explain why they do not. This code is meant to ensure that research and voting recommendations are accurate and reliable and are developed in the client's sole interest. This reform does not act to reduce SMST via Option 2, by cutting off SMST transmission mechanisms. Although better transparency and accountability in the proxy advisory process is worthwhile to ensure prudent management of investments, it is difficult to see how the proxy advisor code of conduct could act to reduce excessive discounting as per Option 1(a), as it does not increase asset owner/asset manager confidence that company managers will deliver on long-term performance objectives. Similarly, there is no indication that such code of conduct will 'improve' asset owners towards longer-term perspective. Therefore, this reform is not included in Appendix 'C', Table 6 as a conceptually effective SMST reform.

Of the implemented intermediary-oriented reforms analyzed in this Sect. B.2, as illustrated in Appendix 'C', Table 6, only one reform actually addresses the SMST issue by employing one of the options identified in Option 2 as necessary for SMST reform. This reform is the 'hard' law

[89] Johnston and Morrow (2014, 1).

[90] See Chapter 4, Sect. B.7.

[91] EU Amended Shareholder Rights Directive, Article 3j.

changes made to the EU UCITS Directive, which restrict certain forms of short-term compensation payable to asset managers of EU UCITS. This reform may reduce SMST by cutting off the transmission of SMST from asset owners in accordance with Option 2(b) as SMST transmission is cut off through the legislative restrictions on short-term focused compensation structures. In theory at least, this implemented intermediary reform could act to effectively reduce SMST concerns, albeit on a limited basis as the reform only applies to asset managers of EU UCITS.

There are also a number of implemented intermediary reforms including UK/Japan Stewardship Code, UK NAPF Stewardship Framework, UK Investor Forum, BlackRock Letters and FCLT, UK NAPF Stewardship Framework/IMA and financial industry guidance which may also act to reduce SMST via Option 1(b)—'improving' asset owners. However, each of these SMST reforms is voluntary or 'soft' law, and to be at least conceptually effective, will also need to coincide with improved quality longer-term reporting by company managers.

3. *Analysis of Company Manager Oriented Reforms*

The following Sect. B.3 analyzes each of the implemented company manager oriented SMST reforms summarized in Appendix 'A', Table 3. As with the asset owner and intermediary oriented SMST reforms analyzed in Sects. B.1 and B.2 above, these company manager SMST reforms are assessed on the basis of whether they, at least theoretically, act to address the SMST problem by employing one or more of the necessary options identified in Sect. A above. The results of this analysis are presented in tabular form in Appendix 'C', Table 7. As demonstrated below, as is the case with the asset owner and intermediary oriented SMST reforms, of the implemented SMST reforms meant to address company manager SMST, few of these actually meaningfully address the underlying SMST concerns.

a. Company Manager Remuneration

Executive compensation reform is a significant area of discussion, and the focus of much guidance and regulation, particularly around 'say-on-pay' votes by shareholders of listed companies. As discussed in Chapter 4,[92]

[92] See Chapter 4, Sect. C.1.

the analysis in this book is limited to reforms to executive compensation which intend to address the SMST issue. This does not include 'say-on-pay' voting structures, as these appear to be motivated more by concerns over excessive compensation and linking pay to performance rather than specific SMST factors. SMTS-driven reforms in this space are meant to reduce or limit executive remuneration if such pay is based on short-term performance and unrestricted equity—i.e. no vesting requirements—, as it has been argued that this type of pay results in short-sighted decisions by company managers at the cost of longer-term economic performance of listed companies. Despite the arguments to restrict short-term compensation, implemented 'hard' law SMST-driven reforms have been limited to enhancements of executive compensation reporting enacted in the UK, at the EU level and in the US, and to 'soft' law guidance linking long-term performance to compensation in governance codes.

'Hard' law reforms include the UK Remuneration Regulations enacted in 2013,[93] which changes require a remuneration report to be presented by companies to their shareholders annually setting out each director's pay for the previous financial year, and how such pay is linked to performance. At the EU level, the Article 9a of the EU Amended Shareholder Rights Directive includes a requirement for an executive remuneration policy, which must be in line with a listed company's long-term interests, and Article 9b mandates a remuneration report, which report must specify how executive remuneration is linked to the listed company's long-term performance.

In the US, to some degree in line with Lipton and Rosenblum's proposal for a quinquennial report linked to executive compensation,[94] the US Securities and Exchange Commission (SEC) implemented a change to Item 402 of Regulation S-K in 2015.[95] This change required that, commencing with 2018 registration statements and annual 10-K filings for US regulated entities, US listed corporations must disclose

[93] UK Enterprise and Regulatory Reform Act 2013 and The Large and Medium-sized Companies and Groups (Accounts and Reports) (Amendment) Regulations 2013 (UK Remuneration Regulations).

[94] Lipton and Rosenblum (1991).

[95] Implemented in August 2015 by an amendment to US securities regulation on executive compensation required as part of the Dodd-Frank reforms—SEC, 'Pay Versus Performance', Proposed Rule proposing amendments to Item 402 of Regulation S-K to implement Section 14(i) of the Securities Exchange Act of 1934.

the relationship between executive compensation actually paid for five years and corporate financial performance. However, unlike Lipton and Rosenblum's proposal,[96] this report is retrospective rather than forward looking. SMST-driven executive compensation reform has also seen more general 'soft' law reform in the form of encouraging links between long-term performance and pay in a variety of governance codes, including in Australia, Norway and Singapore.[97]

These reforms do not insulate the board from short-term interests of asset owners or asset managers pursuant to Option 2(a), nor do they act to 'improve' asset owners as per Option 1(b). Of these reporting measures, only the EU reporting measures intend to reduce short-term compensation of company managers and to link executive pay to longer-term performance by listed companies. These measures theoretically could reduce SMST pursuant to Option 2(b), if they cut off the transmission of asset owner and asset manager short-term interests into a listed company. However, the 'hard' law reforms are based on disclosure of the remuneration practices of listed companies, and the 'soft' law reforms only encourage pay to be linked to long-term performance, rather than providing prescriptive restrictions on the types of compensation payable to company managers. Consequently, such measures will not be conceptually effective on their own to cut off transmission of SMST into listed companies, as they will also require insulation of the board. Such reforms insulating the board from the pressures of asset owners and asset managers have not been implemented.

The question remains as to whether the reforms discussed above may be effective in reducing performance uncertainty pursuant to Option 1(a). As discussed in Sect. B.1.a above, strategic reporting in the UK may be considered a conceptually effective SMST reform as it could reduce performance uncertainty by providing asset owners and asset managers with a clear yard stick by which to measure a company's long-term performance. Similarly, it could be argued that the 'hard' law reporting requirements in the UK, EU and US could be seen to assist asset owners and asset managers to better determine whether company managers are meeting long-term performance objectives. Whether these measures will act to reduce performance uncertainty thereby correcting

[96] Lipton and Rosenblum (1991).

[97] See discussion in Chapter 4, Sect. C.1.

SMST in practice remains to be seen, and will require strong, tangible connections between long-term strategic plans and executive compensation. The 'soft' law guidance on long-term compensation included in various governance codes arguably does not go far enough as only general statements are provided rather than specific guidance on reporting. Further, the reporting in the US and the UK does not expressly link to longer-term performance. Consequently, only Articles 9a and 9b of the EU Amended Shareholder Rights Directive are included in Appendix 'C', Table 7 as a conceptually effective SMST reforms, as these reforms theoretically could act to reduce excessive discounting by asset owners and asset managers.

b. Best Practices for Company Managers

Various voluntary initiatives have been put in place encouraging company managers to manage listed companies for the long-term. As set out further in Chapter 4,[98] these initiatives include the recommendations from the Institute of Directors (IoD) in numerous jurisdictions, governance guidance in Australia and South Africa, financial industry initiatives such as Tomorrow's Company and the Generation Foundation, and the specific calls for company managers to focus on the long-term by Larry Fink of BlackRock and others.

These measures do not address SMST through cutting off transmission from asset owners or asset managers via Option 2, nor do they act to 'improve' asset owners as per Option 1(b). As with reforms to company manager remuneration discussed above, the question remains as to whether these efforts could address SMST by reducing performance uncertainty as per Option 1(a). To do so, these voluntary initiatives would need to increase asset owner/asset manager confidence that company managers will actually deliver on long-term performance objectives there by reducing the real or perceived excessive discounting by asset owners. Similarly, adding clarity around the duties of directors to promote the long-term success of a listed company—for example, the language in Section 172 of the UK Companies Act[99]—may act to reduce performance uncertainty as per Option 1(a). Voluntary initiatives and refined scope of directors' statutory fiduciary duties towards long-term

[98] See Chapter 4, Sect. C.2.

[99] UK Companies Act 2006, Chapter 46, (UK Companies Act).

performance objectives may be helpful in demonstrating asset owner—and asset manager—commitment to long-term performance objectives. However, without robust and measurable strategic long-term reporting to asset owners and asset managers, such initiatives will not act to effectively reduce excessive discounting. Consequently, these reforms are not included in Appendix 'C', Table 7 as a standalone conceptually effective SMST reform.

The analysis in this section demonstrates that of the 24 areas of implemented reform identified, only 12—or 50%—conceptually address the SMST issue by employing one of the options set out in Sect. A as necessary for effective SMST reform. Each of these theoretically effective SMST reforms is summarized in Appendix 'C', Table 8 (Conceptually Effective SMST Reforms). This table also indicates the type of reform—i.e. 'hard' law, 'soft' law or voluntary initiative, revealing that six of the ten conceptually effective SMST reforms are 'hard' law changes.

The limitations of these conceptually effective SMST reforms are also identified. The limitations identified are that these SMST reforms are disclosure-based, voluntary, untested or limited in scope, with all of the 'hard' law reforms being disclosure or 'comply or explain' based, limited in scope or 'opt-in'. As discussed earlier in this book, disclosure-based regulation can be a powerful tool in impacting corporate behaviour. However, use of this approach does suggest reform has generally been a much 'lighter' touch from regulators than called for by SMST reformers. Whether such 'light' touch approach is indeed the most feasible means of addressing SMST is considered below.

C. Why a Light Regulatory Touch with a Clear Message May Be the Solution

As demonstrated through the analysis in Chapter 4, minimal regulatory or financial industry SMST-driven reform has been implemented despite a plethora of reform proposals and considerable discussion of the SMST issue. Further, of the implemented reforms identified in Sect. B above that have the potential to address the SMST issue, most are limited in scope or are voluntary or disclosure-based rather than prescribing, or restricting, specific action. This relatively 'light' touch approach may be justifiable due to the complexities involved in defining the SMST problem, and the evidentiary issues around proving the harms caused by such SMST.

Further, accepting that SMST is a problematic issue requiring regulatory correction, the prescriptive regulatory action required to implement Option 2 by cutting off SMST transmission mechanisms raises collateral concerns. As discussed in Sect. B.2 of this chapter, Option 2 necessitates a two-pronged effort to insulate boards and limit short-term focused compensation each of which require significant 'hard' law reforms. Board insultation raises questions about management accountability and whether with such board insulation there would be sufficient constraints on management excess. Legal constraints on management compensation may also have a negative impact by limiting a listed company's competitiveness. Given this landscape, it is not surprising that SMST-driven reform efforts to date have been relatively 'light' touch and focused on reducing performance uncertainty via Option 1(a), and 'improve' or 'enlighten' asset owners via Option 1(b).

I contend that SMST reform efforts should continue to be primarily be 'light' touch, but the focus should continue to zero in on ways to minimize excessive discounting by asset owners via a combination of Options 1(a) and (b). Eliminating, or at least reducing, the short-term bias of asset owners by 'improving' asset owners, while concurrently reducing performance uncertainty of listed companies appears to be the optimal way to reduce SMST. With such bias reduced or eliminated, there would be no need to cut off transmission mechanisms or be concerned about constrains on management. In support of this argument is the proposition considered further in Chapter 5 that the discounting of future returns by asset owners, although excessive, is based in large part on rational concerns about a listed company's future financial performance. Consequently, forcing a reduction of such discounting through 'hard' law measures cutting-off SMST transmission will not address the underlying concerns held by asset owners. Further, assuming that the discounting is excessive to the point where there is a market-wide bias, and asset owners may be considered to be acting sub-optimally, arguments have been made that rather than correction through paternalistic intrusive regulation of financial markets, a 'lighter' touch may be more effective to reduce such market-wide bias.

'Hard' law, prescriptive regulatory measures may be justified and effective in certain circumstances—for example, legal restrictions on gambling which aim to save us from our biases, such as an optimism bias where we over-estimate small probability events, or in the capital market context, such as restrictions on harmful insider trading. US law professors, Christine Jolls and Cass Sunstein, identified this insulation or 'choice-blocking' approach using law, but also articulated another approach, namely 'debiasing through law', which approach may be more appropriate in certain cases of 'bounded rationality'.[100] The concept of 'bounded rationality' was made famous by Herbert Simon and built on by Nobel Prize winner Daniel Kahneman.[101] 'Bounded rationality' essentially means decisions are made rationally, but within the limits of available information,[102] and, as added by Kahneman,[103] mental constraints—such as a intuition and use of heuristics—i.e. mental short-cuts—in decision-making. Rather than insulating legal outcomes from the effects of bounded rationality, Jolls and Sunstein's 'debiasing through law' approach operates directly on the boundedly rational behaviour. This 'debiasing through law' approach attempts to help people either reduce or eliminate negative behaviour.[104] For example, a 'debiasing through law' approach in the capital market context would be requiring specific disclosure for risky investments, such as initial coin offerings, rather than prohibiting such capital raisings entirely.

Jolls and Sunstein articulate the advantages of this 'debiasing through law' approach as "a less intrusive, more direct, and more democratic response to the problem of bounded rationality."[105] Sunstein further advocated for this 'light' touch approach—also termed 'nudging'—in his 2014 book, which he opened by affirming that human beings can be myopic and compulsive, giving undue weight to the short-term.[106] However, Sunstein asserted that "in light of the pervasive risk of government error and the inescapable fact of human diversity, it is usually best to use the mildest and most choice-preserving forms of intervention."[107]

[100] Jolls and Sunstein (2006, 200).

[101] Bollen (2012, 137).

[102] Simon (1955, 99).

[103] Kahneman (2003, 697).

[104] Jolls and Sunstein (2006, 200).

[105] Ibid., 200–201.

[106] Sunstein (2014).

[107] Sunstein (2014, 17).

These softer forms of action include 'nudges', which Sunstein explained as "initiatives that maintain freedom of choice while also steering people's decisions in the right direction (as judged by people themselves)."[108]

This 'nudge' approach draws parallels to earlier work by Sunstein on the expressive function of law.[109] Sunstein argued that the function of law is often to make a statement rather than directly control behavior.[110] Central to this concept is that for law to perform its expressive function, the law must communicate effectively well.[111] Further analysis is warranted on the language and clarity of the regulatory measures meant to correct short-termism as an expression of a desired social norm—i.e. do regulatory reforms that identify and attempt to correct the harms of SMST clearly communicate an intention to do so? However, the 'light' touch approach adopted in reforms identified as conceptually effective appear to attempt to 'nudge' behaviour and be a positive expression of legislative intent to direct market behaviour towards a desired social norm.

Legal researcher Oskari Juurikkala added specificity to assertion that 'nudges' are favourable to 'hard' law in addressing issues of bounded rationality in the context of complex capital market concerns. Juurikkala presented five arguments in favour of simpler and 'lighter' regulation of financial markets.[112] Juurikkala's arguments were that:

1. novel 'light' touch regulations can change behaviour;
2. faulty market perceptions seem to be best corrected by market-based solutions;
3. simple rather than complex regulation may be better at solving problems caused by lack of market discipline, pricing inefficiencies and financial innovation;

[108] Ibid.

[109] Sunstein (1996, 2024).

[110] Ibid., see the summary of the discussion on the expressive function of law at footnote 14 of Sunstein (1996).

[111] Ibid., 2050.

[112] Jurrikkala (2012, 36–38).

4. regulatory rule makers are subject to imperfect rationality reducing the quality of regulatory intervention—an extension of the public choice theory;[113] and
5. regulatory complexity exacerbates the harmful effects of limited rationality.[114]

Applying Juurikkala specific arguments, and Jolls and Sunstein's general position that 'debiasing through law' may be an optimal response in certain circumstances, to the context of the SMST issue supports the conclusion that SMST concerns may be best addressed through a 'light' touch approach. Such approach would use the method of reducing performance uncertainty as per Option 1(a) and 'improving' asset owners and asset managers as per Option 1(b) of the dual pathway.

This 'light' touch regulatory approach also provides guidance and assistance to market participants who are behaving sub-optimally while not restricting the freedom and innovation of other parties.[115] The specific 'light' touch regulatory options identified, in order of increasing intervention, include default rules, framing and information disclosure rules, cooling-off periods and limitations on choice.[116] Four of the ten conceptually effective regulatory SMST reforms identified in Sect. B and summarized in Appendix 'C', Table 8 (Conceptually Effective SMST Reforms) involve targeted disclosure. Particularly, these reforms require disclosure around future performance objectives and results of such strategy, or disclosure on the links between executive compensation and long-term performance of listed companies. There may be questions on whether the language in such reforms is sufficiently targeted towards long-term performance. However, this approach may in theory be an effective means of 'nudging' market behaviour away from a short-term bias.

[113]Public choice theory is a widely accepted theory in economics that challenges the assumption of rational and well intentioned law-making. See the summary in Jurrikkala (2012, 37) and generally in Lucas and Tasic (2015), in which the authors consider behavioural public choice theory, which expands traditional public choice theory to encompass research in behavioural economics.

[114]Jurrikkala (2012, 36–38).

[115]Ibid., 51.

[116]Ibid., referring to Camerer et al. (2003).

Another argument raised is that the market is best left to the task of debiasing.[117] As demonstrated in this book, there have been numerous calls for regulatory intervention in order to debias equity markets from their supposed current short-term focus. There are, however, significant concerns about regulatory debiasing, and resources and incentives to do so are weak in comparison to the private sector.[118] The argument that the financial industry is best placed to carry on with such debiasing is strengthened by the likelihood that policymakers are themselves not free from behavioural biases and self-interest. In the case of SMST, as discussed in Chapter 3, the swell of public interest and corresponding pressure to address the SMST may have caused regulators to adopt measures in the name of SMST correction, many of reforms which on rigorous analysis, actually appear not to even conceptually address the SMST issue. Rather than implementing reactionary regulation meant to appease an interested public, short-termism debiasing may be more effective if it develops from the market itself, with clear direction from regulators.

Accordingly, in the context of SMST, it may be more valuable for policymakers to start the ball rolling through an assessment of their relevant market place—as was done in the UK with the Kay Review, and in the EU with the EU Governance Green Paper,[119] and to continue monitoring SMST in the context of specific equity markets, essentially a reflexive law position—as discussed further below—that emphasizes self-regulation with regulatory guidance. However, the reform baton should then pass to participants in financial industry who have been 'enlightened' as to the harms of SMST and the benefits of longer-term approach to continue to press for corrective measures.

This process is currently seen in several financial industry initiatives including the UK Investor Forum, LTVC Index, the FCLT project initiated by McKinsey, and the call to company managers to focus on long-term value generation by prominent CEOs including BlackRock's CEO,

[117] Jurrikkala (2012, 36).

[118] Ibid., 60.

[119] European Union Green Paper. 2011. "The EU Corporate Governance Framework." COM (2011)164. 5 April 2011 (EU Governance Green Paper).

Larry Fink. There is merit to this approach—particularly with respect to the continued 'enlightenment' of equity market participants—but, there continues to be a material role for policymakers to play in reducing excessive discounting, particularly on disclosure reforms related to long-term performance. Therefore, SMST reform should not be left exclusively in the realm of the financial industry.

The conclusion that markets should be self-regulated with guidance from regulators in the context of SMST is bolstered by the theory of reflexive law. The theory of reflexive law was articulated by German social theorist Gunther Teubner building on the theories developed by Philippe Nonet and Philip Selznick.[120] Teubner's reflexive law concept perceives the evolution of modern law from the simple formal rational systems of the nineteenth century that stressed universal rules to the more complex and intrusive substantive systems—i.e. laws as an instrument for purposive goal oriented intervention—introduced with the welfare and regulatory state in the subsequent century.[121] Teubner identified an emerging evolutionary stage of law, which he termed "reflexive law."[122] Teubner posited that in modern society, law has become 'reflexive' and essentially a system for the coordination of action within and between semi-autonomous social subsystems.[123]

Reflexive law essentially fosters self-regulation. Although the goal of reflexive law is self-regulation, the legal system still has a role to play in facilitating such self-regulation. Applying a reflexive law approach means that SMST should be corrected through legal standards and regulatory policies that push private firms to: (1) internalize social goals—e.g. reduce short-term bias—and adopt such goals as their own; and (2) creatively self-manage their operations so as better to achieve these goals.[124] This is not achieved through 'hard' laws. Rather a reflexive law approach

[120] Teubner (1983).

[121] Ibid., 240.

[122] Ibid., 242 and 245.

[123] Ibid., 242.

[124] This approach is adapted from the analysis of reflexive law in the context of environmental regulation—see Hirsch (2010).

uses tools such as information disclosure and stakeholder involvement to motivate companies to undertake their own, self-directed improvement efforts, while leaving it up to the firms to determine the most effective means of SMST reduction.

Finally, an argument has been made that simple—e.g. guidance-based—, rather than increasingly complex—e.g. prescriptive—, regulation is more effective at solving problems caused by a lack of market discipline, pricing inefficiencies and financial innovation, and regulatory complexity may actually exacerbate the harmful effects of bounded rationality.[125] The crux of this argument is twofold. First, excessive regulation may result in 'box ticking' rather than substantive compliance.[126] Second, market phenomena, which arguably include the intricate issue of SMST, are complex and multi-faceted. Interfering with such complex phenomena via invasive regulation arguably is unlikely to work and may have significant costs and unintended consequences.

Detailed 'hard' law regulation is justified and effective in certain circumstances in capital markets where the harms associated with non-intervention are considerable—e.g. restrictions on insider trading. But where the harms are less clear and the complexities greater—such as with SMST—simple and less prescriptive measures are in all probability a better approach. Noted economist, Robert J. Shiller, made this point in the context of regulating against stock market bubbles, arguing that "most of the thrust of our national policies to deal with speculative bubbles should take the form of facilitating more free trade, as well as greater opportunities for people to take positions in more and freer markets."[127] Consequently, market driven initiatives led by 'enlightened' asset owners and asset managers and supported by 'light' touch targeted regulatory disclosure reforms meant to reduce performance uncertainty and clear messaging to the financial industry may be the most feasible, if not ideal, way to 'nudge' the market away from the potential harms of SMST.

[125] Jurrikkala (2012, 36–38, 66–74 and 86–90).

[126] Ibid., 82 referring to Bardach and Kagan (1982), describing compliance culture, and Ayres and Braithwaite (1992), providing examples of compliance culture and possible strategies to reduce it.

[127] Shiller (2015, 237).

References

AGM Trends. 2017. *Ernst & Young*. September. http://www.ey.com/Publication/vwLUAssets/ey-agm-trends-2017/$FILE/ey-agm-trends-2017.pdf.

Ambachtsheer, Keith. 2014. "The Case for Long-Termism." Fall. 7:2 *Rotman International Journal of Pension Management*. 6–16.

Aspen Institute. 2009. "Overcoming Short-termism: A Call for a More Responsible Approach to Investment and Business Management." 9 September.

Aspen Institute. 2010. "Short-Termism and U.S. Capital Markets: A Compelling Case for Change." https://assets.aspeninstitute.org/content/uploads/files/content/images/Compelling%20Case%20for%20Change_August2010.pdf.

Ayres, Ian and Braithwaite, John. 1992. *Responsive Regulation: Transcending the Deregulation Debate*. Oxford University Press: New York and Oxford.

Bainbridge, Stephen M. 2006. "Response, Director Primacy and Shareholder Disempowerment."119 *Harvard Law Review*. 1735–1758.

Bardach, Eugene and Kagan, Robert A. 1982. *Going by the Book: The Problem of Regulatory Unreasonableness*. Transaction Publishers: New Brunswick, NJ.

Barton, Dominic and Wiseman, Mark. 2014. "Focusing Capital on the Long Term." January–February. *Harvard Business Revie*. 44–51.

Bebchuk, Lucien. 2013. "The Myth That Insulating Boards Serves Long-Term Value." 113:6 *Columbia Law Review*. 1637–1694.

Bollen, Rhys. 2012. "Bounded Rationality in the Sale and Purchase of Managed Funds." 9 *Macquarie Journal of Business Law*. 125–144.

Bolton, P. and Thadden, E.-L. von. 1998. "Blocks, Liquidity, and Corporate Control." February. 53:1 *Journal of Finance*. 1–25.

Bratton, William W. and Wachter, Michael L. 2010. "The Case Against Shareholder Empowerment." 158 *University of Pennsylvania Law Review*. 653–728.

Camerer, Colin, Issacharoff, Samuel, Loewenstein, George, O' Donoghue, Ted, and Rabin, Matthew. 2003. "Regulation for Conservatives: Behavioral Economics and the Case for "Asymmetric Paternalism'." January. 151:3 *University of Pennsylvania Law Review*. 1211–1255.

Cheffins, Brian R. 2002. "Corporate Law and Ownership Structure: A Darwinian Link?" 25:2 *University of New South Wales Law Journal*. 346–378.

Cho, M. H. 1998. "Ownership Structure, Investment, and Corporate Value: An Empirical Analysis." 47 *Journal of Financial Economics*. 103–121.

Dasgupta, Amil and Piacentino, Giorgia. 2015. "The Wall Street Walk When Blockholders Compete for Flows." December. 70:6 *The Journal of Finance*. 2853–2896.

Demsetz, H. 1983. "The Structure of Ownership and the Theory of the Firm." 26 *Journal of Law and Economics*. 375–390.

Demsetz, H. and Lehn, K. 1985. "The Structure of Corporate Ownership: Causes and Consequences." 93 *Journal of Political Economy*. 1155–1177.

Demsetz, H. and Villalonga, B. 2001. "Ownership Structure and Firm Performance." 7 *Journal of Corporate Finance*. 209–233.

Dent, George. 2010. "Essential Unity of Shareholders and the Myth of Investor Short-Termism." 35:1 *Delaware Journal of Corporate Law*. 97–150.

Dobbs, Ian M. 2009. "How Bad Can Short-Termism Be?—A Study of the Consequences of High Hurdle Discount Rates and Low Payback Thresholds." 20 *Management Accounting Research*. 117–128.

Drucker, Peter F. 1986. Editorial. "A Crisis of Capitalism." 30 September. *Wall Street Journal*.

Fink, Larry. 2018. CEO Letter, BlackRock, Inc. January. https://www.blackrock.com/corporate/investor-relations/larry-fink-ceo-letter.

Fox, Justin and Lorsch, Jay W. 2012. "What Good Are Shareholders?" 90:7 *Harvard Business Review*. 48–57.

Glosten, Lawrence and Milgrom, Paul. 1985. "'Bid, Ask and' Transaction Prices in a Specialist Market with Heterogeneously Informed Traders." 14 *Journal of Financial Economics*. 71–100.

Grossman, Sanford J. and Hart, Oliver D. 1980. "Takeover Bids, the Free-Rider Problem, and the Theory of the Corporation." 11:1 *Bell Journal of Economics*. 42–64.

Hirsch, Dennis D. 2010 "Green Business and the Importance of Reflexive Law: What Michael Porter Didn't Say." Fall. 62:4 *Administrative Law Review*. 1063–1126.

"Implementation of the Kay Review: Progress Report." 2014. Department for Business Innovation & Skills. October.

Jensen, Michael C. and Meckling, William H. 1976. "Theory of the Firm: Managerial Behavior, Agency Costs and Ownership Structure." October. 3:4 *Journal of Financial Economics*. 305–360.

Johnston, Andrew and Morrow, Paige. 2014. "Commentary on the Shareholder Rights Directive." University of Oslo Faculty of Law Research Paper No. 2014-41.

Jolls, Christine, and Sunstein, Cass R. 2006. "Debiasing Through Law." 35:1 *Journal of Legal Studies*. 199–242.

Jurrikkala, O. 2012. "The Behavioural Paradox: Why Investor Irrationality Calls for Lighter and Simpler Financial Regulation." 2012/2013. 18:1 *Fordham Journal of Corporate and Financial Law*. 33–93.

Kahneman, Daniel. 2003. "A Perspective on Judgement and Choice." Anderson, Norman B. (editor). 58:9 *American Psychologist*. 697–720.

Kay, John. 2012. 'The Kay Review of UK Equity Markets and Long-Term Decision Making." Final Report. July.

Lin, Yu-Hsin. 2017. "Controlling Controlling-Minority Shareholders: Corporate Governance and Leveraged Corporate Control." 2 *Columbia Business Law Review*. 454–510.

Lipton, Martin and Rosenblum, Steven A. 1991. "A New System of Corporate Governance: The Quinquennial Election of Directors." 58:1(3) *University of Chicago Law*. 187–253.

Lucas, G. M. and Tasic, S. 2015. "Behavioral Public Choice and the Law." Fall. 118:1 *West Virginia Law Review*. 199–266.

Martin, Roger. 2011. "How to Make Companies Think Long-Term." 3 October. *Harvard Business Review*.

Maug, Ernts. 1998. "Large Shareholders as Monitors: Is There a Trade-Off Between Liquidity and Control." 53:1 *The Journal of Finance*. 65–98.

Nguyen, Bang Dang and Nielsen, Kasper Meisner. 2013. "When Blockholders Leave Feet Firm: Do Ownership and Control Affect Firm Value?" 26 June. https://ssrn.com/abstract=2285453.

Nocera, Joe. 2011. "What Is Business Waiting For?" 16 August. *New York Times*.

Oyedele, Akin. 2017. "Here Is the Letter the World's Largest Investor, BlackRock CEO Larry Fink, Just Sent to CEOs Everywhere." 24 January. *Business Insider UK*. http://uk.businessinsider.com/blackrock-ceo-larry-fink-letter-to-ceos-2017-1?r=US&IR=T.

Porter, Michael E. "Capital Choices: Changing the Way America Invests in Industry." June. 5:2 *Journal of Applied Corporate Finance*. 4–16.

Shiller, Robert J. 2015. *Irrational Exuberance*. Princeton University Press: New York.

Shleifer, Andrei and Vishny Robert W. 1986. "Large Shareholders and Corporate Control." 94:3(1) *The Journal of Political Economy*. 461–488.

Simon, H. A. 1955. "Behavioral Model of Rational Choice." 69:1 *The Quarterly Journal of Economics*. 99–118.

Sorkin, Andrew Ross. 2013. "Shareholder Democracy Can Mask Abuses." 25 February. *New York Times*.

Stout, Lynn. 2012. *The Shareholder Value Myth: How Putting Shareholders First Harms Investors, Corporations, and the Public*. Berrett-Koehler Publishers: San Francisco, CA, USA.

Sunstein, Cass R. 1996. "On the Expressive Function of Law." 144 *University of Pennsylvania Law Review*. 2021–2053.

Sunstein, Cass R. 2014. *Why Nudge: The Politics of Libertarian Paternalism*. Yale University Press: New Haven.

Teubner, Gunther. 1983. "Substantive and Reflexive Elements in Modern Law." Spring.17:2 *Law and Society Review*. 239–285.

Turner, Matt. 2016. "Here Is the Letter the World's Largest Investor, BlackRock CEO Larry Fink, Just Sent to CEOs Everywhere." 2 February. *Business Insider UK*. http://uk.businessinsider.com/blackrock-ceo-larry-fink-letter-to-sp-500-ceos-2016-2?r=US&IR=T.

Wolf, Daniel E. 2014. "Controlling Stockholders in Delaware—More Than a Number." 12 November. *Harvard Law School Forum on Corporate Governance and Financial Regulation*. https://corpgov.law.harvard.edu/2014/11/12/controlling-stockholders-in-delaware-more-than-a-number/.

CHAPTER 9

Conclusion

The research in this book has been undertaken primarily because allegations of harmful 'crisis' level short-termism in public equity markets have increased dramatically since the global financial crisis (GFC). Allegations of stock market short-termism (SMST) have instigated a flurry of reform proposals in financial markets around the world. These proposals have resulted in some implemented reforms by policymakers and the financial industry meant to correct SMST, primarily in the United Kingdom (UK), the European Union (EU) and the United States (US). This wide-ranging burst of activity and high-level attention to the SMST issue, coupled with the increasing interconnectedness of modern equity markets, presents the need for a broad ranging study of such SMST-driven reforms, and a detailed examination on the causes and effectiveness of such implemented reforms. It is logically expected that the significant level of discussion and attention given to the perceived problem of SMST has resulted in substantial implemented regulatory and financial industry reforms. Based on the review in this book, I conclude, however, that despite much discussion, there has not been much prescriptive 'hard' law reforms aimed at correcting SMST, and of the reforms implemented, few effectively address the probable causes of SMST.

The problematic short-termism behaviour considered in this book has been reviewed and defined as asset owners and intermediaries in the equity ownership chain weighing near-term financial outcomes too heavily at the expense of potentially more profitable longer-term

K. M. Willey, *Stock Market Short-Termism*,
https://doi.org/10.1007/978-3-030-22903-0_9

investment opportunities. This weighing is reflected in share pricing as short-term financial actions by company managers have positive impacts on share price and longer-term objectives are undervalued. This impact to share prices causes company managers of listed companies to take actions that prioritize the short-term financial returns of the listed company to the detriment of listed companies, which by extension includes their investors and broader constituent elements.

This definition of stock market short-termism necessitated further analysis of whether short-termism is problematic and, in particular, if SMST is evident in the share pricing of listed companies, as share prices are an important communication mechanism between the market and listed companies. This book accepts that stock markets are generally informationally efficient. However, the basis of share pricing as a measure of fundamental efficiency was questioned based on evidence suggesting that asset owners and intermediaries are at least perceived to excessively discount future returns of listed companies. Such actual or perceived discounting results in company managers prioritizing short-term financial returns. In other words, relying on share prices as an indicator of fundamental firm value is questionable as share prices increase unduly based on short-term returns and do not adequately value longer-term returns. Such excessive discounting appears to be transmitted into listed companies mainly via shareholder activism and executive compensation structures. Consequently, any remedy to the SMST problem requires either: (1) completely cutting off these transmission mechanisms; or (2) addressing causes of excessive discounting issues around share pricing.

This book also considered the evidence on whether SMST is actually detrimental, as short-termism in stock markets only matters if it results in a demonstrable harm. SMST is a complex and nebulous issue, meaning that it is difficult to empirically isolate the harms arising from excessive discounting of long-term financial returns. However, as discussed in Chapter 7, research suggests that SMST results in a reduced trust in the stock market as a capital raising venue, and there appears to be a wealth transfer from future to current asset owners. Regardless of whether these arguments may be conclusively proven, they appear compelling enough to drive regulatory and financial industry reform.

As considered in Chapter 3, SMST rhetoric has long overlapped with the financial market concerns of the day, but appears to be connected to the increasing financial intermediation of public markets and the corresponding increased reliance on short-term performance of asset managers rather than the underlying performance of a listed company. Therefore, a real SMST issue is weavings its way into the fabric of listed company corporate governance, and it is highly probable that SMST will continue to motivate financial industry and regulatory reform for years to come. It remains important to understand the most plausible causes of SMST, and to properly assess whether implemented reforms, at least from a theoretical perspective, effectively address SMST.

The implemented financial industry and regulatory reforms which claim to be motivated at least in part by SMST concerns were considered in Chapter 4 and summarized in Appendix B (Table 4). The results of this analysis indicate that despite the significant level of discussion and many reform proposals, the actual output of SMST reform in all jurisdictions surveyed has been relatively modest. Additionally, of the implemented reforms most are generally 'light' touch rather than prescriptive 'hard' law reforms. The assessment of such implemented reforms in Chapter 8 further narrowed these results and revealed that of the implemented SMST reforms few addressed the most probable causes of SMST.

Such analysis was based on the conclusion reached in this book that any reform efforts to address SMST must do so via a dual pathway for reform, which requires either: (1) minimizing the excessive discounting of future returns; or (2) cutting off the transmission mechanisms of SMST into the listed company. Of the implemented reforms that do not conceptually address the SMST issue, they appeared to either merely use SMST as rhetoric or, worse, contain flawed logic and have the potential to increase the SMST issue. Of the remaining few conceptually effective implemented reforms as identified in Appendix C (Table 8) most were 'hard' law but were limited in that they were disclosure-based, meaning that they were 'light' touch rather than prescriptive in their application. However, this may not diminish the conceptual effectiveness of the implemented reforms, as such a 'light' touch approach could be the most feasible, if not the ideal, means of addressing the SMST issue, provided that such 'light' touch is properly focused on the identified causes of SMST.

While there undoubtedly will continue to be questions around whether SMST is a real and harmful phenomenon, it is highly probable that policymakers and the financial industry will maintain their drive for longer-term sustainable investment in and by listed companies, and that SMST will continue to be viewed as a contributing factor hindering such longer-term investment. Consequently, effective SMST reform should be considered in the context of the dual pathway for reform identified in this book. This analysis identifies Option (1) of the dual pathway, and in particular the two sub-paths in Option (1), namely Option 1(a)—reducing performance uncertainty, and Option 1(b) 'improving' asset owners, as the reform methods which employ a 'light' touch approach. Primarily, implemented reforms in this space focus on disclosure, particularly around long-term strategy, measurable long-term objectives, and linking executive compensation to such long-term deliverables. There is significant room for improvement in further targeting and refining such disclosure on long-term performance. However, for a myriad of reasons, including that regulators are themselves subject to bias, cost and resource restrictions, and that complex, paternalistic intrusive measures can result in harmful unintended consequences, such 'light' touch approach guided by policymakers and implemented and supported by the financial industry may be the most effective method of 'nudging' capital markets away from their short-term focus.

Appendix 'A': SMST Reforms by Jurisdiction

See Tables 1, 2, and 3.

K. M. Willey, *Stock Market Short-Termism*,
https://doi.org/10.1007/978-3-030-22903-0

Table 1 Asset owner oriented SMST reforms

Implemented Reforms ('Hard' Law – , 'Soft' Law – and Voluntary Initiatives -)

Jurisdiction[1]	*Measures Favouring Long-Term Share Ownership*	*Taxation Incentives Based on Duration of Share Ownership*	*Disclosure (Removal of Mandatory Quarterly Reporting and 'Better' Quality Disclosure)*	*Direct Communication/ Engagement between Asset Owners and Companies*	*Restrictions on Stock-Lending*	*Long Term Funds*	*Hedge Funds*
United Kingdom	Considered and rejected in Kay Review	Considered and rejected in Kay Review	Kay Review recommends removal of mandatory quarterly reporting and advocates for 'better' reporting	Recommended in Kay Review	Kay Review recommended restrictions	None	None
			UK Government removes mandatory quarterly reporting and enacts Strategic Report and Directors' Report Regulations	UK Government cites EU efforts and Good Practice Statement	UK Government supports finance industry guidelines and UCITS Directive		
			FRC Guidance on Strategic Report	UK Investor Forum			
United States	Dual class shares already permitted	Capital gains revision and excise tax suggested in Aspen Report and by US reformers	Aspen Report/US reformers call for greater transparency in investor disclosure	None	None	LTVC Index	Brokaw Act
	Proxy Access Rules overturned by Court, continue in practice						
European Union[2]	Proposed EU amendments on voting rights to EU Amended Shareholder Rights Directive rejected	Proposed EU Financial Transactions Tax	EU recommendations on governance reporting and CSR/ESG disclosure	EU Amended Shareholder Rights Directive (Articles 3a and 3b)	UCITS Directive restricting stock-lending	None	None
			EU Transparency Directive, EU Non-Financial Reporting Directive				
France	Florange Law	None	None	None	None	None	None
	L-Shares						
Netherlands	L-Shares	None	None	None	None	None	None
Italy	Enacted but not renewed	None	None	None	None	None	None
Singapore	SGX approves dual class listing for secondary market	None	SGX considering removing mandatory quarterly reporting	None	None	None	None
Other	None	None	Proposed IIRC reporting framework	None	None	None	None

[1]All jurisdictions with significant public equity markets were surveyed, but only jurisdictions which have proposed or implemented reforms at least in part based on express short-termism concerns are included in this table

[2]The EU was considered separately as a governing body from each of its member states

Table 2 Intermediary oriented SMST reforms

Implemented Reforms ('Hard' Law – [yellow], 'Soft' Law – [green] and Voluntary Initiatives - [purple])

Jurisdiction[1]	*Stewardship& Disclosure*	*Duty to Further Long-Term Interests?*	*Asset Manager Remuneration*	*Voting Restrictions*	*Direct Shareholding by Asset Owners*	*Metrics and Models*	*Proxy Advisors*
United Kingdom	UK endorsement of Kay Review stewardship and good practice statements	Recommended in the Kay Review	Kay Review recommends structuring remuneration with timescale of asset owners	Amendments to UK Stewardship Code re disclosure/ use of voting powers	Kay Review recommended direct share holding	Kay Review recommended further review	Not addressed in Kay Review
	UK Stewardship Code Amendments	UK Law Commission report/UK Government recommends minimum standards	UK Government endorses Good Practice Statements		UK Government supporting of EU CSD Regulation (to be implemented in 2023)	UK Government commissioned research on models and metrics	
	UK NAPF Stewardship Framework		NAPF Stewardship Framework				
	UK Investor Forum		IMA and other finance industry guidance on fund disclosure				
United States	None	Aspen Report and other reformers call for 'fiduciary' duties for intermediaries	Aspen Reports recommends regulation to base compensation on long-term performance	None	None	None	SEC confirms onus is on asset managers
European Union[2]	EU Amended Shareholder Rights Directive re voting rights (Articles 3h and 3i)	MiFID II	EU UCITS Directive limiting remuneration	EU Amended Shareholder Rights Directive re voting rights (Article 3c)	EU CSD Regulation (to be implemented in 2023)	None	EU Amended Shareholder Rights Directive (Article 3j)
Switzerland	None	None	None	Minder Initiative restricts voting by intermediaries	None	None	None
Canada	Focusing Capital on the Long-Term	None	None	None	None	None	None
Japan	Stewardship Code	None	None	None	None	None	None
Others	Various voluntary Stewardship Codes	None	None	None	None	None	None
	PRI, UNEP and UN Global Compact	None	None	None	None	None	None

[1]All jurisdictions with significant public equity markets were surveyed, but only jurisdictions which have proposed or implemented reforms at least in part based on express short-termism concerns are included in this table

[2]The EU was considered separately as a governing body from each of its member states

Table 3 Company manager oriented SMST reforms

Implemented Reforms ('Hard' Law – [yellow], 'Soft' Law – [green] and Voluntary Initiatives - [purple])

Jurisdiction[1]	*Company Manager Remuneration*	*Best Practices of Company Managers*	*Mergers and Acquisitions*
United Kingdom	Kay Review recommends structuring executive compensation to relate incentives to long-term performance and for longer-time frames for compensation	Kay Review Good Practice Statement for Directors endorsed by UK Government	Kay Review recommended M&A activity be kept under review
	UK Government approved the Kay Review 'Good Practice Statement for Directors' UK Government adopted Remuneration Regulations with new reporting requirements	Institute of Directors recommends strengthening boards	UK Government felt M&A sufficiently regulated and CMA has long-termism built into its strategy
United States	US Amendments to Item 402 of Regulation S-K	Various finance industry initiatives including BlackRock CEO Letters	None
European Union[2]	EU Amended Shareholder Rights Directive Articles 9a and 9b includes similar new reporting requirements to UK Remuneration Regulations	Various finance industry initiatives	None
Switzerland	Minder Initiative reforms on executive compensation	None	None
Brazil	None	Brazilian Institute of Corporate Governance, 'Sustainability Guide for Companies'	None
Australia	Governance Code (pay should link to long-term strategy)	None	None
Norway	Governance Code (pay should link to long-term strategy)	None	None
South Africa	None	King Report on Governance	None
New Zealand	None	New Zealand IOD, "The Four Pillars of 'Governance Best Practice'	None
Singapore	Singapore Code of Governance remuneration reporting requirements and dual class listings	None	None

[1]All jurisdictions with significant public equity markets were surveyed, but only jurisdictions which have proposed or implemented reforms at least in part based on express short-termism concerns are included in this table

[2]The EU was considered separately as a governing body from each of its member states

Appendix 'B': Implemented SMST Reforms

See Table 4.

K. M. Willey, *Stock Market Short-Termism*,
https://doi.org/10.1007/978-3-030-22903-0

Table 4 Implemented SMST reforms

'Hard' law (statutory)		*'Soft' law (non-statutory)*	*Financial industry initiatives (voluntary)*
Mandatory/prescriptive	*'Comply or explain'/'opt-out'/ disclosure-based*		
UCITS Directive (limited to EU UCITS)	Florange Law (France)	FRC guidance re disclosure (UK)	L-Shares (e.g. L'Oréal France)
Minder Initiative (Switzerland)[1]	Removal of mandatory quarterly reporting (UK)	Recommendation 2014/208/EU and Directive 2014/95/EU re disclosure (EU)	UK Investor Forum
EU non-financial reporting directive[2]	EU Amended Shareholder Rights Directive (Article 3c, 3h, 3i, 3j, 9a and 9b)	UK Stewardship Code Amendments (UK)	LTVC Index
Remuneration Regulations (UK)	EU Transparency Directive	Singapore Code of Corporate Governance (remuneration reporting)	Voluntary organizations (e.g. PRI, 300 Club, etc.)
Strategic Report and Directors' Report Regulations (UK)		Governance Codes (Australia and Norway)	Governance and professional organization best practice guidance
US Amendments to Item 402 of Regulation S-K			BlackRock CEO letters
EU Amended Shareholder Rights Directive (Articles 3a and 3b)			Focusing Capital on the Long-Term
			NAPF Stewardship Disclosure Framework (UK)
			IMA and other finance industry guidance on remuneration of asset managers (UK)
			Various Stewardship Codes (e.g. the Stewardship Code (Japan))
			UNEP and UN Global Compact

[1]Only with respect to limits on intermediary voting. Although the stated purpose of the reforms is to 'counter the culture of short-termism', there is little detail to support how the reforms actually do so with respect to executive compensation reforms

[2]Not yet implemented but entered into force on 9 June 2017 and EU Member States have until 10 June 2019 to implement these changes into national legislation

Appendix 'C': Conceptual Effectiveness of SMST Reforms

See Tables 5, 6, 7, and 8.

K. M. Willey, *Stock Market Short-Termism*,
https://doi.org/10.1007/978-3-030-22903-0

Table 5 Conceptual effectiveness of implemented asset owner oriented SMST reforms

SMST reform	*Measures favouring long-term share ownership*			*Disclosure (removal of mandatory quarterly reporting and 'better' quality disclosure)*			*Direct communication/ engagement between asset owners and companies*		*Restrictions on stock-lending*	*Long term funds*
	Florange Law	*Financial industry use of l-shares*	*SGX dual class shares*	*Removal of mandatory quarterly reporting (UK & EU)*	*Strategic report and directors' report regula-tions (UK)*	*Recommendation 2014/208/ EU, EU Non-financial Reporting Directive*	*UK Investor Forum*	*EU Amended Shareholder Rights Directive (Articles 3a and 3b)*	*EU UCITS Directive*	*US LTVC Index*
Option 1(a)—reduce performance uncertainty	×	×	×	×	✓	✓	×	×	×	✓
Option 1(b)—'improve' asset owners/ asset managers	×	×	×	✓	✓	✓	✓	×	×	✓
Option 2(a)—insulate board	×	×	×	×	×	×	×	×	×	×
Option 2(b)—reduce short-term compensation	×	×	×	×	×	×	×	×	×	×

Table 6 Conceptual effectiveness of implemented intermediary oriented SMST reforms

SMST reform	*Guiding principles/Stewardship*			*Asset manager remuneration*		*Voting restrictions*			*Proxy advisors*
	UK/Japan Stewardship Code / UK NAPF Stewardship Framework	*EU Amended Shareholder Rights Directive (Articles 3h ad 3i)*	*BlackRock Letter and FCLT & UK Investor Forum*	*UK NAPF Stewardship Framework/ IMA and financial industry guidance*	*EU UCITS Directive (asset manager compensation)*	*UK Stewardship Code*	*EU Amended Shareholder Rights Directive (Article 3c)*	*Swiss Minder Initiative*	*EU Amended Shareholder Rights Directive—proxy advisory code of conduct (Article 3j)*
Option 1(a)—reduce performance uncertainty	×	×	×	×	×	×	×	×	×
Option 1(b)—'improve' asset owners/asset managers	✓	✓	✓	✓	×	×	×	×	×
Option 2(a)—insulate board	×	×	×	×	×	×	×	×	×
Option 2(b)—reduce short-term compensation	×	×	×	×	✓	×	×	×	×

Table 7 Conceptual effectiveness of implemented company manager oriented SMST reforms

SMST reform	*Company manager remuneration*			*Best practices for company managers*			
	UK Remuneration Regulations	*US Item 402 Regulation S-K Amendments*	*EU Amended Shareholder Rights Directive (Articles 9a and 9b)*	*Governance codes*	*IOD recommendations to strengthen boards*	*Governance guides*	*BlackRock Letter*
Option 1(a)—reduce performance uncertainty	×	×	✓	×	×	×	×
Option 1(b)—'improve' asset owners/asset managers	×	×	×	×	×	×	×
Option 2(a)—insulate board	×	×	×	×	×	×	×
Option 2(b)—reduce short-term compensation	×	×	×	×	×	×	×

Table 8 Conceptually effective implemented SMST reforms

SMST reform	*Method of addressing SMST*	*Type of reform*	*Limitations*
Removal of mandatory quarterly reporting (UK and EU)	Option 1(b)—'improve' asset owners	'Hard' law	'Opt-In'
Strategic Report and Directors' Report Regulations (UK)	Option 1(a)—reduce performance uncertainty & Option 1(b) 'improve' asset owners	'Hard' law	Disclosure-based
Recommendation 2014/208/EU, EU non-financial reporting directive	Option 1(a)—reduce performance uncertainty & Option 1(b) 'improve' asset owners	'Hard' and 'soft' law	Disclosure-based
UK Investor Forum	Option 1(b)—'improve' asset owners	Voluntary initiative	Voluntary
US LTVC Index	Option 1(a)—Reduce performance uncertainty & Option 1(b) 'improve' asset owners	Voluntary initiative	Untested and limited buy-in
UK/Japan Stewardship Code/UK NAPF Stewardship Framework, UK Investor Forum, BlackRock Letter and FCLT, UK NAPF Stewardship Framework/IMA and Financial Industry Guidance	Option 1(b)—'improve' asset owners	'Soft' law and voluntary initiative	Voluntary
EU Amended Shareholder Rights Directive (Articles 3h and 3i)	Option 1(b)—'improve' asset owners	'Hard' law	Disclosure-based and 'comply and explain'
EU UCITS Directive (asset manager compensation)	Option 2(b)—reduce short-term compensation	'Hard' law	Limited to EU UCITS
EU Amended Shareholder Rights Directive—Article 9a and 9b	Option 1(a)—reduce performance uncertainty	'Hard' law	Disclosure-based

Index

K. M. Willey, *Stock Market Short-Termism*,
https://doi.org/10.1007/978-3-030-22903-0

CPSIA information can be obtained
at www.ICGtesting.com
Printed in the USA
LVHW072256210719
624811LV00018B/608/P

9 783030 229023